W9-DBS-544

NOTES ON THE MINOR PROPHETS

By

H. A. IRONSIDE, Litt.D.

Author of NOTES ON JEREMIAH AND LAMENTATIONS; NOTES ON EZEKIEL THE PROPHET; LECTURES ON DANIEL THE PROPHET; NOTES ON THE MINOR PROPHETS, etc., etc.

LOIZEAUX BROTHERS, Inc., BIBLE TRUTH DEPOT

A Nonprofit Organization, Devoted to the Lord's Work and to the Spread of His Truth

Neptune, New Jersey

FIRST EDITION, AUGUST 1909
NINTH PRINTING, DECEMBER 1966

PRINTED IN THE UNITED STATES OF AMERICA

PREFACE

It was with no definite purpose of writing a series of Notes on the Minor Prophets as a whole, that I first began to take up various books of the twelve, in monthly installments in HELP AND FOOD FOR THE HOUSEHOLD OF FAITH. But after penning some notes on Habakkuk, Jonah, and Obadiah, I found my own soul helped, and an interest developed in the further study of these much-neglected portions of Scriptures, and so took up Hosea and the books following. I have sought to impress their practical application as giving important teaching for a remnant people in a day of decline, while not neglecting their dispensational bearing. This, I am persuaded, is what is greatly needed at the present moment. If God be pleased to use the Notes for the stirring of His people's consciences and the comfort of their hearts, the desired end will be realized.

H. A. IRONSIDE.

INDEX

NOTES ON HOSEA

NOTES ON MICAH

NOTES ON NAHUM

NOTES ON HABAKKUK

NOTES ON ZEPHANIAH

NOTES ON HAGGAI

NOTES ON ZECHARIAH

NOTES ON MALACHI

Notes on the

PROPHECY OF HOSEA

CHAPTER I

THE BLOOD OF JEZREEL*

HOSEA, whose book is the first of the so-called Minor Prophets, was a contemporary of Isaiah throughout almost his entire ministry, as also of Amos in his earlier years. A comparison of the first verses of each of their books with the one before us makes this evident. During the long reign of Jeroboam II, king of Israel, and those of Uzziah, Jotham, Ahaz and Hezekiah, kings of Judah, there was much to rebuke in the two nations. Hosea seems to have confined most of his direct messages to Judah, speaking rather *of* the ten tribes than to them; but the scope of his prophecy embraces both, and that very fully. In fact, no other messenger gives

* It is essential the reader should first read with care, in Scripture, the chapter under consideration in these "Notes." To derive profit and blessing, the subject must be familiar.—[Ed.

so complete an outline of the ways of God with His earthly people as does Hosea, even Daniel not excepted. Read in connection with the visions of the latter, the one throws much light on the other.

Of Hosea's personal history it has not pleased God to give us any particulars, save in relation to his marriage, and the issue therefrom. His father's name is given as Beeri, but neither the prophet's tribe nor the place of his nativity is mentioned. Hosea means *help,* or *salvation.* With a single vowel-point added it becomes Hoshea, *salvation of Jah.* Beeri is said to mean *The well of Jehovah.* The two names together remind us of the Lord's words to the woman of Samaria. He offered her living water from Jehovah's well, which would result in her assured salvation.

"The beginning of the word of the Lord by Hosea" was a command for the prophet himself, bidding him do what would be obnoxious to mere nature, and which must have tested the heart of Jehovah's servant in a very marked way. As in the case of Isaiah, he and his were to be for signs in Israel; so he is told to unite himself in marriage to a woman devoid of character—a harlot; thus signifying the wretched condition of unfaithful Israel, who nevertheless remained the object of Jehovah's love, despite their iniquity, and the filthiness that was in them. What more wonderful picture could we have of grace, not only to the *undeserving,* but to those who had *deserved* the very opposite? It is important to remember that grace is not merely *un*merited favor, but it is favor spite of *merited* judgment.

Such is the marvelous loving-kindness of our God that He finds the objects of His love, not among the righteous and the holy, but among sinners lost and ruined, deserving naught but judgment, stained with guilt and polluted by sin, having all gone out of the way and become unprofitable; nevertheless He sets His love upon wretches so vile and unworthy, and redeems them to Himself. Jehovah's dealings with Israel of old picture His ways of grace with believers now. "All these things happened unto them for types, and they are written for our admonition upon whom the ends of the ages have arrived."

In obedience to the voice of the Lord, Hosea "went and took Gomer the daughter of Diblaim" as his wife; thus giving to her who before had no standing the place and honor of a wife in Israel. Of her he had several children. Having died to her old wretched life, of which she might well be ashamed, she brings forth fruit unto him who has set his love upon her and given her his name and protection. It is easy to see in all this a lovely illustration of the words of the Holy Spirit in Rom. 6:21, 22: "What fruit had ye then in those things whereof ye are now ashamed? for the end of those things is death. But now being made free from sin, and become servants to God, ye have your fruit unto holiness, and the end everlasting life." As also in verse 4 of the following chapter: "Wherefore, my brethren, ye also are become dead to the law by the body of Christ; that ye should be married to another, even to Him who is raised from the dead, that we should bring forth fruit unto God."

Hosea had to bear the shame of having espoused one of so wretched a character, but he did not have to die for her. It was far otherwise with our blessed Lord Jesus. He not only came where we were in our sin and shame, but on Calvary's cross He was made sin for us that we might become God's righteousness in Him. There He purchased us with His own precious blood, "that He might redeem us from all iniquity and purify unto Himself a peculiar people, zealous of good works" (Titus 2:14).

Of His all-conquering love, the kindness shown by Hosea to Gomer is but a very faint picture; as also of Jehovah's undying affection for Israel, the earthly bride. For the cross was where the purchase-price was paid for both the heavenly and the earthly people.

When the first son was born, "the Lord said unto him, Call his name Jezreel; for yet a little while, and I will avenge the blood of Jezreel upon the house of Jehu, and will cause to cease the kingdom of the house of Israel. And it shall come to pass at that day, that I will break the bow of

Israel in the valley of Jezreel" (vers. 4, 5). The name Jezreel itself speaks of blessing, yet here it is used to tell of judgment. Jezreel means "sown of God," and in chapter 2, as also in the last verse of this present chapter, it is used in a very different connection from that in which it is here found.

God was about to cast Israel, the northern kingdom, out of His sight among the Gentiles, in order that they might be chastened for their iniquities. He had redeemed them in grace and brought them to Himself; but they had proven false and treacherous. Therefore they must learn by judgment what they would not learn by lovingkindness. He connects their destruction with "the blood of Jezreel." This is most significant, for the reigning house of Israel had succeeded to the throne through that very "blood of Jezreel." It was when Jehu became the instrument for the destruction of Ahab's house, at Jezreel, that he ascended the throne, and Jeroboam II was of his dynasty.

But neither Jehu nor his house had profited by the lesson of Ahab's judgment. They had themselves walked in the ways of the nations, and followed false gods; therefore the blood of Jezreel would be avenged upon them, and they too should be cut off.

But there is more yet connected with Jezreel. It will be remembered that this was originally the inheritance of the righteous man Naboth. In 1 Kings 21 we learn that this Naboth "had a vineyard which was in Jezreel." Ahab coveted the vineyard, and sought to buy it, that he might transform it into a garden. Naboth rightfully refused to sell his inheritance, saying, "The Lord forbid it me, that I should give the inheritance of my fathers unto thee" (ver. 3). Heavy and displeased, Ahab "laid him down upon his bed, and turned away his face, and would eat no bread." The proud and wilful monarch could not brook the thought that one so insignificant as this Jezreelite should thwart his wishes. Jezebel, his heathen wife, however, wrote letters in his name, saying, "Proclaim a fast, and set Naboth on high among the people: and set two men, sons of Belial, before him, to bear witness against him, saying, Thou didst blaspheme God and the king. And then carry him out, and stone him, that he may die" (vers. 9, 10). The ungodly plot was duly perpetrated. False witnesses swore away the life of the righteous one, and "they carried him forth out of the city, and stoned him with stones, that he died" (ver. 13).

His inheritance was declared forfeited, and Ahab went down to take possession of it. But on the way he was met by Elijah the prophet, who was sent with a message of judgment upon his lips. Jehovah's eye had been looking on, and He commanded His servant to declare to the godless king that his doom was sealed, and his house should fall. The blood of Jezreel should be his ruin, for, "Thus saith the Lord, In the place where dogs licked the blood of Naboth shall dogs lick thy blood, even thine" (ver. 19).

"And of Jezebel also spake the Lord, saying, The dogs shall eat Jezebel by the wall of Jezreel" (ver. 23). All this was literally fulfilled. Ahab was slain in the battle of Ramoth-Gilead; and we read, "So the king died, and was brought to Samaria; and they buried the king in Samaria. And one washed the chariot in the pool of Samaria; and *the dogs licked up his blood;* and they washed his armor; *according unto* the word of the Lord which He spake" (1 Kings 22: 37, 38). This was in the portion of Jezreel, Ahab's summer home.

Ahab was succeeded by his ungodly son Joram, or Jehoram, as he is sometimes called. Jehu having been anointed king of Israel by Elisha, the man of God, set out first of all to put Joram to death. The latter had "returned to be healed in Jezreel of the wounds which the Syrians had given him, when he fought with Hazael king of Syria" (2 Kings 9: 15). In the portion of Naboth the Jezreelite the two met; Ahaziah king of Judah also being with the Israelitish monarch. "And it came to pass, when Joram saw Jehu, that he said, Is it peace, Jehu? And he answered, What peace, so long as the whoredoms of thy mother

Jezebel and her witchcrafts are so many?" Joram attempted to flee, but Jehu pierced him through with an arrow, and, in fulfilment of the word of Jehovah, cast his bleeding corpse into the plot of Naboth. Ahaziah too was smitten, but fled to Megiddo to die. It was against the house of Ahab the Lord's vengeance was to fall in the portion of Jezreel!

Here too Jezebel met her dreadful fate, as the prophet had predicted. "When Jehu was come to Jezreel, Jezebel heard of it, and she painted her face, and tired her head, and looked out at a window." As she taunts Jehu as a regicide, he calls for one upon his side to throw her down. At once several eunuchs lay hands upon her, and "they threw her down, and *some of her blood was sprinkled on the wall,* and on the horses: and he trode her under foot." Afterwards Jehu sent his servants to bury her, but they found that dogs had devoured her in the portion of Jezreel, as the Lord had spoken (2 Kings 9:30-37). The present dynasty (Jehu's) had therefore come to the throne through this blood of Jezreel; but, alas, they had failed to profit by the solemn lesson of God's hatred of sin, and abhorrence of idolatry in particular! Therefore this same valley of Jezreel should be the scene of *their* judgment; as it was some few years later, when in that very spot (called then Esdraelon) the Assyrian defeated Israel, and their captivity began.

Dispensationally, all this is fraught with truth of a solemn and important character. Israel, according to Isa. 5, is Jehovah's vineyard. Of Israel therefore the vineyard of Jezreel speaks. They were "sown of God" in the land of Canaan, to be Jehovah's portion. But they hired false witnesses against the Lord of the vineyard, the Righteous One, who would not give to the enemy His rightful inheritance. By wicked hands they slew the Husbandman, and claimed the vineyard as their own. Because of this the Gentile oppressor was permitted to overturn the kingdom, and power was transferred to the nations. The awful prayer, "His blood be on us, and on our children!" has been terribly answered, as the antitypical blood of Jezreel witnesses. In the very place where they slew the Lord of glory *their* blood has been poured out as wine bursting from the winepress, and they have been devoured by the dogs—the unclean Gentiles.

Have the Gentiles, on their part, profited by the dreadful lesson of the blood of the seed of God? Far from it. High-minded and indifferent to God's claims upon them, they have gone on in their own ways, and refused to hearken to His word. Therefore they too shall be cut off, and thus God will avenge upon them the blood of Jezreel.

Coming back to the literal application of the passage in Hosea, we note that Jehovah was about "to break the bow of Israel in the valley of Jezreel" (ver. 5). Because they had not taken to heart the fact that Ahab's evil house was destroyed because of sin, but had walked in the same unholy paths, the ten tribes were to be carried into Assyria; a prophecy which, as we well know, came to pass about fifty years later, in the days of King Hoshea, who was imprisoned by Shalmaneser the Assyrian ruler, and his people taken captive.

In the next verse we learn that a daughter was borne by Gomer, who was called Lo-ruhamah, in obedience to the word of God. The name means, "Not having obtained mercy," and sets forth the present state of Israel since they have been cast out of their land. On Judah the Lord would still have mercy, and would save them from their enemies. They had not yet openly revolted, as had the ten tribes (ver. 7).

A third child, this time a son, was named Lo-ammi; that is, "Not My people:" for the Lord now declared, "Ye are not My people, and I will not be your God." They had broken the covenant, entered into long ago at Sinai and ratified in the plains of Moab. From the beginning they had been treacherous and rebellious; therefore on the ground of merit they can claim nothing. Hence God gives them up for the time being, and refuses to own them as His people. This Lo-ammi sentence remains unrepealed to the present day. At the Babylonian captivity Judah also came under it, and all Israel have been in its shadow ever since. This accounts for the omission of the name of God in the book of Esther, which sets forth His providential care over them while they are scattered among the nations, and when He cannot publicly identify Himself with them.*

With verse 9 the first chapter ends, according to the Hebrew arrangement; the two verses that follow being the introduction to chapter 2. They speak of mercy yet to be manifested, and tell us that though all is forfeited on the ground of works, God still has in reserve boundless stores of grace, the enjoyment of which they are to enter into in the latter day. "Yet the number of the children of Israel shall be as the sand of the sea, which cannot be measured nor numbered; and it shall come to pass, that in the place where it was said unto them, Ye are not My people, there it shall be said unto them, Ye are the sons of the living God.† Then shall the children of Judah

---

* This has been gone into at some length in the author's "Notes on the Book of Esther," to be had of the same publishers. Paper covers, 30 cts.; cloth, 75 cts.

† It will be observed that, in justifying from Scripture the present work of God in showing mercy to the Gentiles, this is one of the passages to which the apostle Paul appeals in Rom. 9: 25; while his brother-apostle Peter applies the same words to the present remnant of Israel in 1 Pet. 2: 10. Both Jew and Gentile stand now on the same ground before God; therefore the same passage may well apply to both, for the salvation of either is on the ground, not of legal works, but of pure grace.

and the children of Israel be gathered together, and appoint themselves one head, and they shall come up out of the land: for great shall be the day of Jezreel" (vers. 10, 11).

The reference to the sand of the sea carries us right back to the original covenant of pure grace made with Abraham, and confirmed by the oath of El Shaddai. God will not forego the promise made to the fathers, however great the failure of the children. A numberless host of reunited Israel and Judah shall yet be brought into blessing, never more to be forfeited, in the very land pledged to Abraham, to Isaac, and to Jacob, and stained with the blood of Jesus. This is not the return that took place under Cyrus. Very few from the ten tribes came back at that time, and all have since been driven out of their land because of the rejection of Messiah when He came, in accordance with prophecy, to offer Himself as King. When the Lord's set time has come, they shall return from all the lands whither they have been scattered, and shall no longer be divided, but be one happy, united people, under one Head, the once-rejected Jesus—the Christ of God. That will be the true day of Jezreel, when the field of blood will become again the vineyard of Jehovah, and they shall be sown of God in the land of their fathers, never to be rooted up again.

CHAPTER II

THE VALLEY OF ACHOR

GOD'S ways of grace and government are marvelously blended in this first recorded instance of the prophet's ministry, which follows closely on the promise in the last two verses of the previous chapter. In accordance with the assurance of future restoration and blessing, Jehovah cries, "Say ye unto your brethren, Ammi, and to your sisters, Ruhamah" (ver. 1). It is faith's anticipation of the time when the "Lo" (not) shall be removed, and they shall again be owned as His people, who have obtained mercy. This, of course, looks on for its accomplishment to the Millennium, when "all Israel shall be saved."* But it becomes true even now whenever a soul of either Israel or the nations turns to God in repentance, trusting the once-rejected Messiah.

It is to lead Israel to this place of self-judgment and abhorrence of her past ways that He so searchingly outlines her grievous sin in departing from Himself in verses 2 to 5. As a

---

* That is, the *remnant* of Israel: "Because a short work will the Lord make upon the earth." See Rom. 9: 27-29; Isa. 10: 20-23. The remnant then becomes the righteous seed for the millennial kingdom.—[Ed.

wretched harlot—nay, worse than such, an adulteress—He had to put her away. For, after all the love and grace lavished upon her, she had turned from Him to idols, in spiritual harlotry.

Because of this He will see that she eats of the fruit of her own devices. His dealings with her in His holy and righteous government are solemnly portrayed in verses 6 to 18. This is in full accord with Jeremiah's words, "Thine own wickedness shall correct thee, and thy backslidings shall reprove thee: know therefore and see that it is an evil thing and bitter, that thou hast forsaken the Lord thy God" (Jer. 2:19). It is in this way He makes sin to serve. If His people do not refrain their feet from evil, but persistently take their own course, and refuse to obey His voice, then they must be taught by their own sin the lesson they would not learn from His words of warning and admonition. Israel had forsaken Him for idols: she should be given up by Him for a time, and left to the idols of her own choosing for her correction; and in her trouble she would find none to answer (ver. 7). Broken-hearted and world-weary at last, chastened and disciplined by her experiences, she would cry, "I will go and return unto my first husband, for then was it better with me than now." Amazing the grace that, after such heartless abandonment on her part, would yet cause Him to open His arms to her again in the day of her genuine repentance.

It is the same love and grace that every weary sinner and every failing saint is made to know when he seeks God's face, confessing the sin and shame of his evil ways. No transgression is too great for Him to pardon, no evil-doing is too much for His mercy, if there be but a breaking-down before Him, and He be justified by the erring one, while the wrong-doer condemns himself.*

Touchingly Jehovah points out the insensibility of Israel as to the true source of all her past blessing. "She did not know," He says, "that *I* gave her corn, and wine, and oil, and multiplied her silver and gold, which *they* prepared for Baal" (ver. 8). The treasures He bestowed with lavish hand she had poured out upon the altars of her shame! Therefore He would withhold His favor until she learned that her false gods could bring her no good, but only sorrow and want of all things. One by one, all she valued would be stripped from her till she should learn that in Jehovah, whom she had so dishonored, was all blessing to be found. His gifts she had attributed to her idols, saying, "These are my rewards

---

* It is a sad and significant fact that the three words, "Condemn not thyself," form an oft-repeated motto among so-called Christian Scientists of our day. Thus they lock against themselves the door to all true blessing; for God can only justify the one who condemns himself and his ways.

that my lovers have given me" (ver. 12): but, bereft of all, she shall learn that she had been deluding herself and dishonoring Jehovah.*

When at last her lesson has been learned, Jehovah has purposes of grace in store for her which will be fully revealed upon her repentance. This is the precious and tender theme of the balance of the chapter. "Therefore, behold, I will allure her, and bring her into the wilderness, and speak comfortably unto her" (Heb., speak to her heart). "And I will give her her vineyards from thence, and the valley of Achor (Trouble) for a door of hope: and she shall sing there, as in the days of her youth, and as in the day when she came up out of Egypt" (vers. 14, 15). He loves to remember the days of her first betrothal to Himself, when she went after Him into the wilderness, into a land that was not sown; when she was holiness unto the Lord, and her heart was fixed upon Him alone. Those happy days of her first love are to be renewed. Once more He will allure and draw her away from the scenes of her captivity and dishonor. Alone with Himself in the wilderness of the peoples (see Ezek. 20:35), He will plead with her face to face. Her vineyards of joy will He restore, and the valley of

---

* For a striking instance of what is here portrayed, see Jer. 44:15-23. There the remnant actually trace their temporal mercies back to their idolatrous rites.

Achor (of trouble) shall become an opening of expectation. Achor was the scene of Achan's judgment, as recorded in Josh. 7: 24-26. Defiled by her unholy departure from her God and coveting of the accursed thing, Israel's blessing shall begin when the sin that has troubled her is judged and put away. Then, restored to Him from whom she had wandered so long, she shall sing (or, perhaps, respond) as in the days of her early freshness, as in the days of her coming out of Egypt.

The application to the individual soul is simple and natural. For the backslidden child of God who, having learned the folly of departure from the Eternal Lover of his soul, returns to Him, stoning his Achans, and thus putting away the accursed thing, the joy of early days will be restored, and communion, long lost, be once more enjoyed.

In the day of Israel's restoration she shall be owned as the wife of Jehovah. It is important to notice the difference between her place and portion and that of the Bride of the Lamb in Rev. 19 and 21. The one is earthly; the other, heavenly. The former is not called a bride, because she is a restored wife, who had long wandered from her husband. The latter is presented as the bride for the first time at the marriage-supper of the Lamb in heaven. In the Millennium, the Lamb and His heavenly bride will reign over all redeemed creation. On the earth the restored wife of Jehovah will have her place in the land of Palestine. The New Jerusalem above is the capital city of the first; the rehabilitated Jerusalem on earth that of the second. Then will the words be fulfilled, "And it shall be at that day, saith the Lord, that thou shalt call Me Ishi (*i. e.*, my Husband); and shalt call Me no more Baali (*i. e.*, my Lord, or my Master). For I will take away the names of Baalim out of her mouth, and they shall no more be remembered by their name" (vers. 16, 17). These will be the days of Isa. 54: 6, "For the Lord hath called thee as a woman forsaken and grieved in spirit, and a wife of youth, when thou wast refused, saith thy God." Then shall the land become the land of Beulah, and both land and people be manifestly Jehovah's.

Of this joyous period the prophets treat in large measure. It is the day of the glory of the kingdom, when Jesus shall be owned as "the blessed and only Potentate" by the world that once rejected Him.

It will be a time of universal diffusion of spiritual light and blessing. But not only that, the curse shall be lifted from the ground, and the lower creation be brought into the liberty of the glory for which it has groaned so long (Rom. 8: 22). "In that day will I make a covenant for them with the beasts of the field, and with the fowls of heaven, and with the creeping things of the ground: and I will break the bow and the sword and the battle out of the earth, and will make them to lie down safely" (ver. 18). All this is the result of the exaltation of the Son of Man of the 8th psalm, whose beneficent sway all creation shall rejoice in. Isa. 11 strikingly sets forth the blessings of that halcyon age, the true golden age, to be ushered in by the return of the Lord Jesus from heaven, who is to shepherd the nations with a rod of iron (Ps. 2; Rev. 19).

Nor shall Israel ever prove unfaithful again. The blotted history of the past will be forgotten, or remembered only to emphasize the grace that shall have restored. "And I will betroth thee unto Me forever" is Jehovah's word; "yea, I will betroth thee unto Me in righteousness, and in judgment, and in loving-kindness, and in mercies: I will even betroth thee unto Me in faithfulness: and thou shalt know the Lord" (vers. 19, 20). Not to the Church do these words refer, but to literal Israel, who, upon the expiration of the now fast-concluding "times of the Gentiles," will be grafted in again into the olive-tree of promise, restored to God and to their land, and made the inheritors of the promises assured to the fathers. A careful reading of such portions as Rom. 11; Jer. 30; 31; Ezek. 36: 22-38, and 37 should make clear to the least-instructed reader that God has not cast off His ancient people forever. When He restores them, it will be in pure grace, on the ground of the New Covenant, sealed already with the blood of His Son. Nothing shall ever destroy that hallowed union, or again divorce the earthly spouse from Jehovah.

A lovely millennial picture concludes the chapter. "And it shall come to pass in that day, I will hear, saith the Lord, I will hear the heavens, and they shall hear the earth; and the earth shall hear the corn, and the wine, and the oil; and they shall hear Jezreel. And I will sow her unto Me in the earth; and I will have mercy upon her that had not obtained mercy; and I will say to them which were not My people, Thou art My people; and they shall say, Thou art my God" (vers. 21-23). This passage may be a little plainer if we read "respond to" or "answer" in place of "hear." In the soon-coming day of Messiah's glory, heaven and earth shall together be united in the blessing of "the times of restitution of all things spoken by the prophets."

The heavens, in which will dwell the glorified saints who have been raised or changed at the coming of the Lord, will respond to the joy of a redeemed earth, even as God Himself will respond to them. It will be a scene of blissful communion, never again to be broken, despite Satan's last effort to mar and ruin what God shall have wrought (Rev. 20: 7-10).

The earth, freed from the primeval curse, shall no longer yield thorns and briars, but shall respond with overflowing supplies of corn, and wine, and oil. The desert shall rejoice and blossom as the rose. No more in the sweat of his face shall man eat his bread with weariness, but, as though an animate thing, the earth shall ungrudgingly yield her treasures for the redeemed of the Lord.

To Jezreel all shall likewise respond. Israel will be sown as the seed of God in the very land that had once been stained with the blood of the righteous One, and since, in awful retribution, with their own blood.

There they shall take root downward and triumphantly spring upward, and the people called once Lo-Ruhamah shall become Ruhamah, while the Lo-Ammi sentence shall be forever repealed and they shall be called Ammi. In gladsome response they lift their eyes and hearts to Jehovah's throne, and with deepest reverence and self-abandonment exclaim, "My Mighty One!"

This shall be the closing scene of the day of Jezreel. No more shall sin and sorrow, war and desolation, sweep the plains of the field of blood, which shall become the scene of unmingled joy and blessing when Jesus is owned as Sovereign-Lord.

CHAPTER III

ISRAEL'S PRESENT AND FUTURE

THIS chapter, brief as it is, becomes of vast importance if one would understand the ways of God in regard to the earth and the earthly people. It is, one might say, the 11th of Romans of the Old Testament, and, read in connection with that portion, sheds much light on the mystery of Israel's present anomalous condition and the predictions concerning their future glory.

Once more the prophet's relation to his wife is taken up as an illustration. She who had been before denominated a harlot is now an adulteress. The difference in its application is readily perceived. Israel, utterly unworthy before Jehovah took them up in His wondrous grace, had—after their union with Himself had been sealed by covenant—proven more unworthy still, so that they are likened, not only by Hosea, but other prophets also, to an adulteress, following strangers instead of her husband.

Here the language used is significant. The prophet is not told to love his wife. She had forfeited all claim to that relation. She is simply called "a woman," and he adds, "beloved of a friend;" that is, one who had, as we have seen, chosen another in place of her rightful spouse.

Hosea's love for so unworthy and worthless a creature was to be a picture of "the love of the (as shall be made manifest in the day of their restoration), yet they cannot now trace their genealogy; and if they could, there is no temple in which to officiate. Meantime the heavenly Priest ministers in the sanctuary above, but their eyes are holden, and they know Him not.

It might naturally be supposed that, being denied all the consolations of the religion of their fathers, they would have fallen again into the idolatrous practices of the heathen: but no; for we learn they were to abide "without an image," and "without teraphim." The Babylonian captivity cured them of idolatry. Since then, *that* at least has not been one of their national sins. They have no means of access to the true God while they revile and refuse His Anointed. On the other hand, they follow not after idols, but wait, like the redeemed wife of the prophet, till the day when they will again be publicly owned by Jehovah.

When the present dispensation is ended, and the Church has been translated to heaven, God will once more take them up in grace and fulfil the promises made to the fathers.* After passing through the unparalleled tribulation of the latter days, as predicted by Jeremiah (ch. 30), by Daniel (chs. 11 and 12), by Zechariah (chs. 12-

* For a fuller opening-up of Israel's past, present, and future see a book entitled "The Mysteries of God." The same author and publishers. Paper, 30 cts.; cloth, 75 cts.

Lord toward the children of Israel," who, professing themselves to be in covenant-relation with Him, yet "look to other gods and love grape-cakes" (ver. 1). The latter expression is the correct reading, in place of "flagons of wine," which has no specific reference to idolatry. The cakes were expressive of the idolatrous relation they were sustaining, as the reader may see by consulting Jer. 7: 18 and 44: 19. It was thus they honored her who in that day bore the title of "Queen of heaven"— a title which in apostate Christendom has been given to Mary the mother of our Lord, and that in direct defiance of Scripture.

Gomer (for I doubt not she is indeed the "woman" the passage speaks of) seems to have so involved herself that only by paying a redemption price can she be released from her wretched and degrading position; so the prophet "bought her to him for fifteen pieces of silver, and for a homer of barley, and a half homer of barley"—the purchase-price of a common slave, thus illustrating the words of Isaiah, "Ye have sold yourselves for naught, and ye shall be redeemed without money"* (Isa. 52: 3). Tenderly had Jehovah entreated them through the same prophet to "Return unto Me, for I have redeemed thee" (ch. 44:

* I take "without money" to mean that *they* had no money to redeem themselves with—so had to be redeemed by another.

22). But though the purchase-price was paid at Calvary's cross, Judah and Israel are wayward still, and the marriage-covenant has not been renewed.

Hosea says to Gomer, "Thou shalt abide for me many days; thou shalt not play the harlot, and thou shalt not be for another man: so will I also be for thee" (ver. 3); that is, a period of testing, undefined in duration, is to pass ere she shall be restored to conjugal privileges.

The application is made by the Holy Spirit in the closing verses, "For the children of Israel shall abide many days without a king, and without a prince, and without a sacrifice, and without an image, and without an ephod, and without teraphim, afterward shall the children of Israel return, and seek the Lord their God, and David their king; and shall fear the Lord and His goodness in the latter days" (vers. 4, 5). In these two verses we have succinctly set forth their whole state for this entire dispensation, as also the future blessing that is to be theirs in the day of the kingdom, when it is displayed in power and glory.

The "many days" run throughout the whole present period until the fulness of the Gentiles shall be completed.

Ever since the destruction of Jerusalem by the Romans they have answered to the description here given. They have been a nation of wanderers, with no national standing, "without a king, and without a prince." The sceptre has departed from Judah and the lawgiver from between his feet—solemn witness of the fact that Shiloh is already come, but come only to be rejected by them. Thus they are left without a sacrifice, for their temple is destroyed and their altar profaned. From nation to nation, and from city to city, they have wandered through the centuries; a homeless, often-hated people, despised by man and without means of approach to God on the ground of the law which they have broken.

Ritual and Talmudic lore have in large measure taken the place of God's appointed ordinances and the authority of the "Torah" (the law) among them. But from year to year they have to confess in anguish, as they beat their breasts, "Woe unto us, for we have no Mediator!" The smoke of sacrifice ascends not to heaven; the blood of atonement is not sprinkled within the veil in any earthly sanctuary; and blindness in part having wrapped them in judicial darkness, they know not that by the one offering of the Lord Jesus on the cross iniquity is taken away and sin purged, because eternal redemption has been found in that precious blood.

Thus not only are they without a sacrifice, but without a priest also—"without an ephod"—for all records have long been lost: and though many survive who are in the direct line of priesthood

14), and by our Lord Himself in Matt. 24 and kindred scriptures, they shall "return and seek the Lord their God, and David their king; and shall fear [or the Hebrew may be rendered, 'shall hasten to'] the Lord, and His goodness." It will be the fulfilment of that to which all the prophets have looked forward, when Israel's wanderings shall be over, their sins blotted out, themselves renewed, and the kingdom confirmed to them. In that day Jesus will be King over all the earth, sitting upon the throne of His father David, and reigning in glorious power and majesty. It would seem, too, from a careful comparison of this passage with the latter part of Ezekiel's prophecy, that a lineal descendant of David's line (called "the prince") shall exercise regency on earth over the restored nation, under the authority of Him whose capital city will be the new and heavenly Jerusalem, the "city that hath foundations, whose builder and maker is God."

Thus shall the years of Israel's mourning be ended, and the day of Messiah's glory have arrived; for the two synchronize. There can be no full blessing for Israel and the earth till the tragedy of Calvary is repented of, and Jew and Gentile unite in owning their sin in crucifying the Lord of glory and killing the Prince of life.

Till then, the unhappy condition delineated in the next chapter must continue—save that the curse of idolatry has been done away, as we have seen.

CHAPTER IV

JOINED TO IDOLS

THE statement we have just been considering (that Israel should abide many days without an image or teraphim), seems all the more remarkable when we remember the gross idolatry into which they had fallen at the time when Hosea was divinely called to declare the mind of Jehovah regarding their state. Idolatry was then the characteristic condition; and from it, as from a parent-stem, sprang all the other evils for which the prophet was obliged to rebuke them.

Because truth had departed, and with it, mercy and all knowledge of God, Jehovah had a controversy with the inhabitants of the land. His holy eye beheld only swearing, lying, murder, theft, and adultery, in place of holiness and fidelity to Himself. The covenant entered into at Sinai had been broken in every particular. Not one of the ten words remained inviolate on their part. For all this He must set His face against them in His righteous government, as He had warned them He would, through the lips of the law-giver himself (vers. 1-3).

So utterly fallen and wretched were they that none was fit to reprove another. All were alike sharers in the common guilt. The leaven of idolatry openly introduced in the wilderness, though secretly carried from Egypt and even from beyond the Euphrates (Josh. 24:2), had been working unjudged until they were utterly perverted; —so true is it that "evil communications corrupt good manners." They had become like those who "strive with the priest:" that is, they persistently refused to subject themselves when the mind of God was made known (ver. 4).

The lesson for us is a solemn one. Another has well said that evil never dies of old age. Sin unjudged among the people of God becomes like a fretting leprosy or a cancerous sore, ever working and extending its ramifications till the whole mass becomes defiled.

With Israel it was not ignorance that led to their downfall in the first place; though, necessarily, light refused resulted in darkness. They were like those who fall in the day, even their prophets doing likewise. Hence they must be cut off (ver. 5).

"My people are destroyed through lack of knowledge." Such was Jehovah's lament. But the lack of knowledge was the certain result of their own refusal to hearken. He had pressed His truth upon them, but they would have none of it. Therefore He adds, "Because thou hast rejected knowledge, I will also reject thee, that thou shalt be no priest to Me: seeing thou hast forgotten the law of thy God, I will also forget thy children" (ver. 6). Light rejected results in deeper darkness than ever, and involves the offender in sore trouble, and rejection from God.

Often in the history of the Church has a similar state existed to what we have here, and always the issue is the same. When in the 16th century God raised up Luther to sound, with clarion voice, the battle-cry of the Reformation, "The just shall live by faith!" the mass of the professing Church had no ear for the message, and sank into deeper superstition and folly. The Wesleys and their co-laborers, later, were ordained of God to arouse the lifeless profession of their day with a call to repentance, but the majority refused to hearken, and formalism became more formal and ritualism gained its harvest of lost souls.

When at the beginning of the last century the truths of the unity of the Body of Christ and the presence of the Holy Ghost were recovered, the apostles of what were incorrectly called, "The new doctrines," were ridiculed, abused and reproached. As a result, Christendom is rapidly going into apostasy, and the presence of the Holy Ghost is unknown in many places. The Scriptures are rejected as God's revelation and put on a par with human writings, while pride and arrogance are the order of the day. The Lord's words are having a solemn and awful fulfilment,

"If therefore the light that is in thee be darkness, how great is that darkness" (Matt. 6:23).

Is the reader one to whom light has come, which you are afraid or unwilling to obey? Remember that when you act in accordance with the mind of God as made known to you through His Word, your path shines brighter and brighter unto the perfect day. On the other hand, revealed truth wilfully ignored, or still worse, refused, has a hardening effect upon the conscience. We have known of persons who had learned from Scripture certain truths which, if acted upon, would have delivered them from worldly ways and worldly religious associations, and given them liberty to go forth unto the rejected One, bearing His reproach. They hesitated because of possible worldly loss, or of probable family difficulties. Seeking an easier path to that marked out in the Book, they argued down their consciences and quenched the Spirit of God. Behold the sad result! Bereft of spiritual power, shorn of their strength, the truths they once enjoyed have become as a dead letter to them; their consciences are calloused and their testimony for God is over. In vain they may talk of, and endeavor to make sacrifices on other lines, but this will not do for Him who has said, "To obey is better than sacrifice, and to hearken than the fat of rams" (1 Sam. 15:22).

Israel's solemn history may well be a warning

to us of the dire consequences of resisting the truth, "As they were increased, so they sinned against Me: therefore will I change their glory into shame" (ver. 7). Prosperity had not turned their hearts to Him, but the contrary, so He must deal with them according to their deserts. Delighting in their iniquity and ignoring God's word, He would give them up to destruction; and priest and people should suffer together. In their path of self-pleasing they should learn to their cost that there is nothing satisfying apart from going on with Him. Their unholy ways would but "take away the heart," and they should stumble and fall "because they have left off to take heed to the Lord" (vers. 8-11).

They were ready to ask counsel of their idols, but were too haughty and self-sufficient to turn to Him to whom they owed every blessing! It has often been noticed that when people get away from God they can be most punctilious about self-imposed rites and superstitious observances, while counting it a hardship to obey the voice of the Lord. The same is true as to credulity and faith. He who finds it difficult to trust the simplest statement of the Holy Scriptures can accept with amazing ease the most remarkable hypotheses and notions of unbelieving theorists. So was it with Israel at this time. Nothing that their false gods were supposed to demand was too much for them; but the law of Jehovah they could not away with; "Therefore," said He against whom they had so openly transgressed, "the people that doth not understand shall fall" (vers. 12-14). These things are among those "written for our admonition." Oh, for grace to *learn* and act accordingly. It was this the prophet sought to press on Judah. "Though thou, Israel, play the harlot, yet let not Judah offend!" (ver. 15). But, alas, later on we find the southern kingdom in like apostasy to the northern.

Because Israel had been given over to sliding back, "like a backsliding heifer," God would, as it were, give them their way. They should be as a lamb feeding in a large place, left free to go all lengths, but with certain judgment coming: for though they thought they were pleasing themselves, they were like lambs fattening for the slaughter. The word had gone forth, "Ephraim is joined to idols: let him alone!" (vers. 16, 17).

"Joined to idols: let him alone!" Nothing can be more solemn than this. It is as though God had exhausted every possible means for their recovery, save one, and that one the giving them up to learn, by *bitter experience,* what they would not take to heart in any other way. In the New Testament it answers to being "delivered unto Satan for the destruction of the flesh, that the spirit may be saved in the day of the Lord Jesus." (See 1 Cor. 5.) When a soul proves utterly stubborn and wilful, God may at times say of him as of Israel, "he is joined to his idols." Further reproof or brotherly correction is useless. Let him severely alone, till he learns in Satan's sieve how far he has got from God and how low he has fallen. Observe: it is only after the failure of all other means to recover the wanderer that God so deals with souls. It was when His patience had come to an end, as it were, that He gave up Ephraim. From the first He had borne with them, ministered to them, chastened, entreated, and disciplined them; but all had been in vain. They were set on having their own way. At last, because He loved them too much to finally give them up forever, He says, "Let them alone." Now they are where they shall learn by sad experience the full result of departure in heart from Himself. They should be given up to their own hearts' lusts till they should "be ashamed because of their sacrifices" (vers. 18, 19).

How deep the love that breathes through all this unhappy description. How tender the grace that persisted to the end in seeking the restoration of those so worthless and so undeserving!

And for us too, it is precious to know that His grace is unchanging; and if saved by that precious blood of Christ, we are the objects of that

> "Faithful and forbearing love
> That never turns aside."

Surely, nothing should have so powerful an effect upon our ways, as the fact that our waywardness has not, cannot, quench *His* love. No change in us results in any corresponding change in Him. Therefore we are bidden, "Grieve not the Holy Spirit of God, whereby ye are sealed unto the day of redemption." It is not to grieve Him *away*, as people often mistakenly insist it means, for then the words would be in the nature of a threat, instead of the exhortation to every child of God, which comes home to us with the force of so tender an entreaty. How base the soul who would take advantage of love so immeasurable to follow its own bent, and thus do despite to the Spirit of grace!

CHAPTER V

I WILL HIDE MYSELF

THIS chapter is replete with searching ministry for the consciences of the people of God in all ages, which we of the present latitudinarian times will do well to lay to heart. It may be part of a single discourse of which the previous chapter is the introduction, and the balance of the book the remainder; or the various sections may have been penned at different intervals, as the prophet was led of God to write them. In either case the moral value is the same, and the object is one throughout, namely, to bring the backslidden people into the presence of God, that they may be restored in soul, and taste the sweets of companionship and communion with the Everlasting One.

Priests, people, and the royal house, are all alike addressed in ver. 1, and told that judgment is toward them. It had not yet come; but it was as an angel of wrath with drawn sword facing their way, and naught but repentance could cause that sword to be sheathed.

In vain they had been rebuked by Him to whose eyes all things are naked and open. Their iniquity was ever before Him; but though He had sought their recovery so long, they persistently refused to "frame their doings to turn unto their God." A malignant demon, "the spirit of whoredoms," seemed to possess them, and they knew not the Lord (vers. 1-4).

Nor was this the worst. Despite their wretched condition, they were puffed up with haughtiness. "The pride of Israel doth testify to his face." Because of this they must be brought low. "Therefore shall Israel and Ephraim fall in their iniquity; Judah also shall fall with them" (ver. 5). Failing to learn by the sin of her sister, Judah had followed in the same path, and she too must be cast out of the land under the judgment of God.

The sentence of Lo-Ammi, referred to in the first chapter, cannot be turned aside. Even though there *seem* to be a desire after God, they shall not find Him; for they had hated knowledge and despised all His reproof.

When people refuse light, the light is withdrawn, and they are given up to judicial darkness. So here we read: "They shall go with their flocks and with their herds [for sacrifice] to seek the Lord; but they shall not find Him; He hath withdrawn Himself from them" (ver. 6). Thus should be fulfilled the word spoken through Moses long years before: "I will hide My face from them, I will see what their end shall be: for they are a very froward generation, children in whom is no faith" (Deut. 32:20).

Observe, God would not forget them, nor should they be finally cast out of His presence; but He would withdraw Himself from them, leaving them to spiritual famine and desolation till they realized their true condition, and owned it before Him.

In the present dispensation of grace we are not without instances of similar dealing. It was thus the Lord acted in the case of the Gadarenes. Finding them bent upon going their own way, He left them for a time, but was welcomed by them on His return. And indeed this incident pictures to us His rejection when He came at first, but points too to the day when He shall return in glory, and shall be welcomed by the cry, "Blessed is He who comes in the name of Jehovah!" All this is in full accord with Hosea's prophecy.

Till repentance ensues, He will not publicly manifest Himself on their behalf. They may go on in their pride, begetting strange children and boasting of progress and enlargement, but all is hollow and empty, for the Judge is at the door (ver. 7).

From vers. 8 to 14 the prophet seems to have the invading army in sight. "The day of rebuke" is almost upon Israel. In vain they blow the trumpet and seek to defend themselves. In vain they attempt an alliance with Assyria. It is but leaning on a broken reed. God has become as an enemy, and He it is with whom they have to do. To both Ephraim and Judah He will be as a destroying lion, from whose power none shall deliver them.

But, be it noted, in all this He is seeking their blessing still. So He says, "I will go and return to My place, till they acknowledge their offence, and seek My face: in their affliction they will seek Me early" (ver. 15).

How clearly is the Spirit of Christ here discerned to be speaking in the prophet. The same conditions prevailed when the Lord Jesus presented Himself that were characteristic of Hosea's day. True, idolatry was done away; but pride, arrogancy and self-will abounded on every hand. Consequently, "He came unto His own, but His own received Him not." Therefore He had to say, "I will go and return to My place." If they had no room for Him here, the Father had a seat for Him on His throne. So He left their house desolate, and has gone up on high, where He waits till they acknowledge their offence. The great tribulation—the time of Jacob's trouble—will result in a remnant seeking His face in contrition of heart. Then He will no longer hide Himself, but shall appear as their Deliverer in manifested glory.

CHAPTER VI

WHAT SHALL I DO UNTO THEE?

THE opening verses (1 to 3) connect intimately with what we have just been considering, while the balance of the chapter is another appeal to the consciences of Ephraim and Judah.

Nothing could be more suited than the expression of these first three verses upon the lips of the restored remnant in the coming day of His power whose face has so long been hidden from them: "Come, and let us return unto the Lord: for He hath torn, and He will heal us; He hath smitten, and He will bind us up. After two days will He revive us: in the third day He will raise us up, and we shall live in His sight. Then shall we know, if we follow on to know the Lord: His going forth is prepared as the morning; and He shall come unto us as the rain, as the latter and former rain unto the earth."

It is the cry of the returning residue who have learned to know the Lord in the smoking furnace of the tribulation period, and who now ask the way to Zion, and with chastened spirits return unto the One so long despised. The awakening in the 12th chapter of Zechariah links closely with what we have here. Like Naomi, they recognize that He it is who has torn and smitten them; but faith counts on Him for healing and enlargement.

After two days of solemn testimony to their consciences, leading to manifest repentance, He revives them on the third day; answering to the day upon which the water of separation was sprinkled upon the unclean man (Num. 19), that he might be declared clean upon the seventh day. Thus they who once were defiled by the dead are made to live in His sight. So when He descends in glory like showers upon the grass, they find revival and blessing, with daily growth in the knowledge of Himself in His kingdom throughout the age to come.

But, alas, though this shall indeed be when they are made willing in the day of His power, they were far from being in that happy state when the prophet Hosea was sent among them. The lovely millennial picture is presented but for a moment ere the Spirit of God goes on to deal with them because of their wretchedly fallen condition, and to plead in tenderest beseechings that they turn from their evil ways.

There had once been what seemed like a desire to be true to Himself, but it had proven to be but transitory. "O Ephraim," He cries, "what shall I do unto thee? O Judah, what shall I do unto thee? for your goodness is as a morning cloud, and as the early dew it goeth away" (ver. 4). Like Ephesus of a later day, it was but for a brief season that they clung to their first love. The tender feelings of those early days, when they went after Him into the wilderness, had been evanescent indeed, and had now vanished like the dew when the sun rises in its strength. Because of this, in place of sending prophets to gladden their spirits, He had been obliged to give them a ministry like that afterwards given through John the Baptizer, laying the axe unto the root of the trees, which in their pride rose up in such loftiness (ver. 5). The distinction might be made that the prophets of old were more like men sent to prune and hew away all excrescences, thus endeavoring to trim the trees and purge them, with a view to fruitfulness. But all their efforts were in vain; so John came to lay the axe unto the *root* of the trees. All must come down. Recovery was hopeless. The first man could bring forth nothing for God. He must be superseded by the Second! This is the great difference between the closing books of the Old Testament and the opening message of the New.

Mere outward correctness and attention to forms and ceremonies would not do for God. His word is, "I desired mercy, and not sacrifice; and the knowledge of God more than burnt offerings" (ver. 6). Isaiah similarly declared the incompatibility of mere ritualistic observances when the heart was far from the Lord. See Isa. 58, *et al.* God must have reality. All else is but hollow mockery in His sight who is of purer eyes than to behold iniquity.

Like Adam (see margin, ver. 7), they had transgressed the covenant. God had made known His will to them, but they had violated His every command, following the lust of the flesh, the lust of the eye, and the pride of life. Thus had they dealt treacherously with Him whose servants they professed to be.

And Gilead, so greatly favored naturally, had become a city of iniquity, and stained with blood (ver. 8). A priestly city, it should have been holy to the Lord; but these godless sacerdotalists were but as troops of robbers, plundering those they should have led in the right way; living in uncleanness too, instead of in God's holy ways. The leaders of the people caused them to err, and led them astray from the paths of truth.

Who can fail to see the same ungodly conditions developing now in Protestantism, so-called? The open debauchery of the well-named "Dark Ages" has been checked by the light of an open Bible, which has made men ashamed of what they once dared to revel in, in the darkness and ignorance of Romanism and medieval times. But now Satan's supreme effort is to poison the minds of men by the unholy speculations of infidel clerics who give free rein to the filthiness of the spirit, and use their positions as "leaders of Christian thought" to enrich themselves while starving the true flock of Christ and poisoning those who, while bearing the name of Christians, are destitute of divine grace! Terrible must be the end when false religion is judged in the day of the Lord's anger!

In vain the warning voice was raised of old. In vain it is raised today. The mass, then and now, went recklessly on their way, heedless of His solemn rebuke. "I have seen a horrible thing in the house of Israel: there is the harlotry of Ephraim, Israel is defiled" (ver. 10).

The last verse seems to admit of a double interpretation. For Judah a harvest is appointed when their captivity shall be brought again. It might mean that God would get His harvest, whatever man's failure, when they are at last restored to Himself; but as Judah alone is mentioned, while the guilt of both had just been proclaimed, I judge the harvest referred to is that awful one of judgment yet to be reaped because of the rejection of Messiah. Judah must pass through this, as we have already noticed, just prior to their restoration and blessing. The ten tribes, as such, had no part in the rejection of the Lord Jesus. It was not on them the rabid elders invoked the curse when they cried, "His blood be on us, and on our children!" Consequently, for *Judah* a terrible harvest is yet to come. They sowed the wind: they shall reap the whirlwind, when the vials of the wrath of God are poured out upon the prophetic earth.

CHAPTER VII

A CAKE NOT TURNED

JUDGMENT is God's strange work. He had no desire to punish the people He had taken into covenant-relation with Himself, but who had violated the covenant from the first. On the other hand, blessing and restoration had ever been offered them, conditioned on repentance. But when He would have healed Israel — had there been any evidence of self-judgment — He had to say "the iniquity of Ephraim was discovered, and the evils of Samaria: for they commit falsehood; and the thief cometh in and the troop of robbers spoileth without" (ver. 1). No sign of contrition for all their offences could His holy eye detect, only sin and lawlessness deliberately persisted in, despite every entreaty to cease therefrom. In carnal security they considered not in their hearts that He remembered all their wickedness, till "their own doings" had beset them round, so that they were openly before His face. Their rulers delighted in the debauched state into which they had fallen, taking an unholy satisfaction in the dishonesty and wickedness prevailing (vers. 2, 3).

In verse four, a most significant picture is presented for our contemplation. "They are all adulterers, as an oven heated by the baker, who ceaseth from raising after he hath kneaded the dough until it be leavened." The leaven of unrighteousness had long since been secretly working in the nation, but now was energetically and openly corrupting the whole. Satan's effort had been only too successful. Idolatry having been early introduced, and never thoroughly judged, had permeated the entire nation. To this passage the apostle Paul doubtless would have directed the minds of the Corinthian saints when he wrote, "Know ye not that a little leaven leaveneth the whole lump?" Upon the Galatians he also pressed the same serious principle (1 Cor. 5:6; Gal. 5:9).

Leaven, in Scripture, never typifies that which is good; it is always significant of some form of evil. Here we see all Israel leavened with the unholy system of idolatry, with its corrupting influences, doing its deadly work for centuries. Once the leaven is inserted in the dough, the baker knows it will act according to its nature; he sleeps now through the night, but the oven is prepared for the morning. The oven was to be the furnace of judgment.

In Christendom we see the same thing. The Lord Jesus told of a woman who hid leaven in three measures of meal till the whole was leavened. Be it noted: there is no such thing as the "leaven of the gospel." Of the leaven of the

Pharisees, of the Sadducees and of the Herodians we are warned. They seem to speak of hypocrisy, false teaching and worldliness. The leaven of malice and wickedness we are told of in 1 Cor. 5; but of the leaven of *grace* there is not a hint in the sacred writings. Consequently we infer that just as, in Israel, the leaven of idolatry was introduced when they made the calf in the wilderness, and, being never fully judged, worked on till it had permeated the whole nation; so, early in the Church's history, did a woman, the false church, insert the leaven of error into the food of the people of God, which has never since been put away, but is rapidly leavening the whole lump: it is identical with the mystery of iniquity of which the Holy Ghost warns us in the second chapter of the second epistle to the Thessalonians, which will soon be headed up in Babylon the Great and the Antichrist.*

Believers are called upon to "purge out the old leaven," whenever it is made manifest in their assemblies. If, however, the mass are already so corrupted that there is no activity in obeying the word of the Lord, he who would be "a vessel unto honor, sanctified and meet for the Master's use," must purge himself from the unholy mixture, walking in separation from that which is

---

* For a fuller consideration of this solemn theme, see chapter eight of "The Mysteries of God." Same author and publishers. Paper covers, 30 cts.; cloth, 75 cts.

opposed to the holiness that becomes God's house, and finding his fellowship with those who "follow righteouness, faith, love, peace," and "call upon the Lord out of a pure heart" (see 2 Tim. 2: 16-22).

For Israel there was no hope. The entire body politic was symbolized in the king at their head, made sick with the wine of fleshly exultation and stretching out his hand with the scorners. Their own hearts were as the oven of the baker, who could sleep in the night while the leaven wrought, and the fire was prepared to heat the oven for the baking of the coming day. Thus they themselves should work out their own judgment, because there were none who called upon God (vers. 5-7).

"Ephraim, he hath mixed himself among the people [as one with the nations]; Ephraim is a cake not turned. Strangers have devoured his strength, and he knoweth it not: yea, gray hairs are here and there upon him, yet he knoweth it not. And the pride of Israel testifieth to his face: and they do not return to the Lord their God, nor seek Him for all this" (vers. 8-10). It is their unconsciousness of their true condition which this section emphasizes. Like a cake placed upon the coals and forgotten by the house-wife, till, left unturned, it is all burned on one side; so they were quite indifferent to their actual state before God. The mass taking no heed to the prophet's warnings, went carelessly on in their own way, taking it for granted that all was as it should be, when, in reality, everything was all wrong. It is this apparently unconscious backsliding that is so sad a feature in many today. Away from the Lord, yet professing, and even supposing, that all is well—how many are thus like a cake not turned! This one-sidedness is what tells the tale to an observant, anointed eye, that something is radically wrong in many a case. Often saints make much of the truth as a matter of doctrine while allowing themselves to become utterly negligent as to walking in that truth from day to day. They are like a cake not turned, all brown on one side and raw dough on the other. Doctrinally, they may be very particular. Practically, they are loose and unconcerned.

At other times the case is just reversed: much is made of experience, with little or no heart for what is slightingly termed "dry doctrine." But it is as necessary to "hold fast the form of sound words," as it is to seek to live in a godly way. In fact, doctrine is the root of all practice; and our experience will prove a very faulty one if it be not the result of a knowledge of the mind of God as revealed in His Word.

Let us never forget that truth and practice go together, even as position and condition must never be divorced.

Ephraim's first grave mistake was in mixing

himself among the people. God had called Israel to dwell alone, and not be reckoned among the nations. Nothing but evil ever resulted from mixing with those from whom they had once been separated. It was "the mixed multitude" who first caused them trouble in the wilderness, and started their murmuring and longing for Egyptian food in place of the bread from heaven —type of our Lord Jesus Christ come down in grace to meet His people's need. See Exod. 16; Num. 11; and compare with John 6. Again, when Balaam could not curse because God had blessed, he taught Balak to cast a stumbling-block before the children of Israel by causing them to mix with the daughters of Moab; the result of which brought dire judgment upon them —stayed only by the javelin of Phinehas.

This mixing among the people was the ruin of Samson, the mighty Nazarite, who gave up the secret of his strength when he lay upon the lap of Delilah. Alas, how many a valiant servant of God has become weak as other men in a similar way since!

And so we might trace the same evil practice all down through the history of the chosen race, until at last it ended in their being cast out by the Lord, in judgment, to mix among the nations till they should have their fill of the society of the strangers who devoured their strength and brought them to desolation.

The lesson is an important and salutary one for us who have been called with a higher calling, and are commanded to walk apart from a godless world and a corrupt Church. Indifference as to this separation of the clean from the unclean has had a lamentable effect upon the testimony and experience of thousands. Yet we learn so slowly. Oh, that there were in us hearts to cleave to the Lord, heeding His word, "Come out from among them, and be ye separate!"

It is as vain to hope to reform and recover what is not of God, by intermingling therewith in fellowship and intimate association, as it would be to try to teach sparrows or linnets to sing like a warbler by placing a canary in a cage with them. The only result would be that the canary would lose its song, while the sparrows would chirp on as before. Alas, how many a once joyous saint has lost his song by mixing among the people of the world and the world-church! Such an one may boast of his liberality and breadth of mind, and be as unconscious as was Ephraim of the true state of affairs; but the spiritually-minded shake their heads in sorrow as they say, "Strangers have devoured his strength, and he knoweth it not: yea, gray hairs are here and there upon him, yet he knoweth not."

The gray hair is the sign of departing strength, and tells the tale that its owner is going downhill—age and decrepitude are coming on. But

Ephraim, like many another backslider in heart, was quite unaware of the true condition of affairs. In such a case others may note the gray hairs "here and there upon him"—the carelessness here—the indifference there—a growing fondness for worldly companionship—less and less time spent in prayer and over the Word of God—increased love for that which is light and frivolous—the name of Jesus less frequently upon the lips, and a growing fondness for conversation that is not for profit. Contrast with this 1 Tim. 4: 15, 16.

Accompanying this, will invariably be found an assumption of easy-going superiority. "The pride of Israel testifieth to his face;" but there will be no turning to God and seeking to get His mind regarding it all, till broken by discipline.

Ephraim, like a silly dove, without affection for Him that had carried them in His bosom, had turned to Egypt, then to Assyria, for help when the hour of trial came. But the Lord loved them too much to permit them to find anything stable in what spoke of the world and its vain pomp and show. So He would spread His net upon them, like one taking a bird in a snare. He cannot allow those who are in covenant-relationship with Him to go on in their own way for long (vers. 11, 12).

They had transgressed against Him, though He had redeemed them; reminding us of some in a later day, who, having drifted away from God, had "forgotten that they were purged from their old sins:" with supreme indifference to their actual state they blamed Him for what had come upon them as though they themselves were blameless; so that He charges them with speaking lies against Him. "I sometimes think," said one,* "that God has been hard with me, when I forget how hard I have been with God!" This is ever the tendency of a heart not before Him in self-judgment (ver. 13).

And so, for long years had they gone on, neither seeking Him when alone in the secrecy of their own chambers, upon their beds, nor when gathering together in what should have been a solemn assembly, but was really a season of godless merriment. "They howled upon their beds," but not in repentance, only bewailing His discipline instead of their own evil ways. Jehovah had indeed trained them to confide in Him, and strengthened their arm against their adversaries, but in recompense they think ill of Him, turning to any expediency rather than turning to God—so incorrigible is the heart of man, even of a saint, when away from God. So they must be left to sound deeper depths of sorrow and disaster, like the incestuous man of 1 Cor. 5, who was "delivered unto Satan for the destruction of the

* G. V. Wigram, a man of much devotedness—now with the Lord.

flesh, that the spirit might be saved in the day of the Lord Jesus." Their princes were to be destroyed, and they themselves would become a laughing-stock to their Egyptian allies, upon whom they had vainly depended (vers. 14-16).

Surely, the way of man is not in himself. It is not in man to direct his own steps. Therefore the need of brokenness of spirit and self-judgment before God, that He may lead in the paths of righteousness for His name's sake.

CHAPTER VIII

A VESSEL WHEREIN IS NO PLEASURE

GOD seems almost to exhaust figurative language in describing the unhappy condition of His deluded people, their hearts set on wandering from Him who was their only real good. We have already contemplated them in their wretchedly fallen estate, under the expressive symbols of an adulterous wife, a wine-inflamed drunkard, a backsliding heifer, troops of robbers, a leavened mass, a cake not turned, a silly dove, and a deceitful bow. Now they are warned that because of their sins they shall be scattered among the nations as "a vessel wherein is no pleasure."

This was the logical result of the covenant at Sinai, where they pledged themselves to obey all the words of the law, which promised blessing to all who kept it, but invoked a curse upon the violators of its precepts. According to this chapter, Israel had broken it at every point. Therefore, on that ground, they had nothing to claim. That God had wondrous resources of grace, yet to be manifested, the final chapter makes abundantly plain; but they would only come into the good of it when they owned their sin and gave up all pretension to merit.

The prophet, as it were, sounds the trumpet to summon the whole congregation into the presence of the Lord, that they may face the reality of their condition as a people who have transgressed the covenant and trespassed against the law (ver. 1).

In the second verse, we might understand a hint of future restoration: "Israel shall cry unto Me, My God, we know Thee." But it seems rather to imply their unconsciousness of their true state at that time, and during the years of their wanderings while under God's hand. With amazing effrontery, they cry, "My God, we, Israel, know Thee," as the R. V. puts it; while all the time they go on in their folly, having cast off the thing that is good, and so are driven before their enemies. They set up kings after their own heart, and make princes without asking Jehovah's counsel. Idolatry too is everywhere flourishing, and the temple service but a mockery (vers. 3, 4). Thus do they profess that they know God, but in works deny Him. How easy it is, alas, to fall into the truly lamentable state of soul here depicted! How many today talk of being the people of the Lord, or being "in the line of the testimony" (to use a vainglorious phrase popular in certain quarters), while all the time condoning unrighteousness and walking in disobedience to the Word of God. In His time our Lord had to say: "The scribes and Pharisees sit in Moses' seat: all therefore whatsoever they bid you observe, that observe and do; but do not after their works: for they say, and do not"—they could preach to others fairly well according to the Law, but their practice was the true indicator of their soul's condition—and how far from God! It should ever be remembered that while it is of prime importance to be in a right position as to ecclesiastical and other lines of truth, a merely correct position is a poor thing if there be not likewise a right condition of soul. Neither can be neglected without loss; but nothing can be worse than to be priding oneself on "maintaining divine ground," and going on "in the line of the testimony," while the life is defiled and the heart is insubject to the truth.

But the soul that turns from the living and true God to idols, of whatever nature, will learn at last what it is to be bereft and forsaken when help is most needed. The calf of Samaria cast them off. As with the priests of Baal in Elijah's day, they cried, but there was none that answered, nor any that regarded. And how could it be otherwise, when the work of their own hands was that in which they trusted! (vers. 5, 6).

Thus, having sown the wind, they had to reap the whirlwind, as many a soul has done before and since. Yet how slow we are to learn! *Theoretically,* all saints know that there can be no real blessing apart from walking with God; but *experimentally,* how easily most of us are lured aside, and led after other gods, when some opportunity seems to present itself for profit or advantage! But at last all have to realize that the only result of such sowing will be disappointment and sorrow. "The bud shall yield no meal: if so be it yield, the strangers shall swallow it up" (ver. 7).

Apply this to every department of life, and it will be found to be a rule to which there are no exceptions. Apparent success may seem to follow upon disobedience, but "the end is not yet." We may fancy God and His Word can be disregarded, but we shall prove in bitterness of soul that it is an evil thing indeed to choose our own path.

How many a broken-hearted wife could be cited as an example of the principle here enunciated; or how often a wretched and unhappy husband becomes a living illustration of it! God has plainly forbidden unequal yokes. The Word is clear, and the young saint has it pressed home upon the conscience. But one who seems to promise well as a suited life-partner crosses the path. Esteem develops into affection. Affection ripens into love. A proposal of marriage is made. Then begins a period of doubt and vacillation. God's Word is plain enough, but its clear precepts are forgotten. Amiable qualities are remembered. The fact that the other party is unsaved is glossed over. A readiness to go to the meetings of Christians, a willingness to listen to the Scripture, is magnified into a persuasion that a work of God has begun in the soul; and at last the other party, only too readily, is drawn into the snare. An unequal yoke is entered into, and a lifetime of regret follows. In by far the majority of cases the seeming interest in divine things passes away with the first few weeks of married life, and then, even if open opposition is not developed, a cold, studied indifference ensues in regard to eternal things that no kindness or consideration can cover up. Thus the child of God is doubly wretched as the sense of disobedience comes home to the, at last, awakened conscience; and the realization presses upon the soul that the one so loved has no concern about God or His Christ, and that, if not soon awakened and saved, two who loved each other on earth must be separated for all eternity.

And so in many other ways the same sad law is fulfilled, whether in business, social, or religious life. Oh that we might learn from what God has so plainly put before us in His Word, and from the unhappy experiences of thousands, the danger of trifling with conscience, and with the truth which sanctifies the obedient soul!

It was because of refusing thus to obey His Word that God had at last to say of His earthly people, "Israel is swallowed up: now shall they be among the Gentiles as a vessel wherein is no pleasure" (ver. 8). This describes in one verse their history for over two thousand years. Driven out of their land, scattered among all nations, they have been as a vessel in which God could take no delight. In this, how opposite to Him who came to save them! "This is My beloved Son, in whom I am well pleased," was the Father's announcement when, at His baptism, He offered Himself as the One who came to "do always those things that please Him," *i. e.*, the Father. He is the vessel of God's pleasure. Israel has become a vessel wherein is *no* pleasure. How marked the contrast!

It was in vain for them to turn to Assyria, or any of the surrounding nations. There could be no help for them while under the curse of the broken law. Like a wild ass, they had shown the untameableness of their nature. They knew not how to obey. So they must sorrow under the power of the Gentile oppressor whom God had made "a king of princes"—that is, Nebuchadnezzar, king of Babylon (vers. 9, 10; compare Ezek. 26: 7)—for God is evidently passing by the Assyrian, and has before His mind him to whom the Gentile dominion was first fully entrusted.

Ephraim had made many altars to sin, by offering sacrifice to demons, and not to God. His sin should return upon his own head (ver. 11).

The pith of all Jehovah's controversy with him is declared in ver. 12: "I have written to him the great things of My law, but they were counted as a strange thing." They were responsible to act in accordance with the written Word. They had failed to do so. Therefore the Judge was at the door. As with them, so it is with Christendom—never more manifest than at the present time—God's Word is despised and set at naught on all sides. The end, therefore, cannot now be far off.

Having despised the Word, it was useless to bring offerings and to sacrifice and eat flesh before the Lord. He could not accept worship from a disobedient and gainsaying people. He remembers their sins, and must deal with them because of their rejection of His law. Morally, they should return to Egypt, as in fact actually a remnant did in the last days of Jeremiah. "For Israel hath forgotten his Maker, and buildeth *temples!*" They cast His commandments behind their back, yet built temples where a pretended worship was offered. History repeats itself. The words might well describe what is so prevalent today. But the day of the Lord is coming; and, as of old, a fire shall be sent forth from God that will consume all the vain works of haughty men when the hour of Jehovah's wrath shall strike (vers. 13, 14).

Be it remembered, responsibility is always increased in accordance as God's truth is revealed. How solemn then the present moment, and how serious must be the results, if truth be held in the mind that does not change the life!

CHAPTER IX

THE DAYS OF VISITATION

EVEN an utter worldling is relatively happy as compared with a saint of God away in heart from Him whose child he is. This is what the opening verse emphasizes. "Rejoice not, O Israel, for joy, as other people: for thou hast gone a whoring from thy God." Nations who had never known the Lord might go on with a measure of rejoicing, in their ignorance and superstition; but for Israel, that could not be. Having once become the object of His loving-kindness, to whom He had revealed Himself as the one true and living God, they could never be happy in their sin again.

The very recollections of past joys, of hours and days when the soul delighted in God and found precious food in His Word, but make all the more cheerless the restless, unhappy experiences of the backslider in heart as he becomes filled with his own devices. And what a mercy to us that it is so! How grateful we may well be to our God and Father that we cannot be in the enjoyment of true peace and genuine happiness while out of communion with Him to whom we are indebted for every good we have.

It is true the soul away from Him may find a certain excitement and pleasurable exhilaration in the follies of earth; but they are only the "pleasures of sin for a season," and not to be compared to those precious realities which were before the soul of the psalmist when he sang, "At Thy right hand are pleasures for evermore!"

And so of fallen Israel, we read that the floor and the winepress should not satisfy them, and the new wine should fail. Nor should they dwell in the Lord's house, but return to Egypt, and feed on the unclean in Assyria. Having despised the service of the Lord, they should be cut off from His temple, and should not eat of His sacrifices (vers. 1-4).

Then he presses home the question, "What will ye do in the solemn day, and in the day of the feast of the Lord?" when, scattered among the heathen, they thought of past seasons of blessing, and remembered that once more a solemn feast-day had come round, but they were cut off from its privileges; what then would they do, and how would they be able to satisfy their souls?

How seldom do the people of God think of these things as they should! Lured on by the world, fired by unholy ambition and stimulated by pride, believers often allow themselves to be drawn away from the simplicity that is in Christ! Soon they who once took sweet counsel together as they wended their way to the gathering-place of those who loved their Saviour and the truth of God, are widely sundered. Souls who once were filled with sweet contemplations as they sat at the table of the Lord, remembering His love to us in His sufferings unto death, are now drifting away in darkness. What must be the feelings of such when, on the Lord's Day, they call to mind, amid scenes of worldly religiousness, or of irreligious worldliness, the sacred seasons once spent before the Lord with holy joy! To remember that, at the very hour when they are engaged in something which cannot have the Lord's approbation, saints once well known and loved are communing one with another, and with Himself, at the feast His loving heart led Him to institute to remind us of Him when He had passed from human sight—surely in such tender recollections there must be mingled a grief and a remorse not easily overcome!

Such, in their measure, should be the nature of Israel's memories as the appointed seasons for the passover, the solemn atonement-day, or the gladsome feast of tabernacles, came round; and they were scattered among strangers, and unable to participate in privileges once held so lightly. Gone from their land, a spoil to Egypt (typical of that world from which the believer has once been delivered), their precious things would be a prey to their enemies ("their silver shall be desired," see margin), and they themselves wounded by thorns and nettles—pierced through with many sorrows (ver. 6). What a desolate, yet graphic, picture of that which every backslidden soul must prove!

And in all this they would be but reaping as they had sown. They had said (and in solemn irony they are reminded of it), "The prophet is a fool, the spiritual man is mad!" So they had tried to quiet their consciences because of the multitude of their iniquities. Now, when all these things would have come to pass, they should know that "the days of visitation are come, the days of recompense are come" (ver. 7).

The watchman of Ephraim, who had sought to turn them from their evil way, was with God. But they had said, "The prophet is a snare of a fowler in all his ways," because of their hatred against the house of his God* (ver. 8). So easy is it to denounce one who faithfully rebukes sin, and strives to hinder declension in the soul. The leaven of Gibeah's wickedness (the record of which we have in the last chapters of the book of Judges) was still at work among them after these centuries. Sin never dies a natural death; it must be thoroughly *judged.* Like leaven, it is stopped by fire—by "judgment," *self*-judgment

---

* I understand verse 8 should read as follows: "The watchman of Ephraim was with God. [But] the prophet is a snare of a fowler in all his ways! [Because of] hatred against the house of his God."

or God's judgment; for sin ever works on until it is judged. When indulged in by an individual, or permitted in a company, it continues working, though often imperceptibly, until it is judged, either in oneself, or by God's people, or by God Himself. This is the solemn lesson here inculcated. Doubtless those addressed here had forgotten all about the days of Gibeah, or might have pleaded that the trouble at Gibeah happened centuries before they were born, and it was therefore useless to concern themselves about it. But God's holy eye saw deeper than this. He saw that the self-will and corruption manifested at Gibeah were still rampant among them, and called for humiliation and self-judgment before His face. This they ignored. Therefore He must visit them and remember their sins (vers. 8 and 9).

All this is intensely solemn, and may well exercise us in the present season of the Church's deep failure and ruin. Are we not a part of that house of God set up in responsibility upon earth? Do we bear on our hearts the sense of God's dishonor in that house, of which we form a part? May God give grace to both reader and writer to let the truth of it penetrate the heart and arouse the conscience; thus leading to a godly discernment as to what is opposed to the holiness that becometh His house, and self-judgment because of the part one has taken in helping on what is not of Himself. It is easy to judge others. We are called upon to judge ourselves. But true self-judgment will lead one to go back over the path of declension trodden by the people of the Lord with whom I am united in blessing and responsibility. This involves a quickened conscience, and is the very opposite to ecclesiastical pretension and spiritual pride.

In verse 10 God lingers lovingly over the early history of His people, when He found Israel like grapes in the wilderness—precious fruit for Himself in a dry and thirsty land. But, alas, how soon did that early freshness disappear! It was not long till "they went to Baal-peor, and separated themselves unto that shame." Balaam's wretched counsel was only too literally followed when he "taught Balak to cast a stumbling-block" before the separated nation. The daughters of Moab effected what all the enchantments of the false prophets could not do; "and their abominations were accordingly as they loved." Let the reader carefully study the whole account in Num. 25, and 31: 16, compared with Rev. 2: 14.

From the very beginning Ephraim had proven himself untrustworthy. Therefore his glory should fly away like a bird, and they should be bereaved till none were left. "Yea," said God, "woe also to them when I depart from them" (vers. 11, 12).

It should ever be borne in mind that the Spirit of adoption—the indwelling Spirit—who seals all true believers in the present dispensation of grace, will never depart from those whom God thus marks as His own—much as they may fail: but there is what evidently answers to it; namely, the Holy Spirit grieved, communion interrupted, and the Lord ceases to own one as a testimony for Himself when waywardness becomes characteristic.

Ephraim, once "planted in a pleasant place," could no longer be blessed with children. "Fruitfulness" is what the name Ephraim signified. But they should become fruitless and barren; or if children were born they would only be appointed to death (vers. 13, 14). Communion with God and fruit for God go together. Where the first is lacking, the desired result will be absent likewise.

Gilgal, once the place where the reproach of Egypt was rolled away, and the witness to their sanctification to the Holy One of Israel, was now but a testimony to their wickedness. Therefore He whom they had so dishonored would drive them from His house, and disown them, because of their revolt from Himself. When He says "I will love them no more," it is not that *His* heart or purposes had changed, but He would not openly interfere for them. He would give them up to their enemies as One who, so far as they could see, loved them no longer (ver. 15).

Thus, as above noted, Ephraim should belie his name. Smitten in chastisement, "they shall bear no fruit;" and even if they brought forth, His hand would be against them for destruction. In this way would God vindicate His holiness, casting them out of His sight, that they might become wanderers among the nations (vers. 16, 17). Moses had warned them of this from the beginning; but they had given no heed to what should have been ever before them if they had had eyes to see, ears to hear, and a heart to understand. Therefore they must learn by discipline, because they had despised the word of the Lord. Are we, with so much greater light, any wiser than they? Let us search ourselves before Him whose eyes are as a flame of fire, and answer as in His own holy presence.

CHAPTER X

AN EMPTY VINE

WE have already been reminded of Israel's early freshness when God found them like grapes in the wilderness. In those happy days of their first deliverance they bore a little fruit for the Lord (ch. 9:10). Now we have to notice His solemn judgment of them as an utterly failed testimony: "Israel is an empty vine, he bringeth forth fruit unto himself" (ver. 1).

The lesson of the vine is an important one, which we shall do well to trace out through both Testaments. In Psalm 80, beginning at ver. 8, we have a most significant statement. "Thou hast brought a vine out of Egypt: Thou hast cast out the heathen and planted it. Thou preparedst room before it, and didst cause it to take deep root, and it filled the land. The hills were covered with the shadow of it, and the boughs thereof were like the goodly cedars. She sent out her boughs unto the sea, and her branches unto the river." This was Israel according to the mind of God, as His testimony in the earth. Such they would ever have remained, had there been lowliness of mind and subjection of heart, leading to confidence in and dependence upon Him continually. But the very opposite of this was developed, as we well know, and Scripture makes abundantly clear. Therefore "the boar out of the wood doth waste it, and the wild beast of the field doth devour it" (ver. 1 of the same psalm). God came looking for fruit in accordance with Isaiah 5. Gazing down upon His vine, seeking grapes, He found only wild grapes. It was, as described by Hosea, "an empty vine;" there was no fruit for the Lord. All was for self.

Therefore the vine of the earth was set aside eventually, its enclosing wall broken down, and it will be fully judged in the awful vintage yet to come (Rev. 14: 18-20). Meantime upon the rejection of the empty vine, God brings in a vine that *will* bear—one that He will ever find fruit upon. So the Lord Jesus, the Man of God's purpose, tells His disciples in John 15 of "the True Vine," even Himself. He takes the place of Israel to maintain a testimony for God in the earth. In matchless grace He associates His redeemed with Himself in this: "I am the Vine, ye are the branches." Empty branches, with no vital link, may be intruded among the branches as belonging to the vine; but as there is no living connection with the vine there will be no fruit. Such are false professors who are cut off, and cast forth as branches, withered, and whose end is to be burned. The fruit-bearing branches are purged that they may bear *more* fruit. Yea, God the Father is glorified when they bear *much* fruit!

It will be seen from this that the vine refers to the earth. It is God's testimony in the world; once committed to Israel, now maintained by Christ through His beloved people in this scene. The empty vine has been set aside in judgment. The True Vine has taken its place, and shall never be set aside, for it is Christ Himself and His people in Him. Therefore, however individuals fail, we find Him introducing Himself to Laodicea as "The faithful and true Witness" (Rev. 3: 14).

This tenth chapter before us but concludes the proof that Israel had indeed fallen into the sad condition described in the first verse. All hope of recovery was gone for the present. They must pass through affliction and tribulation, and consequent repentance, ere they could again be taken up; and when they are, it will be as branches in the living Vine, linked up with their once-rejected Messiah as God's testimony in the Millennium; no longer as under the old covenant, on the ground of their responsibility (in which position they failed from the first), but under the new covenant of God's pure grace toward them, unmerited and sovereign.

The opening words of the second verse give the root-trouble in a very brief sentence, "Their heart is divided." This was the cause of all subsequent sorrow and failure. They did not cleave to the Lord with purpose of heart. They were double-minded, and therefore unstable in all their ways. A single heart for God's glory is the prime necessity for a holy life. This they had neglected. Therefore they had to eat of the fruit of their own devices.

To walk with God with a divided heart is utterly impossible. He is not asking for the first place in the heart, either—as people often put it. He is far too exclusive for that. His word is, "My son, give Me thy heart" — the whole heart, with no reservation whatever. Only when this is done will the walk and ways be in accordance with His mind. Here Israel failed, as their idolatrous altars testified; and when God chastened them for their sin, instead of owning His righteousness in thus dealing with them, they sought to make a covenant with the nations, that they might escape the merited discipline. Having no prince to save them, they made desperate efforts to secure an arm of flesh elsewhere on which to lean; but that God would not permit (vers. 3, 4).

The inhabitants of Samaria, who, for so long, had "feared the Lord and served their own gods" (2 Kings 17: 33), must now be made to tremble "because of the calves of Beth-aven," upon them they had relied: for at last, after so long a trial, God had written "Ichabod" over the whole northern kingdom. The glory had departed (ver. 5). Therefore they were to be carried as a gift to the king of Assyria, that Ephraim might receive shame and Israel be ashamed of his own counsel. Thus Samaria's king would prove as powerless as the foam upon the water, which seems for a moment substantial and real; but, in the next, has vanished away (vers. 6, 7).

The eighth verse manifestly looks on to a far more solemn fulfilment than its secondary application to the Assyrian victory of old. The expressions used connect it with the awful overthrow of all established order in the last days, as described under the sixth seal of Rev. 6. Then "they shall say to the mountains, Cover us; and to the hills, Fall on us." This will be the time when they shall receive of the Lord's hand double for all their sins, and shall realize, in bitterness of soul, their folly in departing from the living God.

Again He reminds them, as in the previous chapter (ver. 9), that they had sinned from the days of Gibeah. The iniquity then perpetrated had never been thoroughly judged, but rather, as leaven, had wrought throughout all the years since, permeating the mass. Therefore He must chastise them, because of His yearning desire for their blessing. He loved them, and, because of this, He had to discipline them for their sins.

The expression, "When they shall bind themselves in two furrows," is variously rendered, and seems ambiguous. The R. V. gives, "When they are bound to their two transgressions." Might "their two transgressions" be the "two evils" of Jer. 2:13? They had forsaken Him who is the Fountain of living waters, and had hewed out broken cisterns for themselves. The prophet Isaiah similarly charges them with two transgressions—the rejection of God's Anointed, and the setting up of idolatry.

The happy result of the disciplinary ways of the Lord is beautifully portrayed in vers. 11, 12, which here come in parenthetically, ere the subject of their sin and its punishment is continued in the closing verses. Both Judah and Ephraim, as tractable oxen, shall submit to the yoke, and delight to tread out the corn in the days when their lesson shall have been learned in the presence of God. But this will only be when they sow in righteousness and godliness. Then they shall reap in mercy. The fallow ground must be broken up by the power of the Word ministered in the energy of the Holy Ghost. Thus will there be response when the set time has arrived to seek the Lord that He may come and rain righteousness upon them. For us, all this has its present application, if we have hearts to bow to it.

But though, for Israel and Judah, such blessing is in store, the last three verses describe their unhappy state till they are made willing in the day of His power.

Plowing wickedness, they but go on reaping iniquity and eating the fruit of lies; because their trust is not in Him, but in their own way and the multitude of their mighty men. Consequently breaking up and spoiling, in place of repairing the breach and restoration, must be their portion. See Isa. 58:12. Bethel, which had become the centre of their idolatry, would prove their undoing; speaking as it did of their grievous apostasy. Judah, we know, was preserved for a time, and a light maintained for David's sake, till Messiah should appear; but the king of Israel was utterly cut off and the throne over-turned, never to be re-established till He shall come whose right it is to reign. Then the breach between Israel and Judah shall be healed, as predicted by all the prophets, when the times of refreshing shall come from the presence of the Lord. No longer will "an empty vine" be descriptive of the earthly people; but as a vine flourishing they shall take root downward and send forth fruit-laden branches above, to the praise of the glory of Jehovah's grace.

CHAPTER XI

BANDS OF LOVE

"WHEN Israel was a child, then I loved him, and called My son out of Egypt." It is plain, from a consideration of Matt. 2:15, that God had in view His own Son, our Lord Jesus Christ, when the prophet uttered these words. Clearly, and unmistakably, the Holy Babe's sojourn in the land of Egypt is declared to be, "That it might be fulfilled which was spoken *of the Lord* by the prophet, saying, Out of Egypt have I called My Son."

And yet a careful reading of the first few verses of this chapter will make it equally clear that the prophet himself, doubtless, had none other than Israel nationally before him when he spoke the words quoted. He was dwelling on Israel's past deliverance from the house of bondage, when Jehovah loved him and called him, as His son, out of the land dominated by the Pharaohs.

Is there then contradiction here? Far otherwise. There is the most perfect agreement, which another passage at once manifests. In 2 Cor. 3 we learn from ver. 17, read in connection with the entire chapter, that the Lord is the Spirit of the Old Testament. He is everywhere presented to the anointed eye. Hence the apostle wrote by divine inspiration when he declared that Hosea's words prophetically foretold the coming up of God's Son out of Egypt. In wondrous grace He would, as it were, begin as His people began, in regard to His earthly pilgrimage. So, as a Babe whose life is sought by Herod, He is carried over the route taken by Jacob when driven by famine to Egypt; and from that land whence His people had been delivered when oppressed by Pharaoh, He later returns to Palestine. Thus would He be identified with them in their wanderings, that they might understand how the Holy Spirit spoke of Him when He said, "In all their affliction He was afflicted, and the Angel of His Presence saved them" (Isa. 63:9).

Called out of Egypt, He was ever the One in whom the Father found delight. In this how blessedly opposite to Israel! Redeemed by power from Egyptian tyranny, they went far from Him, though He called them in tenderest love. Turning away, they sacrificed unto Baalim, and worshiped images of man's design (ver. 2).

Yet He had taught Ephraim to take his earliest steps, as it were; holding his arms and directing his way. But they soon, like an ungrateful child, forgot Him to whom they owed so much, and knew not that He had healed them. Tenderly He recalls those early days when He drew them with cords of a man and with bands of love, delivering them from the yoke, and providing all that they needed for their sustenance and enjoyment (vers. 3, 4)—what saint but will see in words so lovely the story of his own deliverance from sin and Satan, when first brought to the knowledge of Christ! Long enthralled in worse than Egyptian bondage, how unspeakably precious was the earliest revelation of His grace to our souls, when He drew us to Himself from our wickedness and waywardness by the bands of love; which were indeed the cords of a man—the Man Christ Jesus, who gave Himself a ransom for all! Let us challenge our hearts as to what return we have made to love so deep and tender. What is the Baal that has lured some of us so far from Him who once was everything to our hearts, when we took our first steps out into the wilderness with Him to whom we owed so much? Rest assured, fellow-believer, till every idol is destroyed, we shall never know again the freshness and joy of those early days, if we have allowed other lords to have dominion over us.

Once set free from Egypt, Israel, nationally, could never return there. But because of their sins, they were given into the hand of the Assyrian; as will, in a more awful manner, be the case in the last days, when the sword shall abide upon them, "because of their own counsels" (vers. 5, 6).

Such must be the bitter fruit of forgetting

their God and taking their own foolish and sinful way. From the first they had been "bent to backsliding" from Him, though He had called them again and again to repentance. But they persisted in their folly till there was no remedy (ver. 7).

Yet His yearning heart causes Him to cry, "How shall I give thee up? . . . My heart is turned within Me, My repentings are kindled together" (ver. 8). He could not bear to make them as the cities of the nations upon whom His wrath had fallen without any mixture of mercy. Zeboiim and Admah (see Gen. 14:8) were two of the cities of the plain blotted out in the day when Sodom and Gomorrah fell beneath His judgment (Deut. 29:23). Of a similar doom Moses warned Israel if they failed to keep His holy law. Thus they were righteously under that awful sentence; but God, falling back upon His own sovereignty, declares, "I will not execute the fierceness of Mine anger, I will not return to destroy Ephraim: for I am God, and not a man; the Holy One in the midst of thee: and I will not enter into the city"—*i. e.,* to utterly consume it (ver. 9).

It is most blessed to realize that God, who, once He has given His word in grace, will never repent, or permit that people to be cursed whom He has blessed (as He made known to Balaam), yet reserves to Himself the right to turn from the greatness of His wrath, however richly deserved, and manifest His loving-kindness to the people of His choice upon their repentance. Therefore, though He might righteously have utterly destroyed Ephraim, He preserved a remnant, in grace, who shall yet be to the praise of His glory in the land of their fathers; when "they shall walk after the Lord," in the day that "He shall roar like a lion," causing His once-blinded people to tremble at His word; when He shall "set His hand again the second time to recover the remnant of His people which shall be left, from Assyria, and from Egypt, and from Pathros, and from Cush, and from Elam, and from Shinar, and from Hamath, and from the islands of the sea" (Isa. 11:11). At His call they will come, weeping because of their sin, yet rejoicing in His love; "as a bird out of Egypt, and as a dove out of the land of Assyria," to be placed "in their houses," never again to be removed, according to the word of Jehovah (ver. 11).

This verse completes another distinct division of the prophecy, which extends from their first call out of Egypt to their restoration to the land and to God in the days of the millennial kingdom.

The last verse is properly the introduction to chapter 12, and brings in a new subject, which closes with the end of chapter 13. When Hosea prophesied, as frequently noted, the iniquity of Judah was not yet so manifest as that of the ten tribes whom Jeroboam had led astray from the very beginning, turning them away from Jehovah, and setting up the golden calves for their worship. They had been idolatrous from the first, and all their kings had followed in the steps of "Jeroboam the son of Nebat, which made Israel to sin." Therefore sentence was early pronounced on them because God had to say, "Ephraim compasseth Me about with lies, and the house of Israel with deceit." There had never been any response to the many warnings and entreaties sent them by the Lord.

But with Judah it was far otherwise. Among them, decline was a matter of slow, and sometimes thwarted, progress. Hence we read, "But Judah yet ruleth with God, and is faithful with the Most Holy" (ver. 12, margin). Up to the time when Hosea prophesied, there was still a measure of devotion to Jehovah in Judah. Moreover, revival after revival followed the fervent calls to repentance uttered by the prophets; but it will be observed that as the years went on, they too became less and less responsive to the voice of God, until they lost all concern for His holiness.*

---

* Hypocrisy, therefore, developed especially in Judah—"This people honoreth Me with their *lips,* but their *heart* is far from Me" (Mark 7: 6; Isa. 29: 13). This is the danger where doctrine is right and outward form correct while the heart is away from God. Let every child of God beware of this. See Luke 12: 1.—[Ed.

CHAPTER XII

THE BALANCES OF DECEIT

AS already noticed, a new section of the prophecy began with verse 12 of the previous chapter, in which God most searchingly exposes the hidden corruptions of Ephraim, laying bare the moral springs of their being, which resulted in such open revolting from their God.

Like the royal Preacher of Ecclesiastes, Ephraim, seeking in vain for something to fill the heart apart from God, had been feeding on wind and following the desolating wind of the east, and thus proving that "all is vanity and vexation of spirit" when the heart is estranged from the one true Source of all good. Endeavoring to make a league with the powerful Assyrian whom they dreaded, and sending oil (as a bribe, evidently) into Egypt to buy the help of their old enemy, they thus sought to avert the evil day; but they were following lies and desolation. No human ingenuity could turn aside the day of the Lord's dealings with them for their sins (ver. 1).

With Judah too He had a controversy; for the encouraging word spoken in verse 12 of chapter 11 did not necessarily imply that God was fully satisfied with them. The seed of Jacob, as a whole, were emulating the crookedness of him from whom they sprang; so they must be visited according to their ways, and recompensed according to their doings (ver. 2).

In verses 3 to 6 Jacob is himself before us, as in all respects a picture of the people descended from him. A supplanter from his birth, he manifested his overreaching spirit from the womb, taking his brother by the heel, as recorded in Gen. 25:26. Nevertheless grace had come in, and in his distress he laid hold upon God; or, as the margin says, "He behaved himself princely with God;" thus making good his new name, Israel—a prince with God.

When unable longer to struggle, he clung to Him against whom he had striven; and this was the power in which he prevailed—when he wept and made supplication to Him. It was what another has called "the irresistible might of weakness"—clinging to Him that is mighty, even as the apostle declared, "When I am weak, then am I strong." This was the secret of Jacob's prevailing with God, who had found him in Bethel when he was a fugitive and a wanderer because of his sin. "There He spake with us" implies, I judge, that the word of the Lord to him on the night when a stone was his pillow was intended likewise for all his house to the end of time. Whatever their failings, His eye would ever be upon them; "Even the Lord God of hosts, the Lord

(*Jehovah*—the eternal, the unchanging One) is his memorial."

Oh that Israel would learn from all these things to turn to their God, keep judgment and mercy, and wait on Him continually!

Instead of this, they had but followed in the first ways of Jacob their father; so that God likens Ephraim to a merchantman, or a trafficker, in whose hand are the balances of deceit. He is really a Canaanite—for such is the word rendered *merchantman*. Could anything more aptly describe the Hebrew as he has ever since been known? Conscienceless when business interests were at stake, there can be no doubt that the anti-Semitism of Europe is in large measure the judgment upon his knavery (ver. 7). And so unconscious is he of wrong-doing when he takes advantage of the need or covetousness of his victim, that he congratulates himself on his increasing wealth (as his store grows day by day, swollen with ill-gotten gains), saying, "In all my labors they shall find none iniquity in me that were sin" (ver. 8).

But however dark the picture may be at the present (and that *present* is from Hosea's day to now), the Lord has never utterly cast off the nation whose God He was "from the land of Egypt." In *pure grace* He shall yet restore them to their ancient land, fulfilling all His pledges, and bringing them into the full enjoyment of the true feast of tabernacles; when, their toil ended, their lessons learned, and their warfare accomplished, they shall dwell every man beneath his own vine and fig tree, with none to make them afraid (ver. 9).

To this end God had spoken by His prophets, multiplying visions and using similitudes; thus pressing upon the people's consciences their unhappy condition, and encouraging them by the promise of blessing conditioned upon repentance (ver. 10). In reading the ministry of these prophets, it is important to bear in mind the instruction given us in the New Testament, that no prophecy of Scripture is of its own interpretation, but all must be read in view of the ways of God, as set forth so fully by both Hosea and Daniel. The end of all the burdens of the prophecies of these men of God is the bringing in of the day of the Lord, and the establishment of the kingdom in glory on this earth; when Israel shall return in heart to Jehovah, and own their once-rejected Messiah as David's Son, for whom they have waited so long.

The ministry of the prophets was for the laying bare the true state of affairs. So they discovered the iniquity of Gilead. Vanity was written on all. In Gilgal, where once the reproach of Egypt had been rolled away, they sacrificed, but not to Jehovah. Altars were everywhere, like heaps of stone piled in the furrows of the field, but not to His glory (ver. 11). So they must find their symbol once more in Jacob, who, because of his deceit, fled into the land of Syria, and there kept Laban's sheep, that he might purchase his wife by hard toil (ver. 12). When, of old, the Lord's set time had come to bring Israel out of Egypt, it was by a prophet He did so; and by a prophet he led them through the wilderness, preserving them in all their trials (ver. 13). So the same kind of ministry must be heeded again, ere they would be delivered from the bondage of their sins and brought into the enjoyment of the promised inheritance.

But instead of heeding the word of the Lord, and humbling themselves before Him, when He sent His servants to them, "Ephraim provoked Him to anger most bitterly: therefore shall He leave his blood upon him, and his reproach shall his Lord return unto him" (ver. 14). God-sent ministry, heeded and bowed to, leads to enlargement and blessing; but the Spirit's testimony rejected increases the guilt of him who hardens himself against it, and makes his condition far worse than before. It is ever the case that light refused makes the darkness all the deeper. Hence the need of a tender conscience, quick to respond to every word from God.

CHAPTER XIII

IN ME IS THY HELP

THE opening words, which are really a continuation of the burden begun in the last verse of chapter 11, remind us forcibly of the word of the Lord to Saul when he had turned back from obeying His voice. (See 1 Sam. 15: 17.) "When Ephraim spake trembling, he exalted himself in Israel: but when he offended in Baal, he died" (ver. 1).

These words give us the spiritual history of thousands who have begun well, but ended badly, because of failure to cleave to the Lord with purpose of heart. As we trace out the biographies of many of the kings of Judah, we see the same thing exemplified. And if it is otherwise with the kings of Israel, it is only because not one of *them* began with God at all. They were idolators, all of them; and of the entire number, Jehoahaz is the only one of whom it is stated that he ever sought the Lord, and that only when in deep distress.

But among Judah's rulers there were many who started out well, of whom it might be said that "as long as he sought the Lord, the Lord made him to prosper." With most of them, however, failure came in eventually, to mar their testimony, and bring sorrow and trouble in its train.

When God first took Ephraim up, he "was little in his own eyes," and "he spake trembling;" that is, realizing in some measure his weakness and insufficiency, he was humbled when the word of the Lord came to him. God says, "To this man will I look; even to him that is poor and of a contrite spirit, and trembleth at My word" (Isa. 66:2). Such was Ephraim in the freshness of early days. And when this was his condition, "he exalted himself in Israel. But when he offended in Baal, he died." Alas, that the last sentence had ever to be penned! How much happier had it been for Ephraim, as for untold thousands more, if they had never left their first love! These things are our types, and from them God would have us learn not to trust our own deceitful hearts, but to walk softly before Him, in reverence and godly fear. In no other way shall we be preserved from a moral and spiritual breakdown. Self-confidence is ever the prelude to severe and crushing defeat.

And it is generally found that, the first step taken away from God, each succeeding one becomes easier and easier. Twinges of conscience are less frequent; the strivings of the grieved Holy Spirit attract less and less attention as the heart becomes hardened through the deceitfulness of sin. So was it with Ephraim. "And now they sin more and more," says the prophet, as he proceeds to picture the gross idolatry which everywhere pervaded the land, prevailing among all classes of people (ver. 2). Consequently they are to be carried away in judgment. "They shall be as the morning cloud, and as the early dew that passeth away, as the chaff that is driven with the whirlwind out of the floor, and as the smoke out of the chimney" (ver. 3). In this way the Lord was about to "purge His floor."

But, as so frequently declared, He did not purpose to make a full end of them, the people of His choice. On the contrary, He remained the only true God, the Lord who had been their God from the land of Egypt. The day would come when they should own Him alone, and know no God besides Him; for He only was the Saviour of Israel. In the wilderness—that dry and thirsty land—He had sustained them, till their heart was exalted: and when they were filled with all good things they had forgotten Him, therefore He who had given them all these mercies would be to them as a leopard by the way, and as a bear bereaved of her whelps, who would rend the caul of their heart, and tear them like a lion. The wild beast was appointed to devour them (vers. 4-8).

In the figures here used it would seem that we have more than a hint of the character of the Gentile empires which were to become successively the oppressors of Israel. If the passage be compared with Dan. 7, I think most readers will feel that it is more than a mere coincidence that the lion was there used as the symbol of Babylon; the bear, of Medo-Persia; and the leopard, of Greece. The generic term, "the wild beast," or, "the beast of the field," is possibly a veiled reference to the last beast, "dreadful and terrible," typifying the Roman empire, for long years the persecutor of Israel, and which, though now fallen, is yet to be revived in the first beast of Rev. 13, when the time of the end is come, and the great tribulation shall conclude the sufferings of Jacob.

They alone were responsible for all that had befallen them, and for all that should yet come upon them. "O Israel," God says, "thou hast destroyed thyself; but in Me is thy help" (ver. 9). Their self-will had been their ruin; but He waited still to save, ready to make bare His arm for their deliverance, if there were any sign of repentance and self-judgment. None other could avail for their salvation if they turned not to Him. "Where is thy king?" He asks. (See margin.) Hoshea,* in whom they trusted, was a prisoner in the hands of Shalmaneser, king of Assyria (2 Kings 17: 1-4). Where was any other that could save them, in all their cities? They had asked for a king,

* In so writing, I simply follow the marginal note. There is no positive proof that Hosea prophesied in the days of Hoshea, or that he is the king referred to.

to be like the nations around them; God had granted their request; but where was the power of their king and his judges? They had been trusting in a bruised reed.

It may seem strange, so many centuries after the establishment of the monarchy, and at the close of the history of the ten tribes as such, that God should thus reproach them for the sin of asking a king in the days of Samuel. This but illustrates the remarks already made in seeking to expound chapter 7. The same spirit of independency that led them to desire a king to go in and out before them (when Jehovah Himself was their King), prevailed among them still; and for *that,* judgment must fall. Solemn are the words, "I gave thee a king in Mine anger, and took him away in My wrath" (ver. 11). So may God often allow His children to have what they desire, when their hearts are away from Him; giving them their requests, but sending leanness into their souls. It is well when the will is subject, and in all our prayers and supplications we say, "Thy will be done." He knows so much better than we possibly can what is best for us; and where there is subjection of heart He will reply, not according to our faulty petitions, but according to His own loving-kindness and wisdom. When it is otherwise, He often has to answer our prayers in judgment, and we may have years to regret our folly in not having left all our affairs in His hands.

To all his other failures Ephraim added this. that he kept his iniquity bound up and his sin covered (ver. 12). As long as this is the case with any, God's hand must be on them in discipline: "He that covereth his sins shall not prosper." On the other hand, the moment all is out in the light, and sin is judged and confessed, God Himself provides a covering, and the evil is gone from His sight forever. "Blessed is he whose transgression is forgiven, whose sin is covered. Blessed is the man unto whom the Lord imputeth not iniquity, and in whose spirit there is no guile" (Ps. 32: 1, 2).

Because of Ephraim's persistency in covering his own sin, the sorrows as of a travailing woman must come upon him. This at once suggests another simile. He is an unwise son, remaining where his presence can only be most embarrassing and foolish. So he persisted in his folly when warned and entreated to cease therefrom (ver. 31).

The last two verses continue the general subject, declaring the terrible extent of the disastrous judgments they must undergo. But ere these solemn scenes are depicted, a precious word of grace, like a rainbow of hope in the gloomy, wrath-laden sky, is seen in ver. 14. He who is about to visit them in His anger speaks of mercy and kindness, giving a promise of the triumph of His love at last. "I will ransom them from the power of sheol; I will redeem them from death: O death, I will be thy plagues; O sheol, I will be thy destruction: repentance shall be hid from Mine eyes."

What could be more blessed than such a promise in the midst of so solemn an arraignment? In wrath God will remember mercy. He will yet appear as the Redeemer of His chosen, despoiling death and sheol (synonymous with hades, the unseen world of spirits—not hell nor the grave) of their prey, and saving all who turn to Him in brokenness of spirit, owning their guilt. Of His purposes of grace He will never repent; they shall abide forever in His goodness and mercy.

For centuries now Israel has been like a dead man, buried among the nations, wandering like a shade in sheol; but the hour is not far distant when the closing message to Daniel shall be fulfilled, as also the prophecy of the valley of dry bones in Ezek. 37. "At that time shall Michael stand up, the great prince which standeth for the children of thy people: and there shall be a time of trouble, such as never was since there was a nation even to that same time: and at that time thy people shall be delivered, *every one that shall be found written in the book*. And many of them that sleep in the dust of the earth shall awake, some to everlasting life, and some to shame and everlasting contempt" (Dan. 12: 1, 2). Such also is the testimony of an older prophet, Isaiah (ch.

26:19, *R. V.*). "Thy dead shall live; my dead bodies shall arise. Awake and sing, ye that dwell in the dust: for thy dew is as the dew of herbs, and the earth shall cast forth her dead." All these passages will have their glorious fulfilment when the Remnant of Israel and Judah are awakened from their death-sleep, and shall come forth at the call of God to return to Zion with singing and with everlasting joy upon their heads.

Literally, too, there will be a wondrous fulfilment when "All that are in the graves shall hear His voice, and shall come forth; they that have done good, unto the resurrection of life; and they that have done evil, unto the resurrection of judgment." "Blessed and holy is he that hath part in the *first resurrection!*" (John 5:28, 29; Rev. 20:6).

It would be happy indeed to close our chapter with this precious reminder of the grace of our Saviour-God. But it is salutary and necessary to be reminded that the day of Jehovah's power and Messiah's appearing has not yet come; so we are once more turned back to contemplate the lamentable estate of Israel and the dark days awaiting them ere the glory dawns.

As we dwell upon the solemn words of verses 15 and 16, the "rainbow like unto an emerald" seems to fade away; the dark clouds of doom gather heavier and heavier above the land of promise; while "out of the throne proceeds lightnings, and thunderings, and voices," presaging the dreadful storm about to burst upon those who, having eyes to see, saw not, and having ears to hear, heard not the ominous rumblings of the approaching day of wrath, till it was too late to find a hiding-place. An east wind from Jehovah "shall come up from the wilderness," drying up all the springs of hope and fountains of joy, and spoiling all the vessels of desire. Desolation should enwrap Samaria in midnight gloom and direst woe; "for she hath rebelled against her God." Therefore they should fall beneath the avenging hand of the bloodthirsty Assyrian, who would spare neither age, sex, nor condition.

All this has had a fulfilment in the march of Shalmaneser's hordes through the land. It shall have another and more dreadful one when the last Assyrian sweeps down,* like a resistless flood, till stopped by the breath of the Lord.

With this the body of the prophecy closes. The next, and last, chapter is a tender call addressed to the backslidden people, exhorting them to return to Him, who is their only good and their only hope.

---

* This will take place when they shall be restored to the land of Palestine in unbelief, subsequent to the rapture of the Church, and previous to the establishment of Messiah's kingdom. This has been gone into at length, both in the Author's "Notes on Jeremiah" (chaps. 30 and 31), and in "The Mysteries of God," to which attention has already been drawn.

CHAPTER XIV

RESTORATION AND BLESSING

THE same yearning tenderness that led the rejected Messiah to weep over Jerusalem as He said, "If thou hadst known, even thou, at least in this thy day, the things which belong unto thy peace!" is manifest throughout this final chapter of our prophet. It is one of the most touching yet faithful entreaties to be found in the Book of God, reminding us of the soul-stirring appeals uttered by the Holy Spirit through a later servant, Jeremiah. Not only does it give us the beseechings of Jehovah that His people heed His voice and return to Himself, but it sets forth clearly just how they should go about it, even putting into their lips the words which, if they came from their hearts, He would delight to hear. Abundant promises too are given of blessing to be poured out upon them when they should thus bow before Him in repentance and contrition of heart.

"O Israel, return unto the Lord thy God; for thou hast fallen by thine iniquity!" (ver. 1). How bitterly had they proven that "the way of transgressors is hard!" "Righteousness," we are elsewhere told, "exalteth a nation; but sin is a reproach to any people." Had they followed in the paths of uprightness which their faithful, covenant-keeping God had marked out for them, theirs had been a very different history. But they refused to hearken, and turned away the shoulder. The result was failure and disaster from first to last. They had indeed fallen very low. Yet He, who had been so grievously sinned against, could lovingly entreat them still to return unto Him, who was their God from the land of Egypt.

Let us learn from their unhappy course both to avoid their sins and to know the exceeding grace of our God. The Church, as a testimony for an absent Lord, has failed as fully as Israel. But however dark the day, wherever a true heart turns back to God, judging itself for participation in the common sin of those so highly privileged, He who has been so grievously dishonored will still gladly receive such an one; yea, He waits but for open doors to come in and sup in communion, though the hour be late.

If the soul say, "But I have erred so seriously, I know not how to approach so holy a God after having dishonored Him to such an extent;" then He Himself will put a prayer into the lips of the returning one: thus assuring each seeking soul of His willingness to hear. "Take with you words, and turn to the Lord: say unto Him, Take away all iniquity, and receive us graciously: so will we render the calves of our lips. Asshur shall not save us; we will not ride upon horses: neither will we say any more to the work of our hands, Ye are our gods: for in Thee the fatherless findeth mercy" (vers. 2, 3).

This prayer, indited by God Himself, will repay the most careful consideration. Let us take up its clauses one by one, weighing each in the presence of the Lord. "Take away all iniquity, and receive us graciously," cries the repentant soul. Having long been defiled, till the conscience was almost calloused, the light of God has now shown things up as they really are. This produces an abhorrence of the waywardness so long tolerated as though it were a thing indifferent. Unconcern is succeeded by deep exercise. "Take away all iniquity!" is the soul's longing. Sin becomes hateful the moment one gets into the presence of God. Then the need of grace is felt, and so the cry comes, "Receive us graciously." What a mercy that it is to "the God of *all grace*" we are directed to come!

There can be no restoration so long as one sin is trifled with and remains unjudged; but the instant a full confession is made and all iniquity is honestly turned from, the Word assures us of instant forgiveness. "If we confess our sins, He is faithful and just to forgive us our sins, and to cleanse us from all unrighteousness" (1 John 1: 9). This is the principle that applies to a lost sinner seeking salvation, or an erring saint desiring restoration of soul. Sin judged is sin gone; and the soul may afresh enjoy the communion that has been interrupted from the moment evil was allowed upon the conscience. In the knowledge of this—a knowledge received, not by feelings, but resting on the testimony of Scripture—praise and worship once more spring up in the heart. "So shall we render the calves of our lips!"

Only when the life is right and the conscience pure from defilement can there be worship in spirit and in truth. Then the happy saint can without hindrance pour forth into the ear of God his grateful praises, and his worship, like incense, arise from the heart to which Christ is all. Israel shall enter into this, when, restored to their land after their disciplinary wanderings, they rejoice before Him who shall dwell in the midst of them, having first purged them with the spirit of burning from all that has hindered their full acknowledgment of His grace.

"Asshur shall not save us," is the cry of a people who have learned to "cease from man, whose breath is in his nostrils." We have seen throughout this book how in the hour of their distress they turned, not to God against whom they had revolted, but to Assyria, the proud northern power, who was destined to be their ruin. Thus they learned that "vain is the help of man."

Therefore they will say in the day of Jehovah's might, "Asshur shall not deliver us;"* but in God alone will they find their Saviour.

Nor will they depend in that day upon their own armies, mounted like the cavalry of the nations. "We will not ride upon horses." It is noticeable throughout this history that their strength for warfare consisted not in imitating the manners and customs of the nations, but in reliance upon God in the spirit of praise. When Judah ("praise") led, they conquered, as they counted on the Lord alone for succor. When Jehoshaphat met the enemy, he put *singers,* not cavalrymen, in the van, and a great victory ensued. To this they shall return when humbled before God because of all their failure and sin. "A horse is a vain thing for safety," though it seem to add wonderfully to human prowess. But better far is it to lean upon the arm of Jehovah, and remember that the battle is His, not ours.

Idolatry had been their undoing in the past. But then they shall cry, "Neither will we say any more to the work of our hands, Ye are our gods!" Having learned the impotence of the "gods many and lords many" who have had dominion over them, the Lord alone shall be exalt-

---

* It is usually God's way to cause the very thing in which His people have dishonored Him to become their chastisement—thus to deliver the heart from the idol it has sought after.—[Ed.

ed in that day. It is a lovely picture of a soul who has proven that no power, seen or unseen, can avail for deliverance, but the strength of "the mighty God of Jacob." When everything is thus out in His presence, and no guile remains in their spirit, they can add with assurance, "For in Thee the fatherless findeth mercy." Israel had been Jehovah's son, whom He had called out of Egypt. But they had forgotten Him, and done despite to His Spirit of grace. Therefore He had pronounced the Lo-ammi and Lo-ruhamah sentences upon them, as we saw in the beginning of the prophecy. Thus, when they return, they come in on the ground of pure grace and mercy. They come as "the fatherless;" not to claim the rights of a child, but to be the subjects of that loving-kindness which is better than life. How suited to the lips of the Remnant of the last days will be the words of this prayer!

The gracious response of the Lord immediately follows: "I will heal their backsliding, I will love them freely; for Mine anger is turned away from him" (ver. 4). It is as though His great heart of love had been full, nigh to bursting, but their sins had kept Him from expressing all that was there. Now every barrier is removed, and, like an irresistible torrent, His kindness flows forth, overleaping, or sweeping away, every obstruction that a timid faith might yet raise. Loving them freely, He will set them in paths of righteousness, healing their souls and turning them from all their backslidings. Everything of the dark past forgiven and gone, His wrath has vanished, and His grace knows no bounds.

No longer shall they be as a barren and desolate heath, but like a watered garden, tended and kept by Himself. "I will be as the dew unto Israel: he shall blossom as the lily, and cast forth his roots as Lebanon" (ver. 5). The dew ever, in Scripture, sets forth the refreshing influences of the Holy Spirit, ministering the truth in grace to the soul. The manna in the wilderness fell on the dew—type of Christ ministered in the power of the Holy Ghost. Gideon's signs pictured in a marvelous way God's varied dealings in this regard. At first the dew was on the fleece, while all the ground was dry. Again, the fleece was dry, but all the ground covered with dew. So had Israel been blessed with the Spirit's testimony, while the world lay in ignorance and idolatry. But Israel rejected Messiah at His first coming, and now the chosen nation is dry and desolate, while the Spirit of God is working among the Gentiles. In the Millennium He will be poured out on all flesh; then fleece and ground shall alike be refreshed with the dew. In Psalm 133 "the dew of Hermon" sets forth the same quickening and revivifying power as here in Hosea. God Himself will be as the dew unto His restored people, giving new life and freshness, that they may evermore rejoice in Him. Under His kindly nurture, they shall put on the beauty of the lily, with the strength of the cedar of Lebanon. No fading glory shall again be theirs, but a beauty that shall endure, and a strength that can never fail.

Then "his branches shall spread, and his beauty shall be as the olive tree, and his smell as Lebanon" (ver. 6). Towering up to heaven like a mighty cedar, Israel's branches shall go out in majesty, and their fragrance shall be wafted in the air, that all may know that the Lord has taken them as His own. Nor is it only dignity and fragrance, but there shall be all the loveliness and fruitfulness of the olive tree—the oil tree, as the word might be rendered. This too speaks of the Holy Spirit, who will permeate the nation as the oil permeates the olive, making it a source of spiritual blessing to the whole earth.

"They that dwell under his shadow shall return; they shall revive as the corn, and grow as the vine: the scent thereof shall be as the wine of Lebanon" (ver. 7). Figure after figure is pressed into service to tell the joy of the Lord in His people, and their beauty and preciousness in His eyes. Jacob shall not only be regathered, but others shall find blessing through him, according to the promise to the fathers. Many shall "dwell under his shadow," finding rest through the message committed to him. The corn and wine tell of strength and gladness. It shall no more be said, "Israel is an empty vine; he bringeth forth fruit unto himself." But, planted again in the land, the vine of the Lord shall flourish, and send forth its branches laden with choice clusters, to provide the wine of joy for the whole earth.

Then shall Ephraim say, "What have I to do any more with idols?" Dwelling in fellowship with God, and enjoying His matchless love and grace, the wretched follies of the past will be detested. The new affection will so possess the heart, that the vain idols at whose altars they once bowed will be hated and forgotten. In holy complacency the Lord looks down and says, "I have heard him, and observed him."* In joyous exultation, Israel answers, "I am like a green fir tree!"—not temporary verdure; but, like an evergreen, they will be perennially fresh and lovely in His eyes. But all their goodness is from Himself; so He replies, "From Me is thy fruit found." Apart from Him, all would be barrenness once more, even as Jesus said, "Without Me, ye can do nothing." But, abiding in the uninterrupted

---

* There is good ground here to question the proper construction of this dialogue. I have followed J. N. Darby's suggestion in "The Synopsis of the Books of the Bible." We might understand Israel as saying, "What have I to do any more with idols? I have heard Him, and observed Him! I am like a green fir tree." Then Jehovah's answer, "From Me is thy fruit found."

enjoyment of His love, their fruit shall never fail nor their freshness ever depart.

This closes the prophecy; but pointedly the Lord presses upon every reader the importance of weighing all in His presence. "Who is wise, and he shall understand these things? prudent, and he shall know them? for the ways of the Lord are right, and the just shall walk in them: but the transgressors shall fall therein" (ver. 9). *The ways of the Lord* has been the theme of the book. Happy shall we be if we are, through grace, numbered among the wise and prudent who know and understand, and the just who walk in them!

The Lord give efficacy to His Word for His name's sake! Amen.

Notes on the

PROPHECY OF JOEL

INTRODUCTION

OF Joel the son of Pethuel we know nothing, save what little we can glean from the three chapters forming his message to Israel. Jewish tradition places him in the days of Uzziah; but authoritative proof there is none. His name means, Jehovah is God; and his father's name, Vision, or, Wisdom of God, according to some; or, Be ye enlarged (or persuaded), according to another.

The immediate circumstances of his testimony seem to be these. The land of Israel had been visited by a terrible plague of locusts, which had devoured every green thing, leaving barrenness and famine in their wake. Joel is inspired of God to press home upon the consciences of the nation of *Judah* (for it is in and to the southern kingdom he prophesies) the fact that this visitation was from the Lord, because of the sin of His people.

Then, by the Spirit, he is carried on to the last days, and he beholds in the dire calamity by which they were afflicted a picture of the time of Jacob's trouble, to take place ere Messiah receives the kingdom. Thus the then present desolation becomes the text of a solemn prophetic discourse that is far-reaching in character. This emphasizes what has already been noticed in our study of Hosea, that while prophecy is in many parts, and may have many applications, it is never limited to local matters, but all has its end and complete fulfilment in "the day of the Lord" yet to come.

Another principle of grave moment is likewise brought to our attention by the manner in which the prophet seeks to use the calamity the people were suffering under at the time, to exercise them as to their own state of soul. God would ever have His children recognize His hand in all such visitations. For the believer, there are no second causes. The Lord has said, "I Jehovah create peace, and create evil." And He asks the question, "Shall there be evil in a city, and the Lord hath not done it?" (Isa. 45: 7; Amos 3: 6). Evil, in both these passages, is, of course, calamity—the opposite of a peaceful, quiet condition. If I am called to pass through such experiences, it is because God has seen a need in my soul for just such disciplinary dealings. He has my best interests at heart. Be it mine then to recognize

His actings and to be exercised thereby. This is the lesson of Hebrews 12, and is emphasized in the use Joel makes of Judah's afflictions in this brief but pungent prophecy.

Further remarks will be necessitated on this line as we pursue our study; so we turn at once to consider the teachings of the three stirring chapters of the book itself. May He who alone gives the eye-salve of the Spirit anoint our eyes that we may see wondrous things in His Word now before us!

CHAPTER I

THE LOCUST PLAGUE

THE ancients of Judah are first addressed, and called upon to declare if, in all their recollection, or in all the days of which their fathers had told them, there had ever been so grievous a visitation as that which the land and the people were groaning under at the time when Joel was sent to press home upon their consciences the serious lessons God would have them to learn (vers. 1-3).

"That which the palmerworm hath left hath the locust eaten; and that which the locust hath left hath the cankerworm eaten; and that which the cankerworm hath left hath the caterpillar eaten" (ver. 4). Thus the destruction of every green thing had been complete, so that famine and utter ruin stared them in the face. The various forms of insect-life here spoken of are not generally supposed to be diverse, unrelated creatures, but are probably the various stages assumed by the locust as it advances from the larvæ form to that of maturity.* This much-dreaded plague had

---

* Some scholars dissent from this view; but the position stated is that which commends itself to most.

therefore cut off all the sources of food-supply, and left an appalling scene of desolation behind. And what was so intensely solemn was the fact that it was *God's* voice, and there was grave likelihood that the people might be occupied only with the rod, and fail to hear Him who had appointed it.

Nothing is more natural for us than this. In place of godly exercise, we may give way to self-pity, or hard, stony indifference; thus either fainting under the discipline of the Lord on the one hand, or despising it on the other. Blessing results from being "exercised thereby." This was what Judah was in danger of missing, as with many others before and since.

The pleasure-loving drunkards, who delighted in their wine, were called upon to awake to the realization of their true condition—God's stroke upon them; and to learn the lesson He intended for them. His great army, like a nation of foemen, "strong and without number," had blasted the vine and barked the fig tree, so that the source of their carnal enjoyment was gone (vers. 5-7).

Like a virgin girded with sackcloth, lamenting the untimely death of her betrothed husband, they were called upon to mourn over the sins that had drawn down the judgment of God upon them. His house too was affected; for there that judgment must begin. The meat, or *meal*-offering, and the drink-offering were cut off, and the priests were left to mourn. When God's people are in a famished condition, there is no real appreciation of Christ; hence the oblations cease to be offered. The meal-offering sets forth the manhood of the Lord Jesus. The drink-offering portrays His pouring out His soul unto death. But a spiritual famine dulls the perception and sensibilities of those indebted to His one offering for all their blessing; so the gifts of a worshiping people cease (vers. 8, 9).

The desolate condition of the land is vividly described in verses 10 to 12. All the fruits of the field were gone, and the trees had withered away; even as joy had departed from the sons of men. Therefore the solemn admonition to those whose place it was to minister for them in things pertaining to God: "Gird yourselves, and lament, ye priests: howl, ye ministers of the altar: come, lie all night in sackcloth, ye ministers of my God: for the meat-offering and the drink-offering is withholden from the house of your God" (ver. 13). Insensibility at such a time!—how obnoxious to God, who wished to see a true appreciation of His dealings with His people.

So he calls upon the elders and all the inhabitants of the land to sanctify a fast, and call a solemn assembly, that they may unitedly cry unto the Lord, owning before His face their common failure, and judging their evil ways (ver. 14). The approaching day of the Lord is mentioned as an incentive to this. Not that the day of the Lord (which, in its full, prophetic sense, refers to the revelation of Jesus Christ to usher in the kingdom) was really to occur in their time; but as that day will be for the manifestation of all that has been in accordance with the mind of God, they were called upon to act then in the light of the day that was coming (ver. 15). In like manner are Christians exhorted to walk now in view of the day of Christ, when all our works shall be examined at His judgment-seat. The all-displaying light of that hour of manifestation should ever be shining upon our pathway, that all our steps may be ordered in accord therewith.

Throughout the book of Joel this is the standpoint of the prophet. The day of the Lord is coming. It will be the day of *reality;* when all shams and all hypocrisy will be manifested as what they are. Then, only what is of God will stand. Therefore the prime importance of ordering all their behavior so that it will bear the searching test of Him whose eyes are as a flame of fire.

In verses 16 to 18 the desolate condition of the land is again reverted to. All their hopes have been blasted. The blight is upon all for which they have labored. But serious as their temporal condition had become, it was as nothing compared to the spiritual dearth prevailing, of which their utter insensibility was the saddest feature.

Joel speaks as an exercised soul in the closing

words of the chapter. He takes his place as one who feels the wretched conditions existing to the full: "O Lord, to Thee will I cry!" This alone can be his resource when "the rivers of waters are dried up, and the fire hath devoured the pastures of the wilderness."

CHAPTER II

THE PROMISE OF THE OUTPOURING OF THE SPIRIT

AS we turn to this second chapter we are ushered at once into the solemn and soul-stirring events of the coming day of the Lord; a day which will only come when, the Church having been caught up to heaven, God takes up Israel again as a nation, fulfilling "all that the prophets have spoken."

In so writing, I do not forget that it was the last part of this chapter which the apostle Peter quoted in explaining the wondrous manifestations of the Spirit on the day of Pentecost, as foretold in Scripture. But we shall see, when taking up the passage in question, that it applies primarily to a far wider outpouring yet to come. That of Pentecost was like it in nature, and a measure of its fulfilment; therefore Peter could say, "This is *that*." But the prophecy was by no means exhausted then, as a careful reading of the whole book of Joel will make plain.

The figure of the trumpet, twice used in the chapter (vers. 1 and 15), connects intimately with Numbers, ch. 10. There we find the "two trumpets of silver" were used for a double purpose—to blow an alarm, and to summon the whole congregation to the presence of the Lord. The first was to arouse; the second, to instruct. We find the same thing here. In vers. 1 to 14 the trumpet of alarm is blown, and the people are warned of the dreadful events about to take place in the day of the Lord, which is declared to be nigh at hand, events so grave that the visitation of the locusts under which they had been suffering was but a feeble picture of what is yet in store for the land and the people of Judah. Then, in ver. 15 to the end of the book, at the sounding of the trumpet to call a solemn assembly, instruction is given in detail regarding the results in blessing which will follow the judgments already depicted. In the first part, the day of the Lord is described as "a day of darkness and of gloominess, a day of clouds and of thick darkness, as the morning spread upon the mountains." As the darkest hour precedes the dawn, so, before the break of the millennial morn, the world in general, and Judah in particular, will pass through the darkest period of tribulation that has ever been known.

For Judah, the chief agency in this is "a great people and a strong," who are likened to the devouring locusts. It is the Assyrian of the last days, the dread northern power, who will overrun the land of Palestine just prior to the glorious appearing of the Sun of Righteousness. Like a devouring fire, they will sweep over the land, ravaging without mercy what was as the garden of delight before them, but which will be left as a desolate wilderness (vers. 2, 3). Like mighty horses running to battle, and as chariots on the tops of the mountains, they shall seem to leap as from mount to mount, and from peak to peak, in their irresistible onslaught, as the devouring flames lick up all that is left in their path. Fleeing before them in terror and anguish, "all faces shall gather blackness" in the mad effort to escape the avenging hordes (vers. 4 to 6). Their orderly progress, as a disciplined army, knowing only the behests of their commanders, is strikingly depicted in vers. 7 to 9. Nothing avails to turn them aside. They enter wherever their prey may hide, and overcome all obstacles as they press on in the fury of their power.

The language of ver. 10 is undoubtedly apocalyptic. So tremendous will be the upheavals and overturnings in that day of Jehovah's wrath, that it will be as the quaking of the earth and the trembling of the heavens. The sun will be darkened, and the moon likewise, while the stars will seem to be blotted out in the midnight sky. As in the convulsions of the sixth seal in Rev. 6, all that men have esteemed sure and stable will be overturned. It is the destruction, not of the material universe, but of the moral, spiritual and political economies.

An appeal to the conscience of Judah is based upon this. Jehovah calls upon them to turn to

Him with all their hearts, bringing forth fruits meet for repentance. He wants reality instead of outward forms: so He says, "Rend your heart, and not your garments;" assuring them of His tender compassion, and His grace that cannot fail, if they thus turn to Him with purpose of heart. Even though the first droppings of the coming storm had already fallen, who could tell if He would not turn from His wrath, and leave a blessing behind Him? Though the hour was late, His loving-kindness might be yet toward them, in preserving them from further sorrow, and maintaining still His house and its services in their midst (vers. 12-14).

The second call is in verse 15. In place of the alarm-trumpet, the command is given to "blow the trumpet in Zion, sanctify a fast, call a solemn assembly." God would gather the people before Him that He might instruct them as to His ways, and direct their feet in a plain path, if they have but a heart to do His will. All classes are summoned, and the priests, the ministers of the Lord, are directed to weep between the porch and the altar, crying to Him before whose house they stand to spare His people, and not give His heritage to reproach.

The position of the priests—between the porch of the temple and the brazen altar outside—is significant: it speaks of approach to God on the ground of that of which the altar speaks—the

Person and work of the Lord Jesus Christ. Only in His name, and because of His finished work, has the failing saint title to draw near. "If any man sin, we have an Advocate with the Father, Jesus Christ the Righteous." Thus the priests are directed to take their stand on the temple-side of the altar, as representing a people who, although in failure, are yet the redeemed of the Lord (vers. 16, 17).

Had there been a responsive heart to God's call to contrition and self-judgment, the avenger would have been turned aside; Jehovah would have arisen in His might as their Deliverer, turning back the judgments, and bringing in blessing and gladness. In the last days, the remnant who are to be preserved for the kingdom will take the place here commanded. Then all that is promised upon their repentance will be gloriously fulfilled. The northern army will be destroyed, and his boasted power annihilated, when the Lord shall drive him into a land barren and desolate. Every enemy shall be overthrown, and the arm of Jehovah made bare (vers. 18-20).

It is manifestly in view of such an epoch of national repentance that the consolatory promises that follow (to the end of the chapter) are given. The land is called upon to rejoice because of the great things the Lord is to accomplish. Even the lower orders of creation shall share in the blessings of the earth's rejuvenation. It will be the bringing-in of the liberty of the glory of the children of God for which the whole creation, groaning and travailing in pain, now waits (Rom. 8: 19-23). In the present liberty of grace creation does not share. But the liberty of the glory will be all-embracing. Then "they shall not hurt nor destroy" in all the holy mountain; but the wolf and the lamb shall dwell together, "and a little child shall lead" the strongest and once-fiercest of beasts. From the vegetable kingdom as a whole the curse shall be lifted; the pastures of the wilderness shall spring into beauty and verdure; and the vine and the fig will yield abundantly—types of all food-producing plants (ver. 22).

In order that the fertility of the land of Canaan may be restored, and even marvelously surpass its ancient fecundity, the former and latter rains will be given in abundance. It is a well-known fact that already the God of Israel has given more than a hint of the literal fulfilment of this prophecy. For long centuries the latter rains had been withheld from Palestine, and the land that was once the garden of the East had become largely barren and desolate, scarcely able to sustain its scattered and meagre population. But, in our own times, the latter rains have returned in such measure that agriculture is once more in a flourishing condition, and vineyards, olive-yards and fig orchards abound. It is as though God were graciously giving to the world in general, and His ancient people in particular (even now returning to the home of their fathers in some measure), an evidence that His eye is ever on the land He chose for Himself, which He covenanted to Abraham's seed forever; where His only begotten Son dwelt in His humiliation—yea, where He was crucified, and which once contained His tomb, but which shall soon be touched by His glorious feet, when He descends to take His great power and reign. Throughout the Millennium of Christ's reign (Rev. 20:6) that country will again become the chief garden-spot of the whole world, blessed with the rain in its season, and so fertile that "the floors shall be full of wheat, and the vats shall overflow with wine and oil" (vers. 23, 24).

Then shall all the past ages of oppression and desolation be forgotten; for He has said, "I will restore to you the years that the locust hath eaten, the cankerworm, and the caterpillar, and the palmerworm, My great army which I sent among you" (ver. 25). How striking the language, "My great army which I sent!" In the visitation referred to in chapter 1, they were in danger of beholding only the plague of locusts, and forgetting the One who sent it. He owns it as *His* army, which He had directed against the land for the discipline of His people. But in the coming day of the Lord, He will abundantly make up for all the loss of the past. Then they shall eat in plenty, knowing no want of any kind; while He who had been their Redeemer from of old will be the object of their praise and adoring gratitude. Dwelling in His love, they shall nevermore be put to shame, for He will dwell in their midst, receiving the homage of their hearts, never again to be displaced by the idols of the past (vers. 26, 27).

Then He says: "And it shall come to pass afterward" (that is, after the people of Judah have been restored to their land, and the nation as a whole brought into blessing) "that I will pour out My Spirit upon all flesh, and your sons and your daughters shall prophesy, your old men shall dream dreams, your young men shall see visions: and also upon the servants and upon the handmaids in those days will I pour out My Spirit. And I will show wonders in the heavens and in the earth, blood, and fire, and pillars of smoke. The sun shall be turned into darkness, and the moon into blood, before the great and the terrible day of the Lord come. And it shall come to pass, that whosoever shall call on the name of the Lord shall be delivered: for in mount Zion and in Jerusalem shall be deliverance, as the Lord hath said, and in the remnant whom the Lord shall call" (vers. 28-32). I have quoted this interesting and important passage in full, in order that the least-instructed reader may have it all before him, noting carefully its connection. It is no isolated fragment interjected without connection with the balance of the book: on the contrary, the order is divinely perfect, and it occurs in its exact and proper place, in line with the events of the day of the Lord which the prophet has been unfolding.

Manifestly all this can never be fulfilled till the people of Israel are restored to their land. Then God will cause His blessing to go far beyond them, pouring out His Spirit upon "all flesh;" thus bringing the spared nations into the glorious privileges of the millennial kingdom! Old and young shall be anointed with the Spirit's unction, and shall be enlightened that they may dream dreams, see visions, and prophesy. Nor shall the males alone share in this, but the handmaidens likewise. But observe, the wonders of vers. 30 and 31 will all take place ere this day of the Lord is ushered in. Then salvation shall be extended to all the Gentiles who had never heard the gospel in this dispensation of grace: "Whosoever shall call on the name of the Lord shall be delivered." But why? The answer is, "*For* in mount Zion and in Jerusalem shall be deliverance;" that is, restored Israel will be a centre of blessing for the whole earth. This is not the same thing as the preaching of the gospel of the grace of God today. Mount Zion and Jerusalem are not now the depositaries of blessing for the Gentiles. The very contrary is true. But when the Church, the Body of Christ, has been caught away to be forever with the Lord (in accordance with 1 Thess. 4:14-18), and God has once more taken up the Jews to make them a means of salvation to the heathen nations, Joel's prophecy will be fulfilled to the letter.

I think it must be evident to every careful reader that this is the only unforced and natural explanation of the passage. But this at once raises the question as to the apostle Peter's use of it on the day of Pentecost. Are we to entertain the wretched thought that he misapplied it? Or, on the other hand, can it be that readers generally have misapprehended his use of it? The latter alternative is, I am persuaded, the correct one.

Be it noted, Peter does not say that "this is the fulfilment" of the prophecy. He simply finds the explanation of the remarkable events of that day of wonder in these words of Joel; and he declares, "*This* is *that!*" In other words, he did not identify the *events*. He did identify the *power*. That which had taken place on Pentecost was the very same thing that Joel said would take place when the day of the Lord had come. That the day spoken of had *not* come, Peter very well knew, and elsewhere has plainly declared it (2 Pet. 3:10). But the very same power of the Holy Spirit was operating in that day which shall operate when the kingdom is introduced by and by. There is here no contradiction therefore, and certainly no misapplication. Pentecost was a *sample* of what Joel foretold; and the apostle uses the passage illustratively, not as declaring its complete fulfilment at Pentecost. His own declaration in 2 Peter 1:20 should keep any from supposing Peter meant to take the last verses of Joel 2 from their connection and apply them specifically to the ushering in of the Christian dispensation.

Taken in its full connection, it will be seen the passage in Joel primarily refers to the bringing in of the kingdom—not the Church. But the same power that will operate in the coming day was manifested at Pentecost when Peter preached his memorable sermon.

CHAPTER III

THE VALLEY OF DECISION

STILL having before his soul the events that are to transpire in the day of the Lord, the prophet goes on to set forth more detailed information as to that long-waited-for season of Jehovah's power.

It should not be overlooked that the expression "the day," or, "that day," so often used in connection with the ushering in of the kingdom, does not refer to any one day of twenty-four hours. On the contrary, according to the passage in 2 Peter 3: 10, already referred to, the day of the Lord covers the entire period from the great tribulation to the passing away of the heavens and earth, thus ushering in the day of God, or the day of eternity.

Four dispensational days are brought before us in Scripture. The present is called "man's day" (1 Cor. 4: 3, margin). The manifestation at the judgment-seat of Christ is in "the day of Christ" (Phil. 1: 6, 10).* Then follows "the day of the Lord," which is the entire period during which the once-rejected Lord asserts and makes good His title to the earth. "The day of God" is the eternal state, and is only mentioned in 2 Peter 3: 12.

---

* "The day of Christ" in 2 Thess. 2: 2 should be "the day of the Lord," as a glance at any reputable critical version will show.

It is therefore to this third great "day" that the present chapter refers, and of which the opening verses treat.

"For, behold in those days, and in that time, when I shall bring again the captivity of Judah and Jerusalem, I will also gather all nations, and will bring them down into the valley of Jehoshaphat, and will plead with them there for My people and for My heritage Israel, whom they have scattered among the nations, and parted My land" (vers. 1, 2). The scene depicted by our Lord Himself in Matt. 25: 31-46 would seem to coalesce with this. He vividly describes the coming of the Son of Man in His glory to sit upon the throne of His glory, there to judge the living nations. It has long since been pointed out by others that this judgment-scene is something very different and distinct from the final judgment of the Great White Throne, as set forth in Rev. 20. There the wicked dead are judged and cast into the lake of fire, the righteous having been raised in glory a thousand years before. On the other hand, the judgment of the sheep and goats, as it may be called, is a tribunal before which appear the nations living on the earth when Christ descends to take the kingdom. It is *pre*-millennial. The Great White Throne is *post*-millennial. In Matt. 25 the sheep are rewarded because of their treatment of Christ's brethren, that is, the Jewish remnant. The goats are condemned for their indifference, and even cruelty, to them. The same discriminative judgment is brought to our attention here by Joel.

The Son of Man will place His throne in the valley of Jehoshaphat. To positively locate this valley is an impossibility, as this is the only mention of it in Scripture. It is well known that there is a deep ravine now bearing this name just outside Jerusalem, separating the holy city from the mount of Olives. But it is likely that the name was given it only in view of this prophecy—not that it was so called when Joel spoke, nor yet for centuries afterward, as we have to come down to the fourth century of the Christian era before it is thus designated. If Jehoshaphat be understood as only an untranslated Hebrew expression, all is clear. Then it would read, "The valley of Jehovah's judgment."

There the Lord will sit to judge the nations who have oppressed and scattered His people, selling them into slavery and rejoicing in their degradation. No doubt it is God Himself who has permitted them thus to persecute Israel for their discipline; but that in no wise lessens the guilt of their oppressors. Therefore Tyre and Zidon, with all who have had a share in humiliating the Jew, will be recompensed according to their works (vers. 3-8).

Unquestionably what is especially brought out in Matthew 25 is the treatment of the remnant witnesses, fleeing from Antichrist's bitter persecutions. Hence to minister to them is practically to own the claims of the true Anointed; while to be indifferent to them is to tacitly consent to the iniquitous sway of the false prophet. Therefore new birth is supposed in the case of those who "go into life eternal." Of this, their works were the proof.

Thus we have detailed information in the New Testament account, which it was not God's pleasure to reveal through Joel; but the identification of the judgment seems clear.

This, the call in vers. 9 to 17 makes abundantly plain. The mighty men of the Gentiles are caused to hear an alarm and to come up to Immanuel's land. Turning the implements of peace into weapons of war, they come in great hordes to surround Jerusalem, as predicted in Zech. 14 and Rev. 19. The whole land will be overrun with them; and all human help for the remnant of Israel, who cleave to the Lord, will be gone. Therefore they cry in the hour of their deepest distress, "Thither cause Thy mighty ones to come down, O Lord." Knowing that the hour has struck when the saints shall take the kingdom, they turn heavenward in their affliction, calling for the descent of their once-rejected Messiah and His glorious train. The answer to their prayer is given in the riding forth of the warrior on the white horse, with all the armies of heaven, as recorded in Rev. 19. He executes summary judgment upon the armed hosts of the nations.

But this is not all. A sessional judgment follows, to which all the heathen are bidden attend. "Let the heathen be wakened, and come up to the valley of Jehoshaphat; for there will I sit to judge all the heathen round about" (ver. 12). This is identified with "the harvest of the earth" of Rev. 14: 14-16. "Put ye in the sickle, for the harvest is ripe." Nor will the Gentiles alone be judged and the wheat separated from the chaff; but the apostate portion of the nation of Israel, who had owned the blasphemous claims of Antichrist, will be cast as grapes fully ripe into the great wine-press of the wrath of God (Rev. 14: 17-20). So we read, "Come, get you down; for the press is full, the vats overflow; for their wickedness is great" (ver. 13).

The fourteenth verse is a graphic depicting of the solemn scene—a verse which has often been utterly misconstrued. "Multitudes, multitudes in the valley of decision [or threshing]: for the day of the Lord is near in the valley of decision!" It is the day of the Judge's decisions; not a time when men are being called upon to decide for Christ. The valley of Jehoshaphat becomes as a great threshing-floor where the Divine Winnower sits to separate all that are to share His kingdom from those who are to go away into everlasting punishment. Then shall every created light fade away into darkness, before the presence of the glory of the Crucified (ver. 15)! He, who will be revealed as Jehovah of Hosts, "shall roar out of Zion, and utter His voice from Jerusalem," overturning and shaking to pieces all the framework of the civil and political heavens and the earth, as also all religious pretension; for the Lord alone will be the hope of His people and the strength of Israel in that day (ver. 16).

Thus shall the long-looked-for kingdom of the Son of Man be ushered in, and all Israel shall know that Jehovah their God dwelleth in Zion, His holy mountain. Then shall Jerusalem's long period of Gentile treading-down be over; and, her iniquity accomplished, she shall become in very deed "the Holy City;" never to be trodden under foot of strangers forevermore.

The final four verses apply to that glorious era; yet for Egypt the desolation spoken of will not be final, as we know from other scriptures. "And it shall come to pass in that day, that the mountains shall drop down new wine, and the hills shall flow with milk, and all the rivers of Judah shall flow with waters, and a fountain shall come forth of the house of the Lord, and shall water the valley of Shittim" (ver. 18). It is a scene of plenty and refreshment which is presented, and concerning which Ezekiel adds fuller details in ch. 47 of his prophecy.

Then judgment will be meted out to Egypt

and Edom for their past treatment of the people of Judah. Edom shall be blotted out forever as a nation. This the prophet Obadiah declares. Egypt on the other hand will be restored after having been punished for her sins. See Isaiah 19: 18-25. Judah's time of trouble shall bear precious fruit, leading to her full restoration and blessing; so she "shall dwell forever, and Jerusalem from generation to generation;" having been cleansed from all their defilements, and made clean in His sight who will dwell in their midst in the city of Zion, His chosen capital. "For I will cleanse their blood that I have not cleansed: for the Lord dwelleth in Zion" (ver. 21). It would hardly be necessary to seek to explain this verse somewhat fully, were it not that in our day a wretchedly grotesque interpretation has been put upon it by deluded advocates of a disgusting modern religious fad,* whose emissaries frequently confuse the simple by using it as their proof-text. The ridiculous notion has been put forth that a certain spared remnant *of this age*, are to have their blood cleansed (!) from all impurities that would result in natural death, so that they shall obtain immortality in the flesh. The context makes plain the fact that the words

* I refer to the so-called "Flying Roll;" the doctrines of which are advocated in the misnamed "Pioneer of Wisdom" which has been extensively promulgated in England and her colonies as also in America.

refer to the cleansing of literal Judah from the defilement of the blood of their enemies, which they have contracted during the unparalleled horrors of the great tribulation. They shall be henceforth holiness to the Lord.

A reference to Isa. 4:4 will make this plain. There God speaks of the same glorious time: "When the Lord shall have washed away the filth of the daughters of Zion, and shall have purged the blood of Jerusalem from the midst thereof by the spirit of judgment, and by the spirit of burning." In Lam. 4:14 the prophets and priests of Judah are described as men who have wandered blindly through the streets, and "have polluted themselves with blood, so that men could not touch their garments." Thus, by the part they took in slaying "the Righteous One," all Israel have become polluted; but in that day the blood of defilement will be cleansed away and God will be able to dwell among them. Many other passages could be noticed; but these are sufficient to show what is really intended.

With this, Joel's burden is concluded. He has carried his hearers, and readers, on to the full display of Messiah's glory. Beyond that, prophecy, as connected with the earth, does not go. Only in the hitherto secret things of the New Testament do we have unfolded something of those things which God hath prepared for them that love Him, who are to share His eternal rest, after time has run its course and ceased to be.

Notes on the
PROPHECY OF AMOS

INTRODUCTION

OF Amos, we have much more information than is customary concerning the minor prophets. He gives us, by the inspiration of God, several autobiographical notices of deep interest, which it will be well to look at briefly ere entering upon the study of his messages to Israel and the surrounding nations.

His prophecies were given in the reigns of Uzziah king of Judah and Jeroboam II king of Israel. He describes himself as a herdman of Tekoa, a town in the hill-country of Judea, about twelve miles from Jerusalem, of which mention is frequently made in Scripture. Thence came the "wise woman" sent by Joab to persuade David to permit his murderer son to return to his patrimony, in plain violation of all law, both human and divine (2 Sam. 14:2). There too, Ira the son of Ikkesh, one of David's mighty men, was born (2 Sam. 23:26). It is noticed on numbers of other occasions, and even after the return from

Babylon, the zeal of the men of Tekoa is spoken of, though their nobles are reproved in connection with the building of the wall of Jerusalem (Neh. 3: 5, 27). A desert town, surrounded by large solitudes, it was a suitable place for men of pastoral occupation; and there Amos pursued his humble calling till separated by the Lord to the prophetic office.

He tells us that he was neither born into the goodly company of the prophets, nor did he choose that calling for himself. But when he was "a herdman and a gatherer of sycamore fruit" (that is, the fruit of the wild fig), the Lord said unto him, "Go, prophesy unto My people Israel" (ch. 7: 14, 15). This was enough for Amos. He was not disobedient to the voice from heaven, but, leaving behind the pastures of the wilderness, and turning his back on the place of his birth, we soon find him declaring the word of the Lord away up in the capital of the northern kingdom, greatly to the disgust and arousing the indignation of Jeroboam and his false priest Amaziah. When ordered to flee to his own land and do his prophesying there, he boldly gives his divine credentials, and delivers a message more searching than ever.

Of the duration of his ministry, or the time or circumstances of his death, we have no record. But what has been vouchsafed to us is fraught with most important lessons.

It is ever God's way to prepare His servants in

secret for the work they are afterwards to accomplish in public. Moses at the backside of the desert; Gideon on the threshing-floor; David with his "few sheep" out upon the hillside; Daniel refusing to be defiled with the king's meat; John the Baptist in the desert; Peter in his fishing-boat; Paul in Arabia; and Amos following the flock and herding the cattle in the wilderness of Tekoa—all alike attest this fact. It is important to observe that only he who has thus learned of God in the school of obscurity is likely to shine in the blaze of publicity.

Amos had no thought of becoming, or being recognized, as a prophet, as men today select "the ministry" as a profession. He would doubtless have been quite content to pursue his humble avocation as a small farmer, or possibly a mere farmer's hand or assistant, to the end of his life, if such had been the mind of God for him. But as he followed the flock, his soul was communing with Jehovah. As he gathered the wild figs of the wilderness, his heart was meditating on the great issues of the soul's relationship to God and the importance of walking in His ways. As he tended the herds he was learning wondrous lessons of a faithful Creator's love and care. And so, when for him "the fulness of time was come," the Lord, so to speak, kindled the already prepared fuel into a flame, and the humble herdman became a mighty, Spirit-energized prophet of

God, not only to his own people, but to all Israel and the nations around.

We read of no unbelieving hesitation, no parleying with God, no bargaining or questioning as to temporal support; even as before there was no fleshly impatience or desire to be at the front attracting notice as a prophet or speaker. Throughout it is the record of a simple, humble man of God, who can wait or run as his Lord sees fit. In all this how much there is for our souls today! There are many self-made ministers whose inner lives are in sad contrast to their ministry. Many, too, insist on taking the place belonging to a servant of God who have never spent any time in His school, learning His ways, as did Amos. Thus their utterances are empty and disappointing in the extreme, as might be expected when coming from men who had not been sent by the Lord. It is blessedly otherwise with Amos. The more we learn of the messenger, the more we are prepared to listen to his message.

Those hidden years had not been wasted. Not only were they years in which he listened to the voice of God speaking to his own soul, but in them he was acquiring experience, and an insight into men and things which would be invaluable to him later on. Again and again in his public utterances he uses figures, or illustrations, which show how closely and thoughtfully he had observed the many things, animate and inanimate, surrounding him in his early life. This the following passages make abundantly plain: Chapters 2: 13; 3: 12; 4: 9; 5: 8; 6: 12; 7: 1, 2. Others too we shall notice as we proceed.

The theme of the book of Amos is emphatically one of judgment on Israel and Judah, and the nations about them.

In the first two chapters we have eight separate burdens, addressed respectively to Damascus, Gaza, Tyrus, Edom, Ammon, Moab, Judah, and Israel.

The second part of the prophecy includes chaps. 3 to 6, giving the word of the Lord to Israel, that is, the ten-tribed kingdom of the north.

The third and last division takes in chaps. 7 to 9, in which we have a series of five visions, with a considerable parenthesis (ch. 7: 10-17) devoted to the personal history of the prophet, which we have already slightly noticed. The visions close with the declaration of millennial blessing and restoration, as seen in both the preceding books, Hosea and Joel, and generally throughout the Prophets.

For though judgment be the theme, yet judgment is but to prepare the way for glory. The Lord will not cease till He has established righteousness and blessing in all the earth.

CHAPTERS I AND II

THE INDICTMENT OF THE NATIONS

AMOS does not conceal what men might be disposed to call his mean origin. He boldly begins with, "The words of Amos, who was among the herdmen of Tekoa, which he saw concerning Israel in the days of Uzziah king of Judah, and in the days of Jeroboam the son of Joash king of Israel, two years before the earthquake" (ver. 1). Here the prophet's name, his humble calling, the place of his dwelling, and the date of his prophecy, are all plainly set forth.

The earthquake referred to would doubtless mark a time-epoch for more than one generation; but we have no record by which now to locate it. In Jewish traditionary lore it is said to have occurred when Uzziah impiously sought to take to himself the office of a priest of the Lord. Josephus thus connects the two incidents. But of this there is no *proof*.

Having already dwelt somewhat on the other points mentioned in this first verse, in the introduction, we may turn at once to the prophetic messages, of which, as before noted, there are eight in the first two chapters; five in chapter one, and three in the second.

From verse 2 we gather that the nations addressed are regarded in connection with Jerusalem and Mount Zion. There Jehovah had set His name. Thence He would roar in His indignation and utter His voice in judgment, so that the pastures of the shepherds should mourn and the top of Carmel wither.

Notice that each separate prediction begins with the same solemn formula, save for the change of the name: "For three transgressions of Damascus, and for four, I will not turn away [the punishment] thereof; because ——." This the Jewish expositors generally understand to have the force of, "Three transgressions have I forgiven them, but the fourth I will visit in judgment." It at least implies that, in His long-suffering, God had waited again and again, looking for some evidence of repentance ere finally dealing in wrath; but there was none. In three transgressions they had filled up the cup of their wickedness. In the fourth it had overflowed, and declared that all further testing was useless. They were corrupt and abominable in His sight. Judgment therefore must take its course.

The crowning sin of each people is especially set forth in the terrible indictment and sentence combined which proceeded from the seer's inspired lips.

Damascus had "threshed Gilead with threshing instruments of iron." Ruthlessly persecuting the exposed borders of Israel across the Jordan, they showed no mercy to age or sex, but swept over the land, cutting down all alike, and treating them as grain under the flail. For this they should have judgment without mercy meted out by the Moral Governor of the Universe, whose eyes were upon all their ways (vers. 3-5).

Gaza, the ancient Philistine capital, had made His people their prey, taking them captive and selling or giving them to Edom (in type, how graphic a picture of false religion delivering man up to the power of the flesh!), and thus aiding this cruel unbrotherly foe to destroy and enslave his near kinsman. But as they had sought the destruction of the erring people of the Lord, His fire and His hand would be against Philistia, even to its utter destruction (vers. 6-8).

Tyrus, the merchant city by the sea, once in "brotherly covenant" with Israel, in the days of Solomon and Hiram, had forgotten the pledges made, and likewise sided with Edom, delivering up to them the captives they had taken. Therefore the fire should devour the fancied impregnable wall of Tyre and blot out her palaces (vers. 9, 10).

Edom, ever the bitterest enemy of the seed of Jacob, had been unrelenting in his fury, "pursuing his brother with the sword, and casting off all pity." So should the Lord forget to pity him in the day of His righteous wrath, recompensing to

Edom the indignities heaped upon Israel. The prophecy of Obadiah connects intimately with this passage (vers. 11, 12).

Ammon's fiendish display of hatred against Israel, seeking by cruelty of most heinous character to blot out the hope of the chosen nation, that he might enlarge his own border, had called down the divine retribution upon his own guilty head, and he should be exposed to all the fury of the tempest of Jehovah in the day of the whirlwind of His wrath (vers. 13-15).

Moab, on the other hand, is not charged with cruelty to Israel, but with having undertaken to execute judgment on Edom when guilty of the gravest crimes himself. Therefore the judge should "be cut off from the midst thereof," and all their princes slain (ch. 2: 1-3).

Thus far the prophetic messages have been directed against the peoples surrounding the land of Israel. History is the witness of their fulfilment. Gaza, Tyre, Edom, Ammon and Moab are now but *names*. Their glory has long since disappeared. Damascus still exists, but her people have gone into captivity and the Moslem dwells in her palaces. Thus have the predictions of the herdman-prophet been proved to be the word of Jehovah.

But not only against the heathen did he lift up his voice. To Judah and Israel he also had to proclaim the coming of long-delayed judgment, because of their unholy ways.

Judah, privileged above all others, had despised the law of the Lord, and refused obedience to His commandments. The lies of their false teachers had caused them to err—the prophets whom they preferred to the heaven-sent messengers of the God of their fathers. Alas, the fathers had turned away from their Rock, and the children had walked in their ways. Because of this, Jerusalem's palaces, like those of the nations, must be burned with fire, and the place where Jehovah had set His name be given up to His enemies (vers. 4, 5).

The indictment of Israel is the lengthiest of all. The proud northern kingdom is charged with covetousness, licentiousness, idolatry, and yet with utter unconcern as to the mischief wrought. They sold the righteous for silver, and the needy for a pair of shoes. The most commonplace article of commerce was of more value in their covetous eyes than the cause of the poor. Living in the practice of uncleanness of the vilest description, they yet called themselves by the holy name of the Lord, thus profaning it in the sight of the heathen. Idolatry inflamed them, and they drank "the wine of the condemned in the house of their god," laying themselves down upon the pledged garments of the needy by every altar. The law had forbidden the keeping of the garment of the poor as a pledge overnight; but they not only despised the law, but openly devoted the garments thus acquired to the worship of their idols. The judges also, contrary to all law, used the fines of those they condemned for the purchase of wine for their idolatrous festivals. This was "the wine of the condemned." Thus was the Holy One of Israel dishonored by those who boasted in His name.

Yet had He, as He touchingly reminds them, cast out the Amorite before them, having brought them up from the land of Egypt and led them forty years through the wilderness. He had raised up prophets among their sons, and Nazarites, devoted to Himself, among their young men. But they led astray the separated ones by wine, and refused to listen to the warnings of the prophets. It is a sad and pitiful picture, but how often has it been duplicated since! They to whom the greatest privileges appertain are often the greatest offenders.

At last their iniquities had come to the full. The last sheaf had been cast upon the cart, and the mercy of the Lord had come to an end. Therefore none should stand "in that day"—the day of the Lord's anger (vers. 6-16).

How solemn the charges here recorded! Searching too are these words of old. Oh, that we who today are called by the name of the Lord may consider them well!

CHAPTER III

THE CHASTISEMENT OF THE CHOSEN NATION

WITH this chapter the second division of the prophecy begins, going on to the end of chapter 6, embracing the word of the Lord to Israel, a last solemn remonstrance ere carrying out the predicted judgment we have just been noticing.

It is not merely the ten tribes that Amos addresses under the name of "sons of Israel" in this prophecy, but "the whole family which [the Lord] brought up from the land of Egypt" (ver. 1). They are viewed as one nation though divided into two kingdoms at that time. Their special privileges made them far more responsible than their ignorant heathen neighbors. "You only," He says, "have I known of all the families of the earth: *therefore* I will punish you for all your iniquities" (ver. 2). This is a divine principle we should never lose sight of. "Responsibility flows from relationship." Because Jehovah had separated Israel from the nations, and taken them into covenant with Himself, they were expected to yield that obedience which their favored position demanded; otherwise they must be the special objects of His disciplinary dealing. The same is true as to the assembly of God in this dispensation, viewed collectively, and of every individual saint likewise. We are called to walk worthy of our exalted vocation; and if we do not, we incur our Father's discipline. Nor does chastisement prove that God's heart is hardened against us; but the contrary. It is His love that leads Him so to act. The world may go on in its folly, and know little of such governmental care; but it must be otherwise with the people who are called by the name of the Lord.

Verse 3 lets us into the secret of true fellowship. Two can walk together only when they are agreed. It is not a question of seeing all details alike, but of having common thoughts as to the ground of their communion together. God cannot walk with gainsayers in that intimate, happy sense that is here contemplated. Neither can saints walk together in holy association if the one seeks to honor God, and the other has lapsed into loose thoughts and evil ways.

Beginning with verse 4, the prophet declares the reason for his message. Results spring from adequate causes. The trumpet was to be blown, that the people might tremble, for God was about to bring evil upon them. "Shall there be evil in the city, and the Lord hath not done it?" is His challenge. This verse has perturbed some, overzealous for the reputation of the Lord of hosts.

But evil is, of course, *calamity* (not sin), as we have seen in the first chapter of Joel, and which God uses as His rod of discipline. Of this Amos was to warn the careless inhabitants of the cities of Israel.

He has good cause to prophesy. God has revealed His secrets to him. Therefore he must boldly proclaim them. "The Lord God hath spoken; who can but prophesy?" (vers. 4-8). This is high ground indeed; but it is the only proper ground for one who essays to minister divine truth. If God has not spoken, then one man's guess is as good as another's; one philosopher's speculations are as worthy of credence or consideration as those of his fellows. But if God Himself has spoken, as He has in His Word, that at once settles everything for the one who fears Him. His servant has naught to do but proclaim what has been revealed, rejecting "oppositions of science, falsely so called," and all "vain imaginations."

This is the value of Scripture; and of this Satan would subtly seek to rob us at the present time. God has revealed His will in His Word. "The Lord God will do nothing, but He revealeth His secret unto His servants the prophets." Therefore the man of faith accepts the prophetic writings, to which the Lord Jesus has set His seal, as a final court of appeal; knowing that "holy men of God spake as they were moved by the Holy Ghost." Here faith triumphs, where mere reason stumbles in the dark; vainly endeavoring to peer into the future, to explain the past, or to understand the present.

It has often been alleged by opponents of the inspiration of the Bible that unless we were prepared to believe that the writers of the various books were infallible, it was idle to talk of the unerring Scriptures; and this in face of the solemn declaration of the Lord Jesus that "the Scripture *cannot be broken.*" But the question of human infallibility does not come in at all. When God speaks, one needs but to be obedient, not infallible, in giving out what He has made known. So it was with Amos and his fellow-servants of the prophetic band. An amanuensis need not have exact knowledge of the events concerning which he writes at the dictation of another. He hears the word, and transcribes accordingly. Thus can we understand the Old Testament writers, "searching what, or what manner of time, the Spirit of Christ which was in them did signify (or point out) when He testified beforehand the sufferings of Christ and the glories that should follow." It is only unbelief that could make any difficulty here.

The prophetic message is given in vers. 9 to 15. Israel's dispersion is foretold; but that a remnant shall be saved is likewise made known.

In the palaces of Philistia and Egypt it is to be

published that, because of their sins, the Lord God would no longer be a bulwark to His people. The nations that had once been witnesses of His power would now witness His righteousness. When His people walked not with Him, He could only give them up to chastisement.

But as the Eastern shepherd "taketh out of the mouth of the lion two legs, or a piece of an ear; so shall the children of Israel be delivered that dwell in Samaria in the corner of a bed, and in Damascus on a couch." The shepherd who lost one of the flock would have to be responsible for the same, unless he could bring proof that it was torn of beasts; therefore his anxiety to recover a portion, if only the tip of an ear, of the creature devoured. So shall God preserve a portion of Israel, though a very small remnant, from being devoured by the wild beasts of the Gentile empires. Their transgressions must be visited upon them because of their idolatrous practices, of which the altar at Bethel, set up by Jeroboam the son of Nebat, was a standing memorial. Its fall would involve the destruction of those who gloried in their wealth and reveled in luxury, careless of the fallen state of Israel. This is more fully gone into in ch. 6: 1-6, which will be noticed in its place.

CHAPTER IV

YET HAVE YE NOT RETURNED!

IN this chapter they are reminded of the various means whereby God had been speaking, with a view to recalling them to Himself; but the sad result had been that they pursued their ways of sin regardless of warning or punishment. They despised the chastisement of the Lord.

It is probably the great women of Israel who are addressed in vers. 1 to 3; for in place of "kine of Bashan," the feminine form is used in the original. Luxurious, insolent, and self-pleasing, these haughty dames oppressed the poor and crushed the needy, that they might minister to their own carnal desires. Indifferent to the sorrows their ill-gotten pleasures entailed on others, they feasted and rejoiced; forgetting that the Holy One of Israel was looking on. He had sworn by His holiness to visit upon them their sins, taking them away in the midst of their folly, as the angler hooks the greedy fish that fancies not there is danger lurking in the bait so temptingly displayed.

Verses 4 and 5 have been variously understood; some seeing therein a call to repentance seriously addressed to the consciences of the people. In this case they consider "the sacrifice of thanksgiving with leaven," to be according to the word of God, as set forth in Lev. 7: 13, where leavened bread accompanied the sacrifice of thanksgiving as the offerer's acknowledgment of his own personal unworthiness.

But a thank-offering was only in place when the people were in a right state before God. To call them to the schismatic altar of Bethel, there to bring a thank-offering, when they needed a *sin-offering,* would surely be contrary to the mind of God.

I understand the passage, therefore, to be one of solemn irony, after the manner of Elijah's taunts to the priests of Baal. In fact, it would seem as though the prophet were saying, "Bring a sacrifice of leaven as a thank-offering, for so liketh you, O ye children of Israel!" There is no thought of the leaven here accompanying a slain victim or a presentation of first-fruits; but the *leaven* is the offering which they are ironically called to bring. The whole passage is a sad commentary on the pitifully low state of Israel, whose whole system of worship was but iniquity and transgression, while yet they prided themselves on their pomp and ritual.

Does not He who gazes down upon the pretentiousness of a guiltier Christendom regard it with even greater abhorrence? Where conscience is active it will surely lead to departure from iniquity of so glaring a character.

That there was no thought in the mind of God of accepting a sacrifice offered at Bethel or Gilgal is plain from ch. 5: 5. All that circled around these centres of apostasy was abhorrent to Him who had set His name in Jerusalem; though there, alas, it had also been profaned.

Because of what we have been considering, He had sent a grievous famine upon them, "giving them cleanness of teeth in all their cities, and want of bread in all places;" but there had been no evidence of repentance, and He had to say, "Yet have ye not returned unto Me!" (ver. 6). The rain too He had withheld, and that in such a way as to lead to inquiry and exercise, had conscience been at all active, giving rain to one city and withholding it from another; but again comes the solemn refrain, "Yet have ye not returned unto Me, saith the Lord" (vers. 7, 8); and with blasting and mildew He had smitten them, so that their scanty crop was ruined ere it reached perfection; and if the orchards, vineyards and gardens seemed to do well, the palmerworm (the locust in its most voracious form) was sent to destroy them. But there had been no awakening —conscience remained dormant. "Yet have ye not returned unto Me, saith the Lord" (ver. 9).

With pestilence too He had visited them, "after the manner of Egypt;" the putrid carcases of their goodliest sons, together with their horses slain in battle, polluting the air so that they breathed in disease and death. But none seem to have discerned who it was who afflicted them, and so they returned not unto Him (ver. 10).

A great physical catastrophe, possibly an earthquake, with an accompanying conflagration, had added to their woes. He had overthrown some of them after the fashion of the destruction of Sodom and Gomorrah, so that the survivors were as firebrands plucked out of the burning: yet had they not returned unto Him (ver. 11). Failing to discern His hand in all that had befallen them, they sought only to escape the rod, hearing it not, nor yet Him who had appointed it. Such is ever the way of man untouched by divine grace. Shutting his eyes to the most palpable evidences of God's dealing, he pursues his careless way till the pit closes upon him.*

---

* The writer passed through the California earthquake of April 18, 1906, and was an eye-witness of its horrors. Not the least solemn thing noticed was the persistent efforts of the preachers of all denominations to quiet the fears of the populace by assuring them that *God* had no part in the calamitous events that had taken place. Natural causes explained everything! This the Christless were only too ready to believe; and thus were their partially awakened consciences lulled to rest and their ears closed against the voice of Him who through Amos said, "*I* have overthrown some of you!"

From vers. 11 and 12 of this chapter, it was my solemn opportunity to press the truth upon many at that time, and not altogether, I trust, without fruit; but "the day" will declare it.

Because of their utter indifference, there remained only one thing more: they must meet Him in judgment whose warnings and acts of discipline they had despised. "Therefore . . . prepare to meet thy God, O Israel!" (ver. 12).

For though they knew Him not, yet He who formed the mountains and created the winds, declaring unto man his secret thoughts and making the morning darkness, treading on earth's high places, was Jehovah, the mighty God of hosts (ver. 13).

Him they must meet—but how? And you too, my reader, have this before you, if still unsaved. Think well how *you* will stand in that great day of His wrath!

For the believer walking carelessly, this word also has an application. Taking his own way, he may despise the chastisement of the Lord, and fail to hearken to His reproving voice. But not for long can he so continue. Sooner or later God must be met, and all be solemnly gone into in His presence. Oh, then, keep short accounts with Him who knows the secrets of all hearts!

CHAPTER V

A LAMENTATION FOR ISRAEL

SAD and solemn are the dirge-like measures of the prophet's lamentation over the fallen nation that he loved so well. They had utterly broken down as a people in their allegiance and fidelity to God, and on the ground of responsibility could claim no blessing whatever. If God take them up at all, it must be in *pure grace;* otherwise naught but judgment could be their portion.

Thus has everything failed that God has committed to man, not excepting the testimony entrusted to the Church. But God has infinite resources in Himself, only to be displayed upon the failure of the objects of His grace. This may well cheer and uplift the spirits of all who sigh and cry for the unhappy divisions and utter breakdown of what should have been for testimony to Christ and the glory of God in these last days. Still, despondency and gloom need not overwhelm the soul. God may yet be entreated of His people. If there be brokenness and repentance manifested, He is able to do exceeding abundantly above all we ask or think.

The virgin of Israel had fallen so low that she could never rise again—that is, so far as her own volition was concerned; nor were there any of her leaders who could raise her up. But God still entreated, crying in the ears of any who might heed, "Seek ye Me, and ye shall live!" None could deliver but He from whom they had grievously departed. To seek to Bethel, Gilgal, or Beersheba, where the high places that told of idolatrous self-will were set up, would be all in vain, as ironically declared in ch. 4: 4. The fact that a certain sacredness of association was connected with each of the places named would not prevent their going into captivity. Bethel was no longer the house of God, nor did Gilgal now speak of reproach rolled away. Rather had Bethel become a hold of demons, and Gilgal was itself a reproach (vers. 1-5).

There is nothing in "succession," whether it be the dream of apostolicity, or the modern notion prevailing in some quarters as to "the original ground of gathering," and "the continuity of the Lord's table." What was once clearly of God becomes readily corrupted where pride and self-will are at work, and may have to be turned from and refused, in faithfulness to the Lord, despite all former associations of blessedness and the manifest acknowledgment of God in the past.

Scripture must ever be the guide—not human rules and assumption of authority. "That which was from the beginning" is the original ground—and only that!

So Israel are exhorted to seek the Lord and live, "lest He break out like fire in the house of Joseph, and devour it, and there be none to quench it in Bethel" (ver. 6). Alas, the warning was unheeded; so in a very few years the threatened judgment was carried out, and the house of Joseph was dispossessed of their land—never to be regathered till the day of the coming glory.

The herdman of Tekoa soars to loftiest flights of inspired poetry in verses 7 to 9. The "stars in their courses" had, no doubt, often been his contemplation as he watched his flocks on the hillside at night. The book of Job too had evidently been studied, for ver. 8 is closely linked with Job 9:9 and 38:31.

"Ye who turn judgment to wormwood," he cries, "and cast down righteousness to the ground, consider the Maker of Kimah and Kesil (the Pleiades and Orion), even turning the shadow of death into morning, and who maketh the day dark with night; that calleth for the waters of the sea, and poureth them out upon the face of the earth: Jehovah His name; that strengthened the spoiled against the strong, so that the spoiled shall come against the fortress" (7-9). Kimah and Kesil cannot be identified with certainty. That they refer to some of the more important constellations is clear. Both in the two places in Job where the words occur, and in this passage, they are generally translated as "the seven stars,"

i. e., the Pleiades, and "Orion." The Hebrews generally understood them to refer to these brilliant star-groups, which display the majesty and glory of their Creator. The prophet calls the workers of iniquity to contemplate Him who guides the heavenly bodies, and who brought them into being; who causes the sun to rise in his glory, dispelling the darkness; and whose hand likewise controls the planetary movements that bring the night again; and who gives rain to the thirsty ground. With *Him* men have to do, whether they desire it or not. His eyes beheld all the unholy ways of the people who were called by His name.

Wilfully rejecting light, they hated him who rebuked in the gate, and abhorred him who spake uprightly (ver. 10). Many are their successors. It is a most common thing to find those walking carelessly, or sinfully, filled with indignation against any who faithfully rebuke their unholy ways. Easy-going, man-pleasing preachers and teachers are delighted in; but faithful, God-fearing men are abhorred and despised. But he who would stand for God must expect the opposition and evil-speaking of the unspiritual and worldly-minded.

Knowing that he would be hated for rebuking in the gate, Amos nevertheless proclaims his solemn message without excuse or hesitation. He presses home upon their consciences the sins that were about to draw down coming judgment on the guilty nation. They oppressed the poor, thought only of their own comfort, afflicted the just, were bribe-takers, dealt unjustly with the needy in the place of judgment—the gate—and withal were so overbearing and insolent that it seemed the part of prudence to refrain from exposing their wickedness, so evil was the time (vers. 11-13). But God's faithful servant covers nothing, using no flattering words. He manifests their hypocrisy, and then calls on them to "seek good, and not evil," that they might live, and that the Lord of hosts might be with them. If the word was heeded, God might yet be gracious unto the remnant of Joseph (vers. 14, 15).

Men like Amos are never popular with the mass. Better far, however, to have the approbation of One than of the many. Like Paul, he spoke "not as pleasing men, but God, who trieth the hearts." Yet there is no railing, no cutting or abusive language; simply the solemn, earnest recital of their guilt, and a tender, loving call to repentance.

If this call be unheeded, then wailing must supersede their empty songs, as it did very soon, when all joy was darkened, and even in the vineyards of gladness the lamentations of the desolate were heard (vers. 16, 17).

It is remarkable how low people can fall, and yet how religiously and piously they can talk. Wretchedly vile as was Israel's condition, there were still to be found among them those who professed to desire the day of the Lord, hoping thereby to be delivered from their troubles—the fruit of their own waywardness. A woe is pronounced on such. What profit would there be for them in the day of the Lord? It would be as if a man fled from a lion, and was met by a bear. Seeking to escape this second danger, he flees to his house; but as he leans his hand against the wall, a poisonous serpent, concealed in some corner, or behind some drapery, strikes him with its venomed fangs. There could be no escape from judgment. The day of the Lord is to be the day of manifestation, and therefore, for the wicked, a day of darkness, and not of light; "even very dark, and no brightness in it" (vers. 18-20).

Quite in harmony with this pretended desire for the day of the Lord was the unreality of the feasts and solemn assemblies. Outwardly, there seems to have been some pretence to honor Jehovah in the reign of the second Jeroboam, but actually He was dishonored by the unholy practices indulged in. Therefore He hated the feast-days, and would not accept their offerings. He looked for righteousness to roll on as a mighty stream in the land, not for outward forms and ceremonies (vers. 21-24). But, alas, their present unreal course had been characteristic from their beginning. Even in the days of the wilderness they had set up the tabernacle of their false gods beside the sanctuary of Jehovah, and had offered sacrifices and offerings to them throughout those memorable forty years. "Therefore will I cause you to go into captivity beyond Damascus, saith the Lord, whose name is The God of hosts" (vers. 25-27). This is intensely important, and worthy our most serious consideration. Here the Lord declares that the Assyrian captivity was the result of their sinful idolatry "in the wilderness!" Over seven hundred years had rolled by since that first apostasy; but as it had never been really judged, they must be judged for it! How this passage rebukes those who refuse to face the fact that unjudged evil is ever at work, like leaven, leavening the whole lump! Again we have the same lesson enforced which we noted at length in our study of Hos. 7: 4-7. Oh, for hearts to bow to the truth so frequently pressed in Scripture, and thus to be kept from the defilement of unjudged evil!

CHAPTER VI

AT EASE IN ZION!

IT was not alone the house of Joseph who had provoked the Lord. As before noted, Israel refers throughout, not to the ten tribes only, but to the whole nation. Therefore this division of the prophecy concludes with a stirring word to those at ease in Zion, and to those who trusted in the mountain of Samaria (ver. 1). Down in the southern kingdom, the danger threatening the northern one seemed far off, and they took comfort in the fact that Samaria would, as they supposed, withstand a siege long enough to give them plenty of opportunity to prepare if the enemies drew near. Hence they took their ease, and were not concerned about obeying the voice of God calling them to repentance, nor did they afflict their souls for the sorrows of their brethren.

"At ease in Zion" may well speak to us of that unexercised condition in which so many of the professed children of God are found at the present time, unheeding the special message for the moment, and manifesting no concern as to walking in the power of the truth. But if God's people are indifferent to that which is of importance in His eyes, they need not expect Him to act for them when difficulties and afflictions arise.

Philistine cities, once splendid and magnificent, had been destroyed. Calneh, Hamath and Gath were but solemn reminders of past glory, and now in ruins. What better was Israel than these kingdoms? They put far off the evil day, while violence and corruption abounded within their borders. Stretched on beds of ivory and carved couches, they feasted without fear on the choice of the flock and herd. They chanted to the sound of musical instruments, drank wine, and delighted in costly ointments; but God winds up the solemn indictment by declaring, "They are not grieved for the breach of Joseph" (vers. 2-6). And shall not this have a voice for every saint of God today? Are we not in *grave* danger of living to please ourselves, rejoicing in our possessions, and forgetting the breach of Joseph?—forgetting the unhappy state of the assembly, indifferent to the breaches made by self-will, and which have so dishonored the Lord, the Church's glorified Head? Surely true love to Him will result in exercise of soul as to the present state of that which is so precious in His sight. Such exercises will lead to searching the Scriptures, and judging all in their light; to seeking to walk individually in "the old paths" in which the people of God have walked, even if one has thus to walk alone. But, withal, there will of very necessity be a manifestation of that "love to all the saints" which should characterize every one who enters in any degree into the truth that "there is one Body, and one Spirit."

Because of this lack of concern for the affliction, or breach, of Joseph, the Lord could not show Himself strong on their behalf, but would abhor the excellency of Jacob, and deliver up even the city of David to the Gentile oppressor (vers. 7, 8).

When at last the destruction came, the fearful sense of Jehovah's wrath would close every mouth, even as they buried the dead, for the name of the Lord would be unsuited to their defiled lips (vers. 9, 10). It is sad indeed, to be under the rod, and yet to be utterly unable to get into touch with Him who appointed it. Such is the hardening power of the deceitfulness of sin!

Vers. 11 to 14 look on to the Babylonian captivity, which followed the Assyrian invasion of the north over a century later. When the Chaldeans came in like an inundation, overflowing all the land, it should be as by direct command of the Lord, as *His* rod, because of Judah's having turned judgment into gall, and the fruit of righteousness into poisonous hemlock. The Holy One must Himself take sides against His own if they turn His truth into a lie, and walk in uncleanness. So is it still. "The righteous Lord loveth righteousness," and will not connect His name with what is contrary to it.

With this message the second division of our prophet comes to a close.

CHAPTER VII

TEACHING BY SYMBOLS

THE last division of the book contains a series of five visions, symbolically setting forth divine judgment, and embracing chapters 7 to 9, as noted in the Introduction.

In verses 1 to 9 of the present chapter, three of these visions are described; while the balance of the passage gives a most interesting and instructive bit of autobiography. In the first vision, the prophet was shown a plague of locusts (not merely grasshoppers), "in the beginning of the shooting up of the latter growth, after the king's mowings." In Palestine two crops a year were readily harvested. Under favorable conditions, "the latter growth, after the king's mowings," would have reference to the second crop, which would be depended on largely for the winter supplies of food and provender. But the seer beholds devouring locusts destroying every tender shoot, leading to the heartfelt prayer on the part of Amos, "O Lord God, forgive, I beseech Thee: by whom shall Jacob arise? for he is small." And the Lord hearkens to the intercession, and replies, "It shall not be."

Undoubtedly a desolating scourge like an army sweeping all before it, leaving no remnant, was symbolized by the locusts. As in Moses' day, the anger of the Lord was kindled, and would have destroyed the nation; but the intercession of the mediator interposed. God loves to be entreated. He delights to answer when He hears the cry of such as bear His needy people on their heart.

In the second vision (vers. 4-6), Amos beheld a devouring fire of such intensity that it licked up in its fury the waters of the great deep, "and did eat up a part." It is again threatened judgment of the fiercest character, yet not making a full end. Once more the cry comes from the heart of the man of God, "O Lord God, cease, I beseech Thee: by whom shall Jacob arise? for he is small." And again, in grace, the response is given, "This also shall not be, saith the Lord."

It was the awfulness of overwhelming wrath without discrimination, falling on all alike, that appalled the prophet. Therefore in the next vision he is shown that which assures him that each one shall be dealt with according to his own iniquity.

The Lord stood upon a wall, to test its correctness by the plumb-line in His hand; and cried, "Amos, what seest thou?" The answer is given, "A plumb-line." The Lord replies, "Behold, I will set a plumb-line in the midst of My people Israel: I will not again pass by them any more: and the high places of Isaac shall be desolate, and the sanctuaries of Israel shall be laid waste; and I will rise against the house of Jeroboam with the sword" (vers. 8, 9). It was a figure easily understood. No words are needed when a wall is tested by the plumber. If out of the perpendicular, it is at once manifest, to the confusion of the workman. God's unerring word is such a plumb-line. Unmistakably it tests every soul, manifesting every departure therefrom, and calling down judgment on the violator of it. Throughout the whole land of Israel that Word was despised, while the people took their own ways, and asked not counsel of the Lord. Therefore none could rightfully complain when they were visited according to their ways. Every high place in the land was a silent testimony to the gainsaying and disobedience of the nation. Upon them all desolation would fall, in the day that the sword was to be drawn against the house of Jeroboam. It is, of course, the second of the name that is referred to —the monarch in whose reign Amos uttered his prophecies.

Amaziah, the apostate priest of the high place at Bethel, hearing these solemn words, rises in anger to denounce Amos as a traitor to the king. As head of the apostate ritualistic system, established and supported by Israel's wayward kings, he would, if possible, get the pestilent preacher of the truth out of the way, because the craft was in danger if such utterances were permitted in the land. Therefore he sent to Jeroboam, saying, "Amos hath conspired against thee in the midst of the house of Israel: the land is not able to bear all his words. For thus Amos saith, Jeroboam shall die by the sword, and Israel shall surely be led away captive out of their own land" (vers. 10, 11). It was unpalatable truth indeed that Amos had declared. But Amaziah seems to have reported Amos' words incorrectly, either intentionally so, or his own guilty conscience leading him to misunderstand them. We have no record of Amos declaring that Jeroboam himself should die by the sword (which is manifestly not the case, see 2 Kings 14: 23-29), but that the sword should be drawn against his house; which was fulfilled in the violent death of his son Zachariah (2 Kings 15: 10).

We read of no reply on the part of the king. That energetic monarch may have considered the herdman-prophet and his predictions as beneath his notice; or he may have feared to touch one who evidently was sent of God. So the enraged prelate is left to deal with the intrusive preacher himself. He reasons with him, bidding him consider that he is trespassing in a parish that belongs to another! "O thou seer," he says, "go, flee thee away into the land of Judah, and there eat bread, and prophesy there: but prophesy not again any more at Bethel: for it is the king's sanctuary, and it is the king's court (or palace)" (vers. 12, 13). It is an oft-repeated complaint this, on the part of man-made priests and preachers, that Spirit-sent men of God must not fish in the waters which *they* claim, nor touch any of *their* flock. Looking on God's heritage as their particular allotted portion, they cannot brook the untrammeled servant who comes with the plain word of the Lord, seeking not financial or other gain, but simply declaring the whole counsel of God. Being a hireling himself, Amaziah intimates that Amos is the same, when he urges him to go to Judah, and "there eat bread." He cannot conceive of one going forth to proclaim God's word who has not his eye on a good living. His own covetous heart led him to consider the office of high priest as a desirable means of livelihood, and he takes it for granted that Amos, in his way, is as much a professional man as himself.

Then too he arrogates to himself the right to be the supreme minister and spiritual adviser of the king and people at Bethel. It was what we today would call a cathedral city, and Amaziah was its ecclesiastical head. Away with this unlicensed interloper from the south.

Amos modestly and faithfully answers the haughty and indignant priest. "I was no prophet, neither was I a prophet's son," he replies. He was neither a professional seer, nor did he obtain his appointment through human hands, nor by descent. "But I was a herdman, and a gatherer of sycamore fruit (the wild fig of Palestine): and the Lord took me as I followed the flock, and the Lord said unto me, Go, prophesy unto My people Israel" (vers. 14,15). Here were credentials that were as inexplicable to Amaziah as they have been to thousands of others since. Amos entered upon his ministry by the direct call of God. Like the New Testament apostle, it was "not from men, nor through man" (Gal. 1:1), but by divine appointment. In neither Testament do we ever read of one man empowering another to speak the word of the Lord. An Elijah may, at the command of God, anoint an Elisha; or a Paul may choose a Silas; but God alone gives the gift and accredits the servant.

But Amaziah is to hear more. As he impiously attempted to control divinely-given ministry, he must hear his own doom pronounced. "Now therefore hear thou the word of the Lord: Thou sayest, Prophesy not against Israel, and drop not thy word against the house of Isaac. Therefore thus saith the Lord; Thy wife shall be a harlot in the city, and thy sons and thy daughters shall fall by the sword, and thy land shall be divided by line; and thou shalt die in a polluted land: and Israel shall surely go into captivity forth of his land" (vers. 16, 17).

Plain words these; and though we have no record further, we cannot doubt that they were fulfilled to the letter. We read of no reply on the part of Amaziah. His conscience was on the prophet's side; and that may have sealed his lips. How every word must have come back to him when, stripped of all his honors, he lifted his tear-dimmed eyes heavenward in the Assyrians' land!

CHAPTER VIII

A FAMINE OF THE WORD

THE opening verses (1-3) contain the fourth vision, and its application. It will be noticed that, with the exception of the last of these object-lessons, all are of such a character as would readily come before the mind of a young man who had been reared in a rural district, and was familiar with agricultural life. Locusts are the dreaded plague of the Eastern farmer. Often too Amos may have helped combat a brush or forest fire, threatening destruction to crops and herds alike. The use of the plumb-line would be quite familiar to him, as stone walls were used almost exclusively both in dwellings and enclosures under special cultivation. And the subject of this fourth vision would be as familiar as the rest.

The Lord showed him a basket of summer-fruit; that is, overripe fruit, which could no longer be preserved. In reply to His inquiry, "Amos, what seest thou?" the prophet answers, "A basket of summer-fruit." Then comes the explanation of the simple symbol. Israel had become like a decaying fruit. The end was near—the time of being cast away. No longer would grace be extended to those who had rejected it so repeatedly. The temple songs would be changed to woeful cries of anguish and despair, while the dead bodies of the despisers of God's message would fill the cities, and be cast out in silence.

Accompanying this declaration that the end had come, we have a solemn summing-up of the sin of the people. They swallowed up the needy in their covetousness, making the poor of the land to fail, as in the last days of James 5: 1-6, where the word is, "Ye have heaped treasure together in (not *for*) the last days!"

This same covetous spirit made the appointed feasts and the sabbaths a burden. Outwardly they observed them, but they longed for the close of the day to come, that they might buy and sell, and get gain.

For this the Lord sware, saying, "Surely I will never forget any of their works." All were under His holy eye. All were noted in His book. All should be faced at His judgment-seat! If the eye of an unsaved sinner rests on this page, oh, let me press upon you this statement in all its solemnity. You may forget your own works, so great may be the number of your sins; but God has declared He will ever remember them. And if He thus remembers, you must be banished from His presence forever. But of all who now judge themselves and own their guilt, trusting the One who died to save, "Their sins and iniquities will I remember no more" (Jer. 31: 34;

Heb. 10:17). Are *your* sins then, remembered or forgotten, dear reader?

For Israel's sins the land had to tremble, and its people were to be carried away as by the overflowing river of Egypt, when the sun should go down at noon, and the earth be darkened in the clear day. It is a poetic figure for utter desolation; the result of their grasping selfishness, their heartless misconduct toward the poor, and God's displeasure upon their ways. Bitter would be the mourning in that day, when, alas, repentance would come too late to avert the threatened calamity, which was to be as the mourning for an only son, and the end be a day of woe (vers. 4-10).

But more: a famine was to come upon *them*—who would "swallow up the needy," and "buy the poor for a pair of shoes." It would not be a famine of bread, or a thirst for water, but of hearing the words of the Lord, which they had rejected. From sea to sea, as a people forsaken, they should wander, seeking on all sides for the once-despised word of the Lord; but too late now—they "shall not find it"! (vers. 11, 12).

Undoubtedly this prophecy had its fulfilment in measure when the people of Israel were carried into Assyria. But a larger fulfilment awaits them in the days of Antichrist. Nor shall Israel and Judah alone pass through that famine. Guiltier Christendom, so richly blessed with the

Holy Scriptures, will have utterly turned from the truth, and will be turned unto fables. The day will come when the grieved Spirit of God will have left the earth, and when the very Scriptures of truth shall, as it were, be taken from those who have esteemed them so lightly.

Then "shall the fair virgins and young men faint for thirst," because the water of life, which they refused, shall be withdrawn, when they are left to die in despair, and given up to strong delusion, that they might believe a lie, and will all be judged who obeyed not the truth, but had pleasure in unrighteousness. The famine will result, not in their turning to God, but they shall swear by their idols still, only to find, as in Elijah's day, that there shall be none to hear, nor any to regard. So shall they fall, never to rise again (vers. 13, 14).

CHAPTER IX

NOT A GRAIN LOST

THIS final chapter readily divides into two parts. Verses 1 to 10 give the last of the five visions, and Jehovah's recital of the afflictions awaiting Israel in the lands of their wanderings, but with the assurance that not a grain of His wheat shall be lost. Then, in verses 11-15, as is customary with the prophets, the seer looks on to their restoration to glory and blessing in the last days, when their tribulations shall be forever past, and the nation be saved in the recovered remnant.

The vision has to do, this time, with the house of God. The Lord is seen standing upon, or by, the altar. He commands to smite the lintel, or chapiter of the door, that the posts may shake. The fleeing priests and people are devoted to destruction from which there can be no escape (ver. 1). He declares that though they dig into *sheol,* the world of spirits, or attempt to climb to the heavens, His hand will find them out. They might hide themselves on the top of lofty Carmel, or in the depths of the sea, but they should not escape the judgment their sins deserved. Even when in captivity among their enemies, He would send a sword after them, and set His eyes on them for evil, and not for good (vers. 2-4). Such was the vision: Amos uses it as a text in the following verses. He describes the might of the God they had contemned, and calls on nature to witness to His power and wisdom. At His touch the land melts and the dwellers therein mourn. He spreads the clouds over the heavens, and pours the rain upon the earth. Jehovah is His name (vers. 5, 6). Who, then, can withstand such a God, or who could expect to prosper who despised Him? Israel's special privileges would not avail now. They were no more deserving than others. In nothing were they superior to the Ethiopians. The same One who brought Israel out of the land of Egypt had brought the Philistines from Caphtor, and the Syrians from Kir. In His eyes, Israel was now but a sinful kingdom even worse than their neighbors. So He would destroy them from off the face of the earth.

Nevertheless He remembered His promise to the fathers, and His word as to the coming Seed must not fail; so He excepts a remnant. He "will not utterly destroy the house of Jacob" (vers. 7, 8). He will sift them among all nations as wheat is sifted in a sieve, but not the least grain shall fall to the ground. Only the sinners of His people will die by the sword, they who said, "The evil shall neither overtake nor hinder us" (vers. 9, 10). This is the figure the blessed Lord uses when addressing self-confident Peter. He is to go into Satan's sieve, but not for final destruction; only that the chaff may be separated from the wheat.

Such shall be the result of Israel's sifting among the nations. They are not all Israel that are of Israel; that is, not all that are descended from Jacob are children of faith. Only those who bow to the word of the Lord and believe His testimony are the Israel of God. Upon such, a New Testament apostle invokes peace from God. These will be the wheat that will be preserved for the coming kingdom.

In that day, David's tabernacle, long fallen, will be again reared up, and the city of Jerusalem will be rebuilt and raised up on the old ruins. Then shall restored Israel possess the land of Edom, and all the saved nations shall own their sway (vers. 11, 12). It is noticeable that this is the scripture quoted by James in the 15th chapter of Acts to justify the call of the Gentiles, though there is probably more in his use of it than that. It harmonizes perfectly with the thought of grace going out to the nations. It also shows that after the present work of God in taking out from among the Gentiles a people for His name is completed, the Lord will turn His hand once more to Israel, and raise up the tabernacle of David, fulfilling all the promises made through the prophets (Acts 15:16, 17).

In that glorious restoration period, Palestine shall once more be under cultivation, and made to rejoice and blossom as the rose. The captivity of Israel will be settled in their own patrimony. The waste cities shall be rebuilt and inhabited. Vineyards and gardens shall flourish, and God Himself shall plant His chosen people in the land given to their fathers and confirmed by His oath; "and they shall no more be pulled up out of their land," to which He shall restore them, but shall dwell there under the beneficent sway of the Lord Jesus Christ. The words, "Saith the Lord thy God," abruptly close the book. He has spoken, and He will perform His word for His own name's sake.

Notes on the

PROPHECY OF OBADIAH

THE DOOM OF EDOM

IN one chapter God has embodied for us such part of the ministry of Obadiah the prophet as He foresaw would be for our admonition and edification. Brief as it is, its twenty-one verses are fraught with needed instruction, and may well be laid to heart by each saint of the Lord.

Who Obadiah was, where he was born, of what tribe and family in Israel, his occupation, and the exact time in which he lived—all these are matters which God has not been pleased to reveal. There was Obadiah in the court of king Ahab, of whose care for the persecuted prophets of the Lord we have knowledge; but he is not to be confounded with the writer of the little book now before us. Other Obadiahs are briefly mentioned in 1st and 2nd Chronicles; but whether any of them is identical with the prophet, we have no means of determining—nor is it at all important that we should know. It is the message, not the bearer of it, that God would occupy us with.

The first sixteen verses are concerned with the sin and the doom of Edom. The last five verses set forth the deliverance that is to come to the house of Jacob when the house of Esau shall have fallen to rise no more.

Many important lessons are connected with the history of the two sons of Isaac and that of their respective houses. Before either child was born God made choice of Jacob, saying, "The elder shall serve the younger." It was electing grace, and wondrous grace, surely! For who so unworthy as cowardly Jacob; and who, from certain worldly standpoints, more to be admired than the apparently brave and magnanimous Esau? But God *chose* Jacob, and thus manifested His purpose of grace. Let the reader be clear as to what is here spoken of. It was not a question of selecting Jacob for heaven and reprobating Esau to hell. Theologians have so dreamed; but not in this way does Scripture speak. God chose Jacob to inherit the blessing of Abraham, and to be the conservator of the promise. In so doing He made Esau subject to his brother. It was the carrying out of a principle often noticed in the book of Genesis—the setting aside of the elder, and the giving the birthright to the younger; thus reminding us that God ever sets aside the first man to make the Second Man first. For "that was not first which is spiritual, but that which is natural; and afterward that which is spiritual" (1 Cor. 15:46). This mystery is told out in the cases of Cain and Abel, Ishmael and Isaac, Esau and Jacob, Reuben and Joseph, and of Manasseh and Ephraim.

In accordance with this, Esau and the race that bears his name figure in Scripture as types of the flesh; Jacob, as the new man learning to overcome by discipline. When in the last book of the Old Testament God sums up, as it were, concerning the two families, He declares, "I have loved Jacob, and hated Esau."

In reading the prophecy of Obadiah, we may trace throughout a typical as well as a natural bearing. What is said of Edom coalesces with the condemnation and final doom of the flesh—that hateful thing which ever vaunts itself, even in the breast of the believer, against all that is of God, but which shall at last be utterly destroyed, and become as though it had not existed. The future triumph of the house of Jacob, in the day of the glory of the kingdom, bespeaks the final enlargement and blessing when the flesh is overcome forever, and the man according to God alone remains.

From the Lord a report had come concerning Edom, as a result of which an ambassador was sent among the nations, with a view to raising up their armies against the mount of Esau. Though once all-powerful, he was to be made small among them, and greatly despised.

Edom had ever been the enemy of Israel, even as the flesh lusteth continually against the Spirit. When calamity came upon the house of Jacob, Edom had rejoiced. But now upon him judgment unsparing was to fall. This, no doubt, goes on to the time of the end; for it is just before the kingdom is established that Edom's power is to be utterly broken. There will be a people of his lineage dwelling in Idumea in the day of the last great coalition against Israel; but they will be overthrown: and when the rest of the world is brought into blessing under Messiah's rule, they will be blotted out from under heaven.

As with the flesh, so with Edom; his pride was insufferable. Dwelling in his Idumean heights and rocky fortresses, he considered himself invulnerable, and secure against all attack. But Jehovah declares, "The pride of thy heart hath deceived thee. . . Though thou exalt thyself as the eagle, and though thou set thy nest among the stars, thence will I bring thee down" (vers. 3, 4). No power can avail when the Lord's set time for his destruction is come. Edom has fallen into the condemnation of the devil, exalting himself, and seeking his own glory. On the part of the creature this is rebellion against God, and cannot go unpunished.

Nor will his desolation come as though thieves had broken in to steal, for having enough they would have left something remaining; but in the day that Esau's hidden things are searched out, there shall be no gleanings left. His destruction shall be complete (vers. 5, 6). Deceived by his own allies, and betrayed by those in whom he had trusted, the wise shall be destroyed out of the mount of Esau, and the mighty men of Teman shall be dismayed. None shall be spared, but every one cut off by slaughter (vers. 7-9).

His violence against his brother Jacob has well merited such stern dealing. When Israel came out of Egypt, no ties of relationship served to cause the heart of the king of Edom to be kindly disposed to the Canaan-bound pilgrims, but they were forced to compass his land, thus adding much to the toil and weariness of their journey. From that day on, the seed of Esau had ever been the inveterate enemies of Jehovah's favored people.

When the hour of Jacob's calamity struck, Edom stood complacently to one side, delighting in the ignominy to which his brother was subjected. The desolation of Jerusalem caused him, not grief, but joy. He joined with the Babylonians in casting lots for a division of the spoil (vers. 10, 11). All this Jehovah's eye had seen, and it was an offence to Him, as being the very opposite of that love which rejoiceth not in iniquity, but rejoiceth with the truth. His sentence is, "Thou shouldest not have looked on the day of thy brother in the day that he became a stranger; neither shouldest thou have rejoiced over the children of Judah in the day of their destruction; neither shouldest thou have spoken proudly in the day of distress. Thou shouldest not have entered into the gate of My people in the day of their calamity; yea, thou shouldest not have looked on their affliction in the day of their calamity; neither shouldest thou have stood in the crossway, to cut off those of his that did escape; neither shouldest thou have delivered up those of his that did remain in the day of distress" (vers. 12-14). Because of having acted so contrary to every brotherly instinct, he should reap as he had sown, and judgment unsparing would soon overtake him, until of Edom it could be said, "They shall be as though they had not been" (vers. 15, 16). When other nations, such as Egypt, Assyria, and even Sodom and Gomorrah, are restored and brought into blessing in the millennial kingdom, Edom shall have fallen to rise no more.

In this, how suited a picture we have of the carnal mind and its final destruction! Ever the enemy of the new life imparted to the children of God, because not subject to His law, as in its very nature it cannot be; rejoicing in impiety, and lifting up its haughty head in defiance of all that is holy, how much sorrow and secret anguish has its presence cost every conscientious saint! But soon it shall be cast down to rise no more; soon the bodies of our humiliation shall be made like unto the body of Christ's glory; and then shall the flesh and sin have vanished forevermore.

There are those who idly dream of a present destruction of the carnal mind, or a short cut to Canaan across the land of Edom; but it is all a delusion. Esau's doom comes when Christ appears to reign, as the end of the flesh in the believer will come at the redemption of our bodies when made like Himself.

Synchronizing with the fall of Edom shall be the salvation of Israel, when "upon mount Zion shall be deliverance, and there shall be holiness" (or, it shall be holy). Then shall Jacob come into his rightful inheritance, and shall devour the house of Esau as fire devours the stubble, till "there shall not be any remaining of the house of Esau; for the Lord hath spoken it" (vers. 17, 18). In that day the lands of all their former enemies, who had been for so long as thorns in their sides, shall become Israel's possession, "and the kingdom shall be the Lord's" (vers. 19-21).

So may the believer look on with joyful confidence to the hour when the flesh and all that now disturbs and distresses shall be overthrown forever, and Christ alone shall be exalted. "Even so, come, Lord Jesus."

Notes on the
HISTORY OF JONAH

INTRODUCTION

AMONG these so-called Minor Prophets, Jonah is the only one which, in the ordinary sense of the word, does not contain any prophecy at all, except his announcement of the threatened destruction of Nineveh within forty days, which was not fulfilled. Yet the book is distinctly prophetic, and as such is twice referred to by our Lord Jesus Christ. No spiritually-minded person can read it without discerning the fact that Jonah's whole history, or at least that part of it here recorded for our instruction, is in itself a prophecy, setting forth, as it does, the course of Israel, of whom Jonah was a type, or picture, and likewise exhibiting beforehand the wondrous mystery of the Lord's death and resurrection.

Yet this truly sublime and heart-searching book has often been the butt of the ridicule of the worldly-wise rationalist and the puzzle of the unspiritual religionist, who have never learned the importance of bowing to the authority of the

Word of God. Time was when it was fashionable for men of science, themselves unconverted, to sneer at "Jonah's whale" that could devour a man, on the ground that the anatomical structure of the creature forbade such a supposition. But added light has revealed the fact that even if the Bible had declared the "prepared" fish to be a whale— which rightly read, it does not—still, the sperm whale, which in early ages frequented the Mediterranean, could have fully met the requirements of the case. Thus once more it transpires that rationalism is *ir*rational, and the Scriptures in every way worthy of credence.

No thoughtful and conscientious child of God could think of questioning the inspiration of a book upon which the Lord Jesus has set His seal in the particular way that He has on this one. Indeed, it is a significant fact that Deuteronomy, the last part of Isaiah, Daniel and Jonah have been preeminently the books that the critics have sought to dispute the genuineness of; and these four portions of the Word of God have been authenticated in a most remarkable way by Him who could not lie. He who knew all things quotes Deuteronomy as the very word of God when meeting Satan in the wilderness; and when He reads from "the great unknown" in the synagogue of Nazareth, He finds in the words of "Isaiah" the message of the Holy Ghost. In like manner He warns of the "abomination of desolation" spoken of "by Daniel the *prophet,*" and declares unhesitatingly that Jonah was a sign to the Ninevites after having been in the belly of the great fish. How great is the blasphemy of those who, in the face of all this, sit in judgment on these solemn portions of the God-breathed Scriptures, and profess to be wiser than the Omniscient Himself! Ps. 2:4

Just when Jonah flourished we have no means of positively deciding. We learn that in the reign of Jeroboam the Second over Israel, a prophecy of Jonah's was fulfilled; but whether it was made during Jeroboam's lifetime or not, we are not informed. We are simply told that "he restored the coast of Israel from the entering of Hamath unto the sea of the plain, according to the word of the Lord God of Israel, which He spake by the hand of His servant Jonah, the son of Amittai, the prophet, which was of Gath-hepher" (2 Kings 14:25). But this, though it would seem to indicate that Jonah lived and prophesied at that time, does not necessarily prove it, as he might have uttered his prophecy at an earlier date, only to be then fulfilled. Either way, as God has not been pleased to state definitely the time of his birth and death, we can leave it as, for us, a matter of small moment. But the fact that he was born in Gath-hepher *is* of moment, refuting, as it does, the self-confident words of the Jewish doctors, "Search and look, for out of Galilee ariseth no prophet." Gath-hepher was in Galilee, and this is but an instance of how easy it is to carry the day by mere assumption, when disputing with those ignorant of Scripture, without proving one's position by the Word of God. Needful it is to "prove all things," holding fast only to that which is good.

Unquestionably the great theme of this book is the divine sovereignty. The expressions "The Lord prepared" and "God prepared," frequently repeated, would manifest this. Throughout, however man may plan, and whatever he may attempt, it is God who is over all, and working all things in such a way as to bring glory to His own name.

With these few introductory thoughts, we turn directly to the record itself.

CHAPTER I

THE UNWELCOME MESSAGE

"NOW the word of the Lord came unto Jonah the son of Amittai, saying, Arise, go to Nineveh, that great city, and cry against it; for their wickedness is come up before Me" (vers. 1, 2). This was a most unexpected and uncongenial mission for an Israelite to be sent upon. Like the nation for whom he stands, Jonah was called to be the bearer of a message from God to the Gentiles. Israel had been separated from the nations, not to dwell in a cold, formal exclusiveness, in utter indifference to the fate of the peoples about them, but to be a light in a dark world, making known the mind of God and manifesting the character of Jehovah to those who were sitting in darkness and in the shadow of death. In Jonah's subsequent history we see pictured their failure in this respect, and the disasters that came upon them because of that failure, as also the foreshadowing of the day when, restored and brought again into blessing, they will once more be entrusted with a commission from the Most High. For that Jonah was really restored in soul at the end, whatever the unhappy state portrayed here to the last, we can have no manner of doubt; as, evidently, he himself it is who narrates, for our learning, the experiences he had undergone; but the very manner of the relation of them manifests the fact that it is as a recovered and chastened man he does so. It would not be God's way that he should dwell upon this side of things himself. He simply lets us know something of his own pride and self-will, and the manner taken by the Lord to humble and bring him into touch with Him once more.

For that it was pride and bigotry that was at the bottom of all his wilfulness and waywardness is clear enough. He knew that God was long-suffering, and that He delighted in mercy. He tells us that in the end. He therefore feared for his prophetic reputation; and his thoughts were so far from those of the Lord that he could not endure that grace should be shown to a Gentile power. He knew that of old Jehovah would have spared the cities of the plain had there been found but ten righteous. If Jehovah had so acted then, how could he depend upon His now pouring out His wrath upon Nineveh if its wicked inhabitants should bow to the word and fall before Him in repentance?

In all this, what a picture we have of the deceitfulness of the human heart, even in a saint of God! And how often have we had to reproach ourselves for the same evil propensities being allowed to act! How much easier is it to insist upon judgment of a brother, for instance, if he have in any way hurt or injured *me*, than if it be against others, or against God only, that he has sinned! My own reputation must be maintained at all cost, and I must be cleared of all imputation of blame, whatever it may mean to others! Have we not seen whole companies of the people of God thrown into sorrow and confusion in order that one self-willed man might have his way and be justified in his course?—let others suffer as they might. It is just the working of that same miserable pride of heart that is so strikingly portrayed for our admonition in the book before us.

Rather than go to these Gentiles, and risk his reputation, "Jonah rose up to flee unto Tarshish from the presence of the Lord, and went down to Joppa; and he found a ship going to Tarshish: so he paid the fare thereof, and went down into it, to go with them unto Tarshish from the presence of the Lord" (ver. 3). To get away from the pathway of obedience is invariably to go out from the presence of the Lord; that is, so far as the reality of it is concerned in one's own soul. Actually, it would be impossible to get where the eye of God was not upon him; but in his own consciousness of communion and enjoyment, the moment that Jonah made up his mind to act in disobedience, he lost the sense of the Lord's presence in his soul.

As he flees, what a lot of *going down* there is! He went *down* to Joppa; he went *down* into the ship; he went *down* into the sides of the ship: and in the next chapter he has to confess, "I went *down* to the bottoms of the mountains"—*down* till he could go no deeper, unless he had sunk into the pit of woe: but that could not be; for, whatever his failure, he was a child of God still and the Lord was about to restore him in a marvelous manner.

Oh, that we all might lay this to heart! The path of the one who acts in self-will is always a downward one, let the profession be what it may. One may boast of acting for God, and talk of having His approval; but if self is served instead of Christ, the feet will soon slide, and the steps will be down, down, down—till humbled and repentant, the soul turns back to God, and is ready to own the wrong of its behavior.

From the next few verses we learn that God loved His poor, failing servant too well to permit him to prosper as he took his foolish and sinful course. "The Lord sent out a great wind into the sea, and there was a mighty tempest in the sea, so that the ship was like to be broken" (ver. 4). God has begun to act. Now, let man try as he will, he will have to learn that all his power is as nothing when it is with the Almighty One that he has to contend.

All on the ship are at once aroused—at least all save the miserable man for whose sin the storm has come. He is sound asleep, having gone down into the sides of the ship—insensible to the anxiety and distress he has been the means of bringing upon so many others who had no share in his evil way. What a picture of one who has taken the first wrong step, and, though discipline has begun, is sleeping on in self-complacency, utterly unconscious of the fact that the hand of the Lord has been stretched out against him! This is the hardening through the deceitfulness of sin, concerning which the apostle warns us.

Awakened at last by the ignorant heathen shipmaster, who has exhausted every device known to him to appease the fancied wrath of his gods, Jonah is put to shame before them all. The earnest question, "What meanest thou, O sleeper?" followed by the rousing command, "Arise, call upon thy God, if so be that God will think upon us that we perish not," brings him to a realization of the terrible circumstances in which all are placed, but does not suffice to open his lips in confession. Accordingly, the sailors cast lots, and God deigns to use this means to point out the guilty man. "The lot is cast into the lap; but the whole disposing thereof is of the Lord" (Prov. 16:33). "The lot fell upon Jonah."

But even then it is only in reply to the queries of the affrighted men that "he said unto them, I am a Hebrew; and I fear the Lord, the God of heaven, which hath made the sea and the dry land." On his part, the confession seems to have been coolly enough made. He knows that his case is desperate. His feelings are no doubt aroused; but there is no evidence as yet that conscience is really in exercise. He is like one who has hazarded all on a false expectation, and now finds that he must lose, and so determines to lose like a man, as people say, philosophically reminding himself that it cannot be helped.

The terrors of the heathen, when they realize the true state of affairs, might well have gone home to his conscience. "Then were the men exceedingly afraid, and said unto him, Why hast thou done this? For the men knew that he fled from the presence of the Lord, because he had told them." Even *natural* consciences will view with alarm what a backslidden child of God can survey with a measure of equanimity. This is the awful effect of trifling with God and grieving His Holy Spirit.

In desperation, seeing that all their efforts are unavailing, the mariners inquire of Jonah as to what they shall do, in order that the storm may cease. He accordingly directs them to throw him into the sea, owning that he knows the tempest was sent for his sake. Conscience is evidently rousing now, but to what extent it is hard to say. The men hesitate to carry out his word; but when at last all their efforts to bring the ship to land proved unavailing, they prepare to do as he has directed them. Crying to the Lord not to lay it to their charge, and owning that sovereignty which Jonah had virtually denied ("Thou, O Lord, hast done as it hath pleased Thee"), they took up Jonah and cast him into the sea. Immediately the waters became calm, and "the men feared the Lord exceedingly, and offered a sacrifice unto the Lord, and made vows." Dark and ignorant though they were, their hearts responded to the mercy of God who had thus granted them so signal a deliverance.

As for His unworthy servant, for him too there was mercy; but neverthless government must have its way, though the final result shall be that God will magnify Himself in the deliverance and restoration of the wanderer. "Now the Lord had prepared a great fish to swallow up Jonah. And Jonah was in the belly of the fish three days and three nights" (ver. 17). Dispensationally, it is Israel who, because of their failure as God's witnesses in the earth, have been cast into the sea of the Gentiles, but who, despite all their vicissitudes, have been marvelously preserved by the Lord, and are yet to become His testimony-bearers to the whole world.

CHAPTER II

OUT OF THE DEPTHS

WHEN the scribes and the Pharisees hypocritically requested a sign that they might know for certain of the Lord's Messiahship, He significantly replied: "An evil and adulterous generation seeketh after a sign; and there shall no sign be given to it, but the sign of the prophet Jonas: for as Jonas was three days and three nights in the belly of the great fish; so shall the Son of Man be three days and three nights in the heart of the earth. The men of Nineveh shall rise up in judgment with this generation, and shall condemn it: because they repented at the preaching of Jonas; and, behold, a greater than Jonas is here" (Matt. 12: 39-41). In these solemn words He does two important things for us. He authenticates the story of Jonah, and He unfolds a marvelous typical line of truth set forth in that record, which we might otherwise have overlooked. Jonah's experience is sober history. We have the word of the Son of God for it. Moreover, the prophet's entombment in the great fish and his subsequent deliverance were intended as a sign to the Ninevites, and a type of the death and resurrection of the Lord Jesus Christ. It is true that Jonah found his suffering in the path of disobedience, and in Christ we contemplate with adoration the ever-faithful One who suffered to accomplish all His Father's will; but this is only a proof of the fact that God ever causes the wrath of man to praise Him, and what would not do so He restrains. To the Ninevites Jonah was a man who had passed through death and resurrection. In this he portrays the glorious mystery of the gospel. He who is now set forth as the object of faith, is the One who was delivered for our offences and raised again for our justification. He went into death, but could not be holden of it. In a fuller sense than Jonah ever knew, He could say, "The waters encompassed Me about, even to the soul." But God has raised Him from the dead, thereby testifying His satisfaction in the work of His Son. This is the only sign now set before men. All who trust in the risen Saviour are forever delivered from wrath and judgment—that judgment so rightfully theirs.

But in Jonah's experiences we likewise have to trace God's dealings with his own soul; and this has a moral lesson of the deepest importance for us. There is also, as previously intimated, the fact that Israel, the unfaithful witness-bearer, refusing the thought of grace going out to the Gentiles, is here pictured. Their present condition answers to this second chapter, as declared by the apostle Paul when he writes of "the

Jews, who both killed the Lord Jesus, and their own prophets, and have persecuted us; and they please not God, and are contrary to all men; forbidding us to speak to the Gentiles that they might be saved, to fill up their sins alway: for the wrath is come upon them to the uttermost" (1 Thess. 2: 14-16). By and by their deliverance shall come, when they are ready to own that salvation is of the Lord, all undeserved by them. In that day they will become the messengers of the same boundless grace to heathen millions, once hated and despised.

But we turn now to trace out, as intimated above, the exercises of the prophet's soul when in his living tomb.

In his affliction he cries to Him from whom he had been seeking to hide. Divine life, like water, seeks its proper level, or sphere. Because, whatever his failings, Jonah is a child of God still, he turns instinctively to the very One he had been grieving, in the hour that he is brought to realize that he is the subject of divine discipline. A man is a long way on the road to recovery when he is ready to own the righteousness of his chastening, and when he *sees* that he is under the hand of God. Having already acknowledged to the mariners that such is the case, he now cries to Him who hears him even "out of the belly of hell."

The floods have compassed him about, even to

the soul; the weeds are wrapped about his head; all God's waves and billows have gone over him; yet he will look again toward Jehovah's holy temple (vers. 1-5). It is blessed indeed when the soul does not faint beneath the discipline of the Lord, nor yet despise it, but looks up to God and counts upon His grace, however the sense of merited affliction may press upon the conscience.

But for deliverance there must be more than this, and for a time Jonah seems to fail to attain to it. He goes down to the bottoms of the mountains, but is able in the anticipation of faith to say, "Yet hast Thou brought up my life from corruption, O Lord my God." His soul would have fainted within him, but he remembers the Lord, and is assured that his prayers shall be heard, and shall penetrate His holy temple. He is here in the place that the future remnant of Israel shall be in, in their experience, when the blindness of the present condition has passed away; afar off, yet, in accordance with the prayer of Solomon, looking toward the temple of Jehovah, though in ruins, as in the day that Daniel opened his windows toward Jerusalem (vers. 6, 7).

He exclaims, "They that observe lying vanities forsake their own mercy." He had forsaken his own mercy when he sought to flee from the presence of the Lord. He knows therefore the condition of the heathen by his own experience. Now, however, he is confident that he will wander no more; though, as we well know, his confidence was as yet misplaced. His heart was no more to be trusted in after he had been in the belly of the fish than before. When he cries, "I will sacrifice unto Thee with the voice of thanksgiving," and when he adds, "I will pay that that I have vowed," there is still no response on the part of God. He is not yet at the end of himself. As in the conversion of a sinner, so it is with the restoration of a saint: he must get to the end of himself before the Lord will undertake his case. The sinner must learn that he is without strength, and the erring saint must learn that in himself he is not a whit better or stronger than other men, ere God can manifest His grace.

So it is here, that after prayers, pledges and vows have availed nothing, the crisis is reached when he simply owns, "Salvation is of the Lord!" Then, and not till then, "the Lord spake unto the fish, and it vomited out Jonah on the dry land" (vers. 8-10). Jonah has thus, in figure, passed through death and resurrection. He is now ready to go to the great and godless city of the Ninevites and declare the word of God to them.

That he has not yet fully done with self is evident later on; but he is now in God's school, and he will have a patient and gracious Teacher.

CHAPTER III

DEATH AND RESURRECTION

IT is of all importance, in studying the typical characters of the Old Testament, to distinguish between a man in his individual and in his official aspect. In other words, one may be a type of the Lord Jesus, if looked at officially, who, if viewed morally, may be a most marked failure. This is strikingly illustrated in the case of David. As the anointed of the Lord, he is preeminently a type of the true King, the Anointed of Jehovah, yet to be set upon the holy hill of Zion; but actually there is much in his life that is altogether opposed to the holiness and perfections of Him who was truly the Man after God's own heart. In the present instance the same principle applies. Jonah's history is, as we have seen, sad and sorrowful in the extreme; but grace delights to take up just such as he: and so we find the Divine Expositor Himself declaring that His own death and resurrection were set forth in symbol in the experience that the prophet from Galilee passed through. It is as the one who has thus tasted death, but triumphed over it, that Jonah becomes the bearer of Jehovah's message to the Ninevites.

All his waywardness had not altered the thoughts of God as to his being sent to preach to these impious people. The servant might fail, but he is a servant still, as in the instances of Abraham and Job. The former was to intercede for Abimelech, "for he is a prophet," though he had just denied his wife. The latter, restored in soul, no doubt, prays for his friends, though he had justified himself rather than God. There is a solemn and serious lesson here for those put in trust with the gospel, or who have a special ministry to the people of God. They are judged of the Lord, not merely as saints, but as servants. Nor does failure relieve them of responsibility to serve, but calls all the louder for self-judgment, that they may be in a right state of soul to minister in holy things. In so writing, I have no thought of countenancing clerical pretensions, or making of servants of Christ a special class who are supposed to be above the frailties common to men, and even to saints. But I only press what Scripture frequently insists on, that he who serves should do so because called of God to his particular ministry; and when so called, he has a most grave responsibility to walk accordingly. A *one*-man ministry is rightly rejected by many as unscriptural. An *any*-man ministry is equally so. He who runs unsent has failed even in his very start.

Jonah had been called of God to his mission. He is given the command the second time to "Arise, go unto Nineveh, that great city, and preach unto it the preaching that I bid thee." In response there is apparently no hesitation now, for we read, "So Jonah arose, and went unto Nineveh, according to the word of the Lord." His obedience now is as conspicuous as his former lack of it; but we know from the next chapter that he had not yet judged the point of departure from God. It is a serious thing to realize that people may become outwardly correct in their demeanor and zealous in the work of the Lord after a failure, so that none may realize that they are not yet restored in soul, while in reality the evil remains unjudged. The root of the matter is unreached. Certain *acts* may be confessed, and the confession may be real and genuine, so far as it goes; but the state of soul that led to these acts has not been faced in the presence of God. This was the great lack here, and a vital one. But God will have His own way of exposing the true state of His servant to himself, and of restoring his soul.

"Yet forty days, and Nineveh shall be overthrown," is the burden of his message to the voluptuous city. The result is just as he had feared. For himself, he had gladly proven that "salvation is of the Lord." The people of Nineveh shall prove the same; but so perverse is the human heart, even though it be the heart of a saint, that it fills Jonah with anger to see mercy going out to the repentant city. In a few graphic sentences the story of the great awakening is told. "So the people of Nineveh believed God, and proclaimed a fast, and put on sackcloth, from the greatest of them even to the least of them. For word came unto the king of Nineveh, and he arose from his throne, and he laid his robe from him, and covered him with sackcloth, and sat in ashes. And he caused it to be proclaimed and published through Nineveh by the decree of the king and his nobles, saying, Let neither man nor beast, herd nor flock, taste anything: let them not feed, nor drink water: but let man and beast be covered with sackcloth, and cry mightily unto God: yea, let them turn every one from his evil way, and from the violence that is in their hands. Who can tell if God will turn and repent, and turn away from His fierce anger, that we perish not?" (vers. 5-9).

It is an open question if all the annals of revival-history could furnish a scene to parallel this. From the greatest to the least, all are crying to God. It is noticeable that it is not to the Lord—that is, *Jehovah*—that they direct their prayers, nor of whom they speak. Here, as in all Old Testament Scripture, Elohim (God) and Jehovah are used with scrupulous exactness. Foolish men may stumble at the use of the two names: but it is because they are blinded by the god of this age, and thus they fail to see that Jehovah is the covenant name that links God with His people in known relationship, while Elohim speaks rather of sovereignty and Creatorship. Hence the sailors of chapter one rightly use the broader title, or name, until, instructed by the erring prophet, they cry to Jehovah not to hold them accountable for his blood. And so, too, these Ninevites address their petitions to Elohim; and, as a result, we are told that "God saw their works, that they turned from their evil way; and God repented Him of the evil, that He had said He would do unto them; and He did it not" (ver. 10). Would any find a difficulty here? Let them know that He with whom judgment is a strange work is ever ready to repent Himself, and manifest His grace upon the least evidence of a breaking down before Him, and contrition of heart because of sin.

> "His is love, 'tis love unbounded,—
> Without measure, without end.
> Human thought is here confounded,
> 'is too vast to comprehend."

Alas, that Jonah was in no condition of soul to enter into and enjoy such love and grace! His is the spirit of the elder son in the parable, as the next chapter makes manifest.

CHAPTER IV

THE REPENTANCE OF NINEVEH

THE Holy Spirit has declared that "the carnal mind is not subject to the law of God, neither indeed can be." It is a most humiliating truth, but experience and Scripture everywhere corroborate it. It is not that the carnal mind in an unconverted person merely, is so hopelessly evil; but this wretched principle is as unreliable and vile in the greatest saint as in the worst sinner. Indeed, it is when we see the working of the flesh in one who is an example of piety that we appreciate its incurable iniquity as never before. No child of God dare trust the flesh. It will betray him into unholy thoughts and ways every time it is permitted to have control. I say *permitted,* purposely, for no Christian is of necessity subject to its power. Rightly viewed, it is a foreign thing, that should not have place for one moment. The believer is called upon to refuse its sway, and, in place of yielding his members unto it as though it had a necessary authority over him, he is called upon to make no provision for the flesh to fulfil its lusts. He is to reckon himself dead to it, and to yield himself unto God as one alive from the dead. Let it be otherwise, and defeat is certain—the triumph of the flesh is assured. But if we walk in the Spirit, we shall not fulfil the lust of the flesh.

Now in Jonah, here, we see a saint under the power of the flesh; though we cannot doubt that he was enabled to judge his failure at last, while commanded by God to put the record of it in the form it here bears in order that it might prove an admonitory lesson to thousands. No one doubts that it was the flesh that led to his fleeing from the presence of the Lord. It was the same power that was controlling him when he sat down outside the city, after delivering his message, to see what the Lord would do. Instead of his heart being filled with joy because of the repentance of the Ninevites, he was filled with anxiety as to his own reputation.

Probably few of us realize what a strong place self has in our affections till something arises that touches our own personal dignity. It is then that we manifest what spirit we are of. There is more of the Jonah disposition about us than we like even to admit to ourselves. Yet to own failure is one of the first steps to deliverance from it.

When all heaven was rejoicing at the repentance, not of one sinner, but of a vast multitude, we are told that "it displeased Jonah exceedingly, and he was very angry." His state is most wretched, yet he is altogether unconscious of it. Puffed up with a sense of his own importance, the weal or woe of so many of his fellow-creatures is as nothing compared to his own reputation. Yet so utterly unconscious is he of the wretchedness of his state of soul, that he can turn to God and express his shameful failure as though he had not failed at all; or even as though the failure, if there were any, was on the part of the Lord Himself.

"He prayed unto the Lord, and said, I pray Thee, O Lord, was not this my saying, when I was yet in my country? Therefore I fled before unto Tarshish: for I knew that Thou art a gracious God, and merciful, slow to anger, and of great kindness, and repentest Thee of the evil. Therefore now, O Lord, take, I beseech Thee, my life from me; for it is better for me to die than to live." It seems almost unbelievable that a servant of God could be in such a dreadful state of soul; but, alas, it was but an aggravated form of that insidious disease, pride, that so readily finds a congenial place for growth and expansion in the breast of any saint out of communion.

The tender question of the Lord might well have broken Jonah down, had he not been so thoroughly self-occupied. "Then said the Lord, Doest thou well to be angry?" There is no reproach: just the serious and solemn question that ought to have awakened him at once to his true condition of soul.

How often He would press a similar question upon us when cherishing unholy thoughts or feelings, or walking in our own paths and neglecting

His ways! "Doest thou well" to be thus pleasing thyself and dishonoring Him? Surely not! But it is amazing how slow one can be to own how ill he is doing when he has become hardened by the deceitfulness of sin.

On Jonah's part there is no response in words; but, acting in self-will and wounded vanity, he goes outside the city, and, after building a booth, sits under its shadow, to see what would become of Nineveh and of his prophetic reputation.

In grace God prepared a gourd, which, growing very rapidly, soon overshadowed the petulant prophet, and thus sheltered him from the fierce rays of the almost tropical sun. Because it ministered to his comfort, Jonah was exceeding glad of the gourd. This is the first note of joy on his part that we find recorded, and is in fact the last as well. His gladness was as truly from selfishness as was his sorrow.

But God now prepares something that is to blast that joy. A worm is permitted to destroy the gourd, and then a vehement east wind is likewise prepared by Him who has His way in the whirlwind and in the storm. The sickening heat almost overcame Jonah, so that he fainted; and in his chagrin and wretchedness he wished once more that he might be permitted to escape his trials by dying, saying, "It is better for me to die than to live."

Again God speaks: this time to inquire in tenderest tone, "Doest thou well to be angry for the gourd?" Gloomily the offended prophet answers, "I do well to be angry, even unto death." It is the callousness that comes from allowing sin to go unjudged, till all capacity to discern between right and wrong seems to have gone.

The reply of Jehovah is an opening up of His grace that evidently accomplishes its end; for Jonah has no word of self-vindication to offer. He permits God to have the last word, and closes his record abruptly, as though what followed were of too sacred and private a nature for him to publish it abroad. The Lord said, "Thou hast had pity on the gourd, for the which thou hast not labored, neither madest it grow; which came up in a night, and perished in a night: and should not I spare Nineveh, that great city, wherein are more than sixscore thousand persons that cannot discern between their right hand and their left hand; and also much cattle?" The question is unanswerable. Jonah grieved for the loss of the gourd because it had ministered to his comfort. Jehovah yearned over the sinners of Nineveh because of the love of His heart. How opposite were Master and servant! But we must leave the history where God leaves it. The rest we shall know at the judgment-seat of Christ. Meantime may we have grace given to daily judge in ourselves aught that, if left to develop, would lead us as far from Himself as Jonah wandered!

Notes on the
PROPHECY OF MICAH

CHAPTER I

THE SUMMONS TO HEARKEN

MICAH'S prophecy, while simple in structure and clear in the main, yet contains a number of seemingly involved and obscure passages. In taking up its study, one feels more than ever the need of divine illumination to understand aright the dark sayings so frequently occurring. But the theme of the book is plain. It is the wretched estate of all Israel because of their sin, and the wonderful deliverance to be brought in by Him "whose goings-forth have been of old, from everlasting," yet who was to come out of Bethlehem-Ephratah to effect salvation for His people. Hence, though this first chapter begins with their solemn arraignment for "the transgression of Jacob" and "for the sins of the house of Israel," the book concludes with the precious assurance that He whom they have offended will cast all their sins into the depth of the sea. In all this we are on familiar ground, often trodden heretofore, and cast up as a highway by "Moses and all the prophets." It is only as to details there is difficulty, and then nothing of a fundamental character.

Micah is called "the Morasthite," that is, a man of Moreshah; or, as he himself calls it in verse 14, Moresheth-gath; or, again, Mareshah, in the following verse, a town lying to the south-west of Jerusalem, and therefore in the land of Judah.

Micah is cited by the elders of Jerusalem in the days of Jeremiah, a hundred years later, as an example of one who had prophesied ever against Israel, but who was not apprehended therefor by the godly king Hezekiah (Jer. 26: 16-19).

His prophecy might have been all delivered at one time, as there are no clear breaks in its continuity; but it seems more likely that it consists of three discourses and a prayer—each of the former commencing with a summons to hear. In that case the first division would embrace chaps. 1 and 2; the second, chaps. 3 to 5; and the third, chap. 6; while chap. 7 would be the fourth and last.

Coming to the front a little later than Isaiah, Micah is his contemporary for the greater part of his ministry. In verse 1 we find, as also on examination of the book before us, that it embraces all Israel, not merely Judah, where the seer himself dwelt.

"Hear, all ye people; hearken, O earth (or land), and all that therein is: and let the Lord God be witness against you, the Lord from His holy temple" (ver. 2). In spirit the people are called back to the days of Lev. 1:1, when the voice of Jehovah was heard from the sanctuary, setting forth the holiness that was comely in those among whom He dwelt. Now, He speaks again from the sanctuary; but, this time, to convict them of having violated His Word in every particular, and thus forfeited all title to blessing under the covenant of works entered into at Sinai and confirmed in the plains of Moab. They are summoned to let Adonai Jehovah* be witness against them. To do so will be to justify God and to condemn themselves; and for a failed people this is the path of blessing.

It is a great thing to bow to the whole Word of God, even when it judges me and condemns my ways. To do so is the precursor to something better; but to excuse myself at the expense of God's truth is a process most hardening to the conscience.

In verses 3 and 4 the Lord is represented as coming out of His place to inquire into Israel's state. The language used is highly figurative, the

---

* Such is the divine title rendered here "the Lord God."

sublimity of which must be conceded by all. Like volcanic fires bursting forth and rending the earth is the awakening of Jehovah to judge His people.

The transgression of Jacob and the sins of the house of Israel furnish the occasion for this display of power and wrath. Samaria, with her mixture of idolatrous rites and Israelitish worship, is the transgression of Jacob. Jerusalem, in its treachery and apostasy, is the sin of Judah. Therefore Samaria was to become a desolation, as a vineyard given over to destruction. All the graven images and idols of every kind were to be beaten to pieces, and her "hires" (Lesser translates, "her wages of sin") burned in the fire. Nothing shall abide the day of Jehovah's fury (vers. 5-7).

Ver. 8 seems to be language put into the mouth of the despoiled nation; or it may be the prophet's own picture of his bitter sorrow at the fate about to befall Samaria. It is an instance of the peculiar character of this book.

Nothing now could stay the avenging hand, for "her wound is incurable!" It is solemn indeed when God thus has to pronounce upon the malady affecting those who bear His name. Like a spreading pestilence, "it is come unto Judah, [and] hath reached unto the gate of My people, even to Jerusalem" (ver. 9). The whole body was affected, and the whole head sick. See Isa. 1:5, 6.

Alas, that the Philistine enemes of Israel should hear of so wretched a condition prevailing among those who were called "The redeemed of the Lord!" "Tell it not in Gath, weep ye not loudly [there]." But "in Beth-le'-aphrah ('the house of the dust') roll thyself in the dust!" (ver. 10). The prophet plays on the word Aphrah, signifying "the dust." There, might fallen Israel well resort, and roll themselves in the dust because of their sins.

To city after city desolation and woe are assured. Saphir, "the fair," shall be given up to shame. Zaanan, "the place of flocks," was to be without any to come forth of her portals. "The mourning of Beth-ezel (or, Beth-haezel, 'the house at hand') taketh from you its halting-place." Here, again, the prophet is playing on the name. Beth-ezel was evidently what we would call a half-way house. It shall no longer be a halting-place for travelers on their way to the city of the great King (ver. 11).

The dweller in Maroth ("bitterness") finds only the bitter, and bewails the good that comes not. To Jerusalem's gate, evil sweeps down like a flood; and what is so solemn is, that it is "from the Lord." He it is who is judging His people because of their sin (ver. 12).

The 13th verse is difficult of interpretation. For some reason Lachish is declared to be the beginning of sin to the daughter of Zion. Hence her people shall flee before the advancing enemy.

Neither are the two following verses sufficiently clear to dogmatize as to their explanation. They seem to imply an unsuccessful effort to form a Philistine alliance for protection from the common foe; but Achzib ("the lie") shall become indeed that to the kings of Israel. Typically the passage may well point us to the coming day when the lie of Antichrist will be believed, and when he will be confided in to deliver the apostate nation from the onslaught of the last Assyrian; but all in vain. For the Assyrian shall prove to be in very deed the rod of Jehovah's anger.

Unhappy Israel, fallen so low that conscience no longer troubled, may well make herself bald and mourn in anguish for her delicate children, destroyed by the sins of the fathers. "They are gone into captivity from thee" (ver. 16).

The whole chapter is a dirge of unappeasable sorrow because the nation has forsaken Him who would have blessed them so richly had they but walked in His ways. May there be in us a different spirit! Otherwise we too must learn in bitterness of soul the folly of departure from the living God.

CHAPTER II

IS THE SPIRIT OF THE LORD STRAITENED?

IT is the will of God that those whom He has taken into covenant relationship with Himself should ever be overcomers. If it is otherwise, the fault is in them—not in Him. He has abundant resources for the believer to draw upon. But where unbelief and disobedience hold sway, spiritual paralysis must necessarily ensue.

Often had this been proven in Israel's case, and never more so than when Micah was sent to them with Jehovah's message upon his lips. Their state of soul at this time was wretchedly low; consequently their apprehension of divine things was so dulled that they had lost the power to distinguish what was of God, and what was of man. It is ever thus when people do not walk in obedience to revealed truth. They lose the power to distinguish truth from error, and may, under the deadening influence of the deceitfulness of sin, do the most outrageous things, and calmly announce that they were for the glory of God: yea, and be deeply grieved if their high pretensions are not recognized and bowed to.

In this second chapter the unrighteousness prevailing (as detailed in vers. 1 and 2) is given by God as the reason why He devised evil against the whole family of Israel. As they had ignored

His righteous claims in their dealings with each other, He could but measure out to them what they had measured to their fellows. So He told them He would bring evil upon them which no haughtiness could preserve them from. They would fall upon difficult days (ver. 3). Lamentations and mourning were to succeed their careless songs. Their fields were to be divided among strangers, and none of themselves should "cast a cord by lot in the assembly of the Lord" (vers. 4, 5)—that is, none would be left of Israel with authority to divide the land and measure it off, placing the landmarks accordingly.

Unpalatable was this, and so they cry, "Prophesy thou not!" Like many today, they would silence the messenger and forget the message. But God says, "They shall prophesy." His servants were not to be thus refused with impunity. On the other hand, the Word given and rejected, the Lord says, "They shall not prophesy to these, that reproach may not overtake them" (ver. 6).*

For the judgment was now decreed, and must surely fall. Nevertheless, He asks the questions, "Shall it be said in the house of Jacob, Is the Spirit of the Lord straitened? are these His doings? do not my words do good to him that

---

* The A. V. is very confusing here. Verse 6, according to eminent scholars, should read, "Prophesy not! [say they; but] they shall prophesy: they shall not prophesy [indeed] to these, that reproach may not overtake them."

walketh uprightly?" Surely He would have recognized repentance if manifested in any, and shown Himself strong in their behalf, whatever the impending ruin.

This is full of comfort and encouragement for any who in these last days of the Church's history on earth have an ear to hear what God has said in His Word. Nothing can now avert the soon-coming doom of haughty Christendom, nor raise up the fallen assembly of God. But wherever there is individual faithfulness, or wherever a few in weakness seek to heed the Word of God, there will be blessing, and the Lord will own all He can own as of Himself.

God's words will ever "do good to him that walketh uprightly." Spiritual things "are spiritually discerned," and therefore only the upright and godly soul will find real profit and blessing in the Scriptures. But where there is exercise as to this, that Word will be found sufficient for all the needs of the pilgrim-path. There will never be a circumstance so trying, a crisis so serious, that the man of God will be left without furnishing unto all good works, if he be found feeding upon the truth. Scripture, with the Holy Spirit's enlightenment, is all that is required in every emergency.

But if the professed people of God "rise up as an enemy," and refuse to heed His Word (as in vers. 8 and 9), then comes the call for separation from what is unclean and unholy, "Arise ye, and depart; for this is not your rest: because it is polluted" (ver. 10). To continue in fellowship with what is opposed to God's mind will result in desolation. We are called to "buy the truth, and sell it not."

With Israel, any false prophet was more acceptable than a God-sent messenger (ver. 11). An evil man "speaking lies in hypocrisy," and "turning the grace of God into lasciviousness," would have been a suited prophet for them in their fallen condition.

Thus they set at naught the Shepherd of Israel, and would not follow His ways. Hence their casting off. Nevertheless His anger shall not burn forever; for the message closes with a precious promise of restoration and blessing to be fulfilled in a day yet future (vers. 12, 13). God will Himself assemble the lost sheep of Jacob, gathering the remnant of Israel, and placing them together as flocks in His fold. If walls rise before them to bar their return to the land of their rest, He will send His breaker* to open a way for His redeemed, thus leading them in triumph back to Immanuel's land, as it is written, "Their king shall pass before them, and the Lord at the head of them."

Happy ending when all their discipline is accomplished, and they ask the way to Zion!

---

* It is really "wall-breaker."

CHAPTER III

PRINCES AND PRIESTS APOSTATE

THE second division of the book begins with a summons to the heads and princes of Israel to hear the prophet's rebuke.

It is no longer the common people who are addressed, but the princes, or judges, in vers. 1 to 4, and the prophets in vers. 5 to 8. Then both are grouped together, the priests also being included, as "heads of the house of Jacob," in vers. 9 to 12.

It is a solemn thing when the leaders of God's people cause them to err; when those who should have been a bulwark for the truth turn away therefrom, "speaking perverse things, to draw away disciples after them."

They who should have known judgment, and who were raised up of God to rule the nation in righteousness, were the very ones who were leading the mass astray. Often has it been so in the history of the Church, as well as of Israel. Therefore the need to test all that is taught or practised, by the only infallible rule, the unerring Word of God. If Christians are content to be styled "the laity," and leave their spiritual interests in the hands of their guides, they have themselves to blame if they are led in wrong paths. Each is responsible to exercise himself unto godliness, and to try the things that differ.

It too frequently happens that leaders become pretentious and haughty, regarding themselves as "the clergy," whose special province it is to find sustenance in "the ministry," forgetting that to minister is to *serve,* not to lord it over possessions. No pride is worse than spiritual pride. No pretension is more to be abhorred than ecclesiastical pretension. But there are never wanting vain, self-confident men, who are ever ready to arrogate to themselves high-sounding titles and powers if the people love to have it so. And it is solemn indeed to realize that it generally is the people themselves who are responsible for this kind of thing, because of the readiness with which they accept the *ipse dixit* of some gifted uninspired man, rather than to search the Word for themselves, that they may find therein set forth the path for their feet.

Here, the people were indifferent, and the princes lived recklessly, despising the "lower classes," and flourishing in their presumption and avarice. In place of caring for the flock of God, as those who must give an account, they looked upon them as their lawful prey, "flaying the skin from off them" (vers. 2, 3).

One is reminded of the grim jest of Pope Leo X, who, it is said, made the remark to his companion princes of the church, "What a profitable thing this myth about Jesus Christ has been to us!" And all because the Bible had been kept from the people, and they were willing it should be so.

But the hour of judgment is coming, when all such must answer to the great Shepherd of the sheep for their unholy ways. "Then shall they cry unto the Lord, but He will not hear them: He will even hide His face from them at that time, as they have behaved themselves ill in their doings" (ver. 4).

In the second section it is "the prophets that make the people err," who are summoned to hear the Word of the Lord. The princes ruled by sheer power, because of the awe in which they were held. The prophets perverted the very words of the Lord, and gave false burdens, in order to hinder any from inquiring concerning the path of life. Prince and prophet have been blended into one splendid hierarchy in Christendom for centuries, but in our day have been largely divorced, so that we can readily distinguish between those whose power rests on assumption of ecclesiastical character, and those who lead astray because of professed spiritual insight, entitling them to be heard as exponents of the truth, while perverting, or setting aside, the Word of God.

But all alike, however their systems may differ, have one characteristic mark: "They serve not our Lord Jesus Christ, but their own belly; and by good words and fair speeches deceive the hearts of the simple" (Rom. 16:18). This was what marked the false prophets in Micah's day—and in all days before and since. "Who, when they have something to bite with their teeth, cry, Peace; but who prepare war against him who putteth nothing in their mouths" (ver. 5)—such is Leeser's graphic translation of a verse that in the Authorized Version is a little ambiguous.

The true prophet of the Lord is not concerned about financial or other recompense. He goes forth in dependence on Him who has sent him, and is thus free to speak His Word, "not as pleasing men, but God, who trieth the hearts." Every false religious system is marked by greed for filthy lucre, and its advocates act on the thought that so readily found lodgment in Simon's heart, "that the gift of God might be purchased for money." It is the error of Balaam, and is especially characteristic of the last days.

Thus perverting the truth for personal profit, they darken counsel by words without knowledge. But as they have hidden the light from others, *they* shall go into the night at last The sixth and seventh verses are intensely solemn, and may well cause teachers of error to tremble. "Therefore the night shall be unto you, that ye shall not have a vision; and it shall be dark unto you, that ye shall not divine; and the sun shall go down over the prophets, and the day shall be dark over them. Then shall the seers be ashamed, and the diviners confounded: yea, they shall all cover their lips; for there is no answer of God." Unspeakably awful will be the awakening when those who have posed as the very oracles of divine truth before their fellows shall have their eyes opened to see that they are lost and ruined forever; and though they cry out in the anguish of their despair, there will be no answer of God!

How different was the case of Jehovah's true servant! In simple confidence he could say, "Truly I am full of power by the Spirit of the Lord, and of judgment, and of might, to declare unto Jacob his transgression, and to Israel his sin" (ver. 8). Undismayed by the fear of man that bringeth a snare, he could faithfully proclaim the mind of God, as revealed to him by the Holy Spirit. He was the servant not of men, but of Jehovah of hosts; and his ministry was in the energy of faith, hence in the mighty power of God.

The last section is a summing up, ere the glad tidings of future blessing are told, of which chap. 4 treats.

Abhorring judgment, and perverting all equity, the rulers built up Zion with blood; yet, with most barefaced effrontery, they declared the Lord was in their midst and ratified their doings. "The heads thereof judge for reward, and the priests thereof teach for hire, and the prophets thereof divine for money: yet will they lean upon the Lord, and say, Is not the Lord among us? none evil can come upon us" (ver. 11). Thus they made Him the minister of unrighteousness, and made His holy name their answer to any who sought to reach their consciences.

Saints of God are called to "follow righteousness." If this be overlooked, it is the veriest assumption to talk of having the Lord's presence, and declaring themselves in the line of His testimony. This 11th verse may profitably be weighed in connection with Jer. 6: 13, where the condition a few years later is found not to have improved, but deteriorated, as is ever the case when evil is left unjudged.

Because of this hardened condition, Zion was to be plowed as a field and Jerusalem destroyed; the mountain of Jehovah's house being treated as the idolatrous high places of the groves. If righteousness be not maintained by His saints, God will remove their candlestick and annul their pretensions. He who is the Holy and the True will not go on with iniquity.

CHAPTER IV

THE FIRST DOMINION

IT is refreshing indeed, ere the sad story of failure and sin is resumed, to turn our eyes for a little time to the glad scenes depicted in the first half of this chapter.

The three opening verses are an almost exact duplicate of Isa. 2:2-4. We need not inquire whether the charge of plagiarism should be brought against the elder or the younger prophet. We have not here to do with the literature of men, but with the inspired Word of God. He says, "The testimony of two men is true;" and He has given the same promise of millennial blessing through both Micah and Isaiah, that all may know that neither wrote from himself, but as he was moved by the Holy Ghost. It need be no matter of surprise that He chose to use the same language on each occasion.

In the last days, the time to which all prophecy points, "the mountain of the house of the Lord shall be established in the top of the mountains." The future millennial temple will not stand on mount Moriah, but on a magnificent table-land, lifted up above all the surrounding hills, after the land has gone through some remarkable topographical changes, caused by a great earthquake, which will occur when the feet of the Lord Jesus stand again on the mount of Olives. See Ezek. 40: 2 and 48: 8-12; Zech. 14: 4.

There, in commanding position, shall the house of the God of the whole earth be located, and thither shall the nations come up regularly to worship and to inquire the ways of Jehovah. From this sanctuary the law will go forth, and the word of the Lord from Jerusalem, the metropolis of the world in the age to come.

At last all delegated rule shall have ceased in the closing up of the times of the Gentiles. Henceforth our once-rejected Lord Jesus shall "show who is that blessed and only Potentate, King of kings, and Lord of lords." He shall minister unerring justice, and bring in everlasting righteousness. No more will nation lift up sword against nation; but all warlike instruments shall be destroyed, and the implements of peaceful agricultural pursuits take their place.

In that day of universal blessing there will be no curse of poverty to contend with, no vexatious property questions to settle, no struggle to acquire or conflicts to hold what can never be properly administered; but in contentment and comfort "every man shall sit under his vine and under his fig tree; and none shall make them afraid." What men have vainly striven to attain through socialist propaganda, or other equally impracticable economic systems, will then have been reached, and will be maintained for a thousand years by the personal presence of Him whose right it is to reign (vers. 1-4). The statement of the fourth verse is not found in Isaiah, but the call to walk in the ways of the Lord occurs immediately after what is here found in ver. 3. Micah presents the more nearly complete picture, and then gives the remnant's answer to the exhortation of Isa. 2: 5 in the lovely words, "For all people will walk every one in the name of his god, and [or, but] we will walk in the name of the Lord our God for ever and ever." It is faith laying hold of the promise, and the believer walking now by the glory that is coming.

But the nation to whom "the first dominion" is yet to be given must, ere that day of triumph, be scattered among all nations because of their sins. Therefore the Lord Himself will regather them ere the kingdom is set up in power. So the prophet goes on to tell how Jehovah will assemble the halting and afflicted remnant, and bring them back by omnipotent power to the land of their fathers. The nation, *as such* (continuing in unbelief, and accepting the false Christ when he arrives), will never be restored; but a repentant remnant will be found in the last days who will become the nucleus of a new nation in the land. Over them "the Lord shall reign in mount Zion from henceforth, even forever." Then shall the first dominion indeed have come for Israel, when Jerusalem shall be the joy of the whole earth (vers. 6-8).

But much had to elapse ere the glorious vision should be fulfilled. The daughter of Zion, as a travailing woman, should first pass through her hours of bitter anguish. She was to be carried to Babylon, and there made the sport of unfeeling Gentiles who were blind to her beauty and ignorant of her wondrous destiny. Her enemies are to magnify themselves against her till the hour when the set time to favor her has come, and the Lord Himself shall appear, to act the part of her Kinsman-Redeemer, delivering her from her bondage and bringing her into everlasting blessing. In that day their wealth shall be devoted to Him through whom all their joys shall come, and their substance will gladly be held at His bidding (vers. 9-13).

CHAPTER V

THE SMITTEN JUDGE

THE promises we have been considering are all to be made good by Messiah, of whose rejection at His first coming we are now to read. In the Hebrew arrangement of the text, at the present, the first verse is taken from chap. 5, and made ver. 14 of chap. 4—thus divorcing the testimony as to the smitten Judge of Israel from the One born in Bethlehem, whose goings forth have been from the ages of eternity. It is easy to detect rabbinical opposition to the New Testament narratives in this, slight as the difference might seem to the careless reader.

Accepting the Hebrew arrangement, it would seem as though the Judge in question was simply one of the many rulers of Israel who would be treated shamefully by the northern foe. But the light of the New Testament makes it plain that the smitten One is none other than He who could say, "I gave My back to the smiters, and My cheeks to them that plucked off the hair: I hid not My face from shame and spitting" (Isa. 50: 6). He it was who came to His own, but His own people received Him not. In the high priest's house "did they spit in His face, and buffeted Him; and others smote Him with the palms of their hands, saying, Prophesy unto us, Thou Christ, Who is he that smote Thee?" In the Roman pretorium likewise the rough soldiers "spit upon Him, and took the reed, and smote Him on the head" (Matt. 26: 67, 68, and 27: 30).

But of Him it had been declared by the prophet, "Thou, Beth-lehem Ephratah, though thou be little among the thousands of Judah, yet out of thee shall He come forth unto Me that is to be ruler in Israel; whose goings forth have been from of old, from everlasting [or, the days of eternity]" (ver. 2). Thus, in plain language, seven centuries before God incarnate appeared on earth, the place of His birth was distinctly indicated. To David's city should this honor be given. This, as is well known, is the passage to which the scribes turned when they explained to Herod where Christ was to be born. They held prophetic truth, and searched the Scriptures: but the truth held not them, nor did they permit the Scriptures to search them.

The lesson is important for us all. Mere familiarity with the written Word of God will only make us the guiltier if it be not that which controls all our ways. To read the Book; to study its various lines of truth; to be able to speak intelligently of the great doctrinal principles of Scripture—and yet not to have received that Word in an honest heart, to be controlled and guided by it, is dreadful indeed!

One has said, referring to the not uncommon, nor unhelpful, practice of Bible-marking, "It is a small thing how you mark your Bible, but it is of all importance that it mark *you*."

To Bethlehem, then, came the Eternal One, "God manifest in flesh." Over His manger-bed angels hung, adoring their God and ours. A few shepherds and, later, some wise men from distant lands, came to worship likewise; but, for the rest, Israel and the nations around went on in their indifferent, careless way. God the Son had become the Son of Man; but man, in the main, was unconcerned. "He was despised and rejected of men," and the Judge of Israel was smitten on the cheek! Thus was Messiah cut off, and He had nothing. For this, judgment fell on the city that wickedly judged Him, and Jerusalem has for centuries been trodden down of the Gentiles, and shall be, "until the times of the nations are completed"—"until the time that she which travaileth hath brought forth: then the remnant of His brethren shall return unto the children of Israel" (ver. 3). Dispersed among all peoples, scattered into every country, suffering under every sky, Israel endures the awful curse invoked by her own elders, "His blood be upon us and our children."

Unto her a Son was born and a Child given ere she travailed for His birth. But her pains are yet to come. In the great tribulation, under the personal Antichrist, she shall be in anguish to be delivered. Then shall she truly bring forth, apprehending in the Crucified her own Son and her Saviour! Compare Rev. 12:1-5 and Isa. 66:7-9, "Before she travailed, she brought forth; before her pain came, she was delivered of a man child." Therefore her pains are yet future, and she shall be in sore travail ere she recognizes and owns her Messiah.

Then a multitude of sons shall also be hers when "the remnant of His *brethren* shall return unto the children of Israel." The residue, called "His brethren" here, He owns Himself as "My brethren" in Matt. 25:40. Thus shall be fulfilled the word of the elder prophet, "As soon as Zion travailed, she brought forth her children" (Isa. 66:8). He will be revealed as the long-waited-for Shepherd of Israel, who "shall stand and feed [or, shepherd] in the strength of the Lord," and who shall give abiding rest to His regathered flock. His majesty and glory shall be made known throughout the habitable world, "for now shall He be great unto the ends of the earth" (ver. 4). It is a connected prophecy of the rejection of Christ when He came in lowly grace, to be succeeded by His acceptance and world-wide acknowledgment when He comes the second time, in power and dignity becoming His exalted Person.

But the hour of His appearance will be the

hour of Israel's deepest sorrow. Jerusalem shall be compassed with armies. The Antichrist will be reigning, with blasphemous pretensions, in the city. The legions of the revived Roman empire will have entered into a league with him both offensive and defensive. From the south a fierce horde will be pouring into the land. From the north the dreaded power denominated "the Assyrian," of whom Sennacherib was but as a type, will be marching down in exultant triumph, spreading desolation on every hand. "*Then* shall the Lord go forth, and fight against those nations, as when He fought in the day of battle" (Zech. 14:3), and "this [Man] shall be the peace." He who has now made peace with God for guilty men by the blood of His cross; He who, seated as Man on Jehovah's throne, *is* our peace; He shall be the Peace in that day; and in Him weary, distracted Israel shall find their rest.

The haughty Assyrian will be overthrown, and God's chosen people delivered from his cruel power (vers. 5 and 6). Then, freed from all their enemies, "the remnant of Jacob shall be in the midst of many people as a dew from the Lord, as the showers upon the grass," bringing refreshment and blessing to all nations at the Lord's bidding, and tarrying for none (ver. 7).

The lion of Judah's tribe shall arise in His might, subjecting all enemies to His sway. Thus shall Israel have become the head, and nevermore be the tail (vers. 8, 9). Everything that has exalted itself against the Lord shall be put down. Evil of every kind shall be rooted out of the scene, and righteousness will be triumphant to the ends of the earth (vers. 10-15). It is the end to which all the prophets looked forward; so it becomes a fitting end to the second section of our book.

CHAPTER VI

THE LORD'S CONTROVERSY

WE now enter upon the third division of the book. It is no longer the future that the prophet is especially looking forward to, either of joy or of sorrow; but he directs the attention of the people to *their ways,* and presses home upon the conscience moral truth of great moment. In other words, this final message is the practical application of what has gone before, and is, in large measure, of the same character as the major part of the prophecy of Jeremiah and much of Hosea.

The mountains and the hills (an oft-used simile for chief cities and their tributary villages) are called upon to give ear to the searching words of "the Lord's controversy." We are told, "The Lord hath a controversy with His people, and He will plead with Israel" (vers. 1, 2).

God *always* has a controversy with those who walk in disobedience. There can be no fellowship or communion while His Word is not bowed to. He desires truth in the inward parts: nothing else will satisfy "Him that is holy, Him that is true." The moment the conscience is reached, and the heart bows before Him in true self-judgment, controversy ceases, and communion is re-established.

Let the reader note: it is not of union we write, but of something which flows from it, and which should ever be maintained with it—communion.

Union implies being partakers of the common life of all God's children. "He that sanctifieth and they who are sanctified are all of one" (Heb. 2:11). All such are eternally united to Him from whom they derived that new life. This is a link that can never be broken. Otherwise the life communicated would be forfeitable, and not eternal.

But communion is the normal state of one who has thus been made a child of God. It is the practical manifestation of that life in abiding fellowship with the Father and the Son. For the saints of Micah's day it was, according to the revelation then made, enjoyment of Jehovah's favor. This Israel had forfeited by disobedience; and it could only be regained by self-judgment. The principle abides. Only when that which is known to be contrary to the Word of the Lord is unsparingly condemned in my own life and walk, will I enjoy communion with God.

That Israel might be stirred up to desire this, He takes them back over their early days, reminding them of His patient grace with them from the day when He first brought them out of the house of bondage (vers. 3-5). He had led them like a flock through the wilderness, permitting none to curse them, but, in His holy discipline, dealing with them Himself when they sinned, that they "might know the righteousness of the Lord."

All His chastening was with a view to their blessing. Therefore the humbled soul might well ask, "Wherewith shall I come before the Lord, and bow myself before the high God?" Did He demand sacrifices and offerings? Was it these that were lacking? Would He be pleased with thousands of rams and myriads of rivers of oil? Even though one gave upon the altar his dearest and best, his first-born, would that avail for the sin of the soul? Was it by means such as these the interrupted communion was to be restored? (vers. 6, 7).

No! It was righteousness that was lacking. Righteousness, then, must be maintained. "He hath showed thee, O man, what is good; and what doth the Lord require of thee, but to do justly, and to love mercy, and to walk humbly with thy God?" (ver. 8). Only when they bowed before Him, to own the sin of the past, and sought strength to walk as here outlined, could there be that happy sense of the Lord's favor which lifts the soul above all circumstances, and enables it to joy in God Himself.

But that this might indeed be, "The Lord's voice crieth unto the city, and the man of wisdom shall see thy name: hear ye the rod, and who hath appointed it!" (ver. 9). This is the beginning of blessing. When the soul bows before God and owns the righteousness of His disciplinary dealings, then he is in the place where restoring grace can meet him. As long as he kicks against the goads, so long must he go on under chastisement. But when he "hears the rod," confessing his need of it, he has reached the point where restoration begins.

The next three verses itemize the sins to which general reference had been made; that the people may the more readily pass judgment upon themselves and all that is unholy in their ways. Covetousness, extortion, unrighteousness in business dealings, violence, deceit—all these evil things are the evidence of their wrong state of soul (vers. 10-12). Therefore governmental wrath must fall if there be no sign of repentance: they would be made desolate because of their sins. In vain should they seek satisfaction while the will was insubject and the walk opposed to holiness. They might sow, but they should not reap; in fact, all their labor should be for naught. The work of their hands would fail to meet the needs of the body till they came to themselves, like the prodigal, and owned their guilt (vers. 14, 15; see also Deut. 28: 38-40 and Haggai 1: 6).

The chapter closes with the record of the melancholy fact that Jehovah's law was despised;

but "the statutes of Omri are kept, and all the works of the house of Ahab, and ye walk in their counsels; that I should make thee a desolation, and the inhabitants thereof a hissing; therefore ye shall bear the reproach of My people" (ver. 16). Solemnly and tenderly had the Lord pleaded, and set forth the grounds of His controversy with them; but the words fell on deaf ears and calloused consciences. They seemed bent upon their own destruction—and these things are written for our admonition. May we have ears to hear and hearts to understand!

CHAPTER VII

FUTURE REPENTANCE AND BLESSING

THIS last chapter, which forms the fourth division, is closely allied to the book of the Lamentations. It is the prayer of the repentant remnant in the days of the great tribulation, the time of Jacob's trouble. That is, the prophet sets forth the suited utterance of those who no longer walk in pride, but, humbled because of their sin, own the justice of the Hand that smote them. Excuses there are none, nor do they look at second causes, but they accept all as the due reward of their deeds, and yet look up in faith to the God of their fathers, upon whose unfailing grace they count for restoration.

The three discourses, or divisions, that have gone before, were all designed to lead to this desired end: so that this chapter sets forth the future result of the ministry which at the time seemed to fall to the ground. It was the Word of the living God, and could not return unto Him void, but must accomplish that for which it was sent.

In the six opening verses we have a most graphic portrayal of conditions in the fearful days of the Antichrist. To the remnant it seems as though the good have been destroyed out of the earth, and "there is none upright among men." Treachery and deceit shall so abound that one dare not put confidence in his most intimate friend. Even the wife of his bosom may betray him to the unholy inquisition of that fearful time. For those be the days of vengeance described by our Lord in Matt. 24:9-31, when the abomination of desolation shall stand in the holy place; as also in Matt. 10:21-36, where He quotes this very passage when referring to the final testimony ere the appearing of the Son of Man.

Such times have been known already in many places, as in the dark days of Roman Catholicism's power; but for Israel, in a special sense, darker days are yet to come.

The confidence of the remnant and their submission to the will of God are beautifully delineated in vers. 7 to 10. Owning the righteousness of His dealings, they yet look up to Him in faith, crying, "I will wait for the God of my salvation;" and they are assured that He will hear. The enemy may seem to triumph; but though fallen, they shall arise, and the Lord shall be their light when the darkness has become the deepest. In lowliness and humility they say, "I will bear the indignation of the Lord because I have sinned against Him." This is remarkably fine, and shows how truly their exercises have resulted in the peaceable fruits of righteousness. Thus they can count on God for deliverance, and wait in patience till He shall plead their cause and execute judgment for them, that they may glorify Him for His righteousness. Then shall Israel's enemies, who taunted her in her forsaken condition, own that she is indeed the chosen of the Lord.

"In that day" temporal prosperity will return to Jerusalem, and her walls shall be rebuilt. Her children shall be brought back from Assyria and all the places whither they have been carried captive. Though the land shall first be desolated by the armies of the nations, because of the fruit of Israel's doings, yet the old wastes shall be rebuilt, and the flock of Jehovah's heritage shall be brought from their hiding-places and shepherded in the choice pastures of Bashan and Gilead, "as in the days of old" (vers. 11-14).

As once the Lord had brought them up in triumph out of the land of Egypt, He will show marvelous things when He arises for the salvation of His chosen in the last days. The Gentiles, who have despised and hated the Jew, will be filled with astonishment when the remnant are reestablished in the land of their fathers, and the first dominion has returned to Jacob (vers. 15-17). It will be a marvelous exhibition of grace, and of the loving-kindness of the Lord.

No wonder the book closes with so precious an ascription of adoring gratitude. "Who is a God like unto Thee, that pardoneth iniquity, and passeth by the transgression of the remnant of His heritage? He retaineth not His anger forever, because He delighteth in mercy. He will turn again, He will have compassion upon us; He will subdue our iniquities; and Thou wilt cast all their sins into the depths of the sea. Thou wilt perform the truth to Jacob, and the mercy to Abraham, which Thou hast sworn unto our fathers from the days of old" (vers. 18-20).

This will be the happy ending of all God's ways with Israel. Established in the kingdom of the Son of Man, they will be brought into the blessedness of the knowledge of transgressions forgiven and sin covered. And they will trace all that blessing back to the smitten Judge, who came in grace to save, but who was despised and rejected by the very people who held in their hands the Scripture of truth, foretelling the actual things which they in their unbelief fulfilled.

In the hour of their deepest anguish they will turn back to the same sacred books, and learn therefrom that the Nazarene was the long-expected One whose goings forth have been of old, from everlasting. At last convinced of their fearful sin, the remnant will bow in bitterness of soul before God, owning the guilt of their fathers, and judging their own past unbelief. Then grace will act on their behalf, and restoration to their land and their God will follow.

From every renewed heart will burst the cry of worshipful praise, "Who is a God like unto Thee, that pardoneth iniquity?"

Into the sea of His forgetfulness He will cast all their sins, justifying them freely by His grace through the same wondrous redemption which is now the ground of blessing for every Jew and Gentile who trusts in the name of Jesus.

Thus Micah's prophecy reaches the end to which all the prophets pointed; when the oath of Jehovah to Abraham, Isaac and Jacob will be performed, and their seed will be established in their ancient patrimony, never again to be uprooted, and enjoying all the blessings of the new covenant, confirmed by the precious blood of Christ.

Notes on the
PROPHECY OF NAHUM

CHAPTER I

FAITH'S REFUGE

"SEARCH and look," said the prejudiced Jewish doctors, when summarily disposing of the claims of the Lord Jesus, "for out of Galilee ariseth no prophet." We have already seen, in the case of Jonah, that their positive assertion was unsupported by the evidence of Scripture, to which they so coolly appealed. The son of Amittai was unquestionably out of Galilee. There are the best of reasons for believing the same of Nahum. He is called the Elkoshite; that is, a man from Elkosh, or, as it is sometimes written, Elkesi (ver. 1).

It is well known that there was an Assyrian village on the banks of the Tigris by this name; but Jerome states positively, when he retreated to Palestine from the turmoil of an unfriendly world, that he was shown the site of the Galilean

Elkosh where Nahum was reported to have been born.

The prophecy of Nahum bears every evidence of having been delivered in the land prior to the death of Sennacherib, and, therefore, at least a century before the destruction of Nineveh, of which it mainly treats. He was in all likelihood contemporary with Isaiah, and uttered his poetic prediction in the reign of Hezekiah. Nahum was therefore, one can scarcely doubt, a Galilean, who came at the call of God from his northern home to speak words of comfort to the trembling people of the south, whose hearts were in fear because of the Assyrian invasion.

The book seems to divide readily into two parts. Chapter 1 presents the Eternal One as the Rock and Stay of those who confide in Him, whatever the danger that threatens. Locally, it was the army of Sennacherib that seemed about to overwhelm them. But God was above all, as was soon made manifest. Chapters 2 and 3 give the destruction of Nineveh, whence the oppressor had come. The description of the siege and breaking up of the guilty city is a masterpiece of dramatic poetry.

It is of interest to note that both the prophets whose Galilean birth we have commented on had to do largely with Nineveh in their ministry. Jonah was used to the repentance of the generation of his day, about one hundred and fifty years ere Nahum declared the final overthrow of the city because its iniquities had reached unto heaven. In that destruction it is easy to see a picture of the future end of the impious Assyrian of the last days, to which attention has frequently been directed in these notes.

Nahum means *Consolation;* and consolatory indeed are the precious words of cheer which he was inspired to deliver in this first chapter.

Vengeance belongs to God. To the Thessalonian saints Paul writes, "It is a righteous thing with God to recompense tribulation to them that trouble you." He is ever watching over His people; and while He permits many things for their discipline, He will never overlook an indignity done to His redeemed. "He reserveth wrath for his enemies" (ver. 2). Note this: the enemies of His people are His enemies. He makes their cause His own. Faith rests on this, and is thus saved much worry and anxiety. Nature would be alarmed and excited, where faith is calm and quiet. Nature sees the Assyrian armies: faith looks up to the God of battles. The entire 19th and 20th chapters of 2 Kings may be read with profit in this connection, as they describe the actual scenes to which the first part of Nahum's prophecy refers.

The third verse contains much that is precious for the afflicted soul, as well as a solemn warning for him who hardens himself against discipline.

Slow to wrath, and mighty in power, the Lord cannot pass by iniquity. He will not acquit, or hold guiltless, the wicked. Of old, God had declared to Moses that He was "merciful and gracious, long-suffering, and abundant in goodness and truth, keeping mercy for thousands, forgiving iniquity and transgression and sin, and that will by no means clear the guilty" (Exod. 34:5-7). Full of love as He is—yea, though He is love itself—yet He is also light: therefore sin must be judged. This is where the cross comes in. But even for men who have found forgiveness there, God will not tolerate unjudged evil; and if we judge not ourselves, we must be judged by Him; for "when we are judged, we are chastened of the Lord, that we should not be condemned with the world" (1 Cor. 11:32). Exod. 34: 6 is for the sinner's warning. Nah. 1: 3 is for the saint's comfort. Yet the principle is the same; for whether in the case of men in general, or of His children in particular, His holy eye passes over nothing till all is judged. But if the whirlwind and the storm seem about to overwhelm, and for the believer the sky seems black with clouds, it is sweet to know that the Lord has His way in all that seems so terrific, and at times so arbitrary. The stormy wind but fulfils His word, and "the clouds are the dust of His feet."

Look up then, dear tried and perplexed soul;

for He is just above those heavy clouds of sorrow. As the dust in the distance betrays the approach of the traveler ere the form is seen upon the dry roadway, so the clouds tell of His near presence who knows all thy griefs and comes in love to dry thy tears. At His word the tempest-tossed sea is rebuked and the rivers of woe assuaged, even as of old He dried up the Red Sea and rolled back the waters of Jordan. All creation must own His power, and all elements yield to His authority. None can stand before His indignation nor abide the day of His wrath. Yet He is good, a fortress in the day of trouble, "and He knoweth them that trust in Him" (vers. 4-7).

What comfort words like these would be to Hezekiah and his people, shut up in Jerusalem, affrighted and taunted by the arrogant Assyrian, polluting the air with his blasphemies against Jehovah!

Little did Rab-shakeh and Sennacherib know with whom the battle was really to be fought. Little could they realize that Jerusalem would flourish long after Nineveh had become a heap of ruins. In accordance with Isa. 10:5 to 19, Nahum foretold in vers. 8 to 10 the very manner in which the imperial city by the Tigris was to be destroyed. Profane history gives its testimony in the record of Ctesias that while a drunken feast was going on, the flood-gates of the city were swept away by a sudden rise of the river, and the palace foundations were thus dissolved. The army of the Babylonians, who had been besieging it for some time, entered by the breach made, and burned it with fire while the inebriated inhabitants sought in vain to escape. See chap. 3: 11.

Such should be proud Nineveh's end. Meantime one had come from thence, a counselor of Belial, imagining evil against the Lord (ver. 11). This is God's description of haughty Sennacherib, who may well be viewed as a type of the last great Assyrian, so often contemplated in the prophecies.

But all his boasting was in vain: Jehovah had permitted his invasion as a chastisement for the sins of Judah. He had observed the effect. Hezekiah and his princes were humbled before Him. Now God would act for them. Though He had afflicted them, He would do so no more. The Assyrian hosts were blasted by the breath of His mouth, and Sennacherib himself basely murdered a short time afterward, as ver. 14 declared he would be, by the hands of his own sons. See Isa. 37: 36-38.

Freed from the danger that had threatened, Judah could keep her feasts in peace, rejoicing in the appointed ministry of cheer sent by Jehovah. His messengers are spoken of in Isa. 52: 7 in almost the same language. Possibly Nahum and Isaiah feasted together when the enemy was thus destroyed, and enlargement granted to Judah.

Delivered and exultant, they are called upon to perform their vows, for the host that had but a little before struck terror to their souls would pass through the land no more.

Who can fail to see in all this a wondrous picture of the introduction of millennial blessing when the last coalition against Israel has been overthrown, and the Lord Jesus Himself shall descend with feet beautiful upon the mountains to publish peace that shall no more be disturbed!

CHAPTER II

THE DESTRUCTION OF NINEVEH

IT is important, in reading the Prophets, to distinguish between those parts which relate primarily to events long since fulfilled, and those which have to do entirely with what is still future. Fulfilled prophecy is a clinching proof of the divine inspiration of the Scriptures. That which tells of what is yet to come is "a light shining in a dark place," enabling the devout reader to put a proper value on all he sees around him.

On the other hand, all prophecy is one connected whole and must be read in view of that to which it all points—the coming day of the Lord. But for many peoples and nations that day has already come. Their course has been run. Their manifold iniquities have been judged; and their civilizations have passed out of existence.

The glory of Nineveh has been for over two and a half millenniums but a memory. That it should be so was predicted by Nahum a century at least ere his words had their awful fulfilment in the Babylonian conquest. This is given in detail in chaps. 2 and 3, a portion of Scripture (and of literature in general) unsurpassed for graphic delineation and poetic fervor.

"He that dasheth in pieces," the leader of the Chaldean hosts, is seen, in vision, coming up against Nineveh, proudly resting in her glory on the banks of the Tigris. Founded by Nimrod, as was also the rival Euphratean city Babylon, the one sets forth the world in its grandeur and independence of God; the other, the religious world, the home of superstition and traditionary ritual. Necessarily the former must fall before the rising power of the latter, even as, centuries later, paganism had to succumb to an unholy, pseudo-Christianity, which seemed more fully to meet the need of man in his hopeless depravity. Yet it often becomes a question to the thoughtful student, Which was worse, the world without God, or the world with a perverted idea of God, wrapped in the darkness of medieval superstition and ignorance of the Scriptures of truth?

Let Nineveh attempt to defend herself as she may, no power can avail to avert the richly-deserved judgment (ver. 1). She had herself been the instrument used to punish the excellency of Jacob; but now, since they had been punished, the heathen should not escape. It is the principle enunciated in 1 Pet. 4:17, 18—judgment begins at the house of God. What then of those who know Him not? If He will pass over nothing because committed by His own, how solemn the day when the wicked have to answer for all their lawlessness! If the powers of evil are permitted to mar the branches of the vine of Jehovah's planting, who shall prevent the destruction of the wild trees of the wood? (ver. 2).

The terrific character of the final assault on Nineveh is vividly described in vers. 3 to 5. As this passage has often been applied most fancifully, I quote it in full, in order that it may stand out clearly in its true connection. "The shield of his mighty men is made red, the valiant men are in scarlet; the chariots shall be with flaming torches in the day of his preparation, and the fir trees shall be terribly shaken. The chariots shall rage in the streets, they shall jostle one against another in the broad ways; they shall seem like torches, they shall run like the lightnings."

It is a striking portrayal of the wild disorder that necessarily prevailed when the Babylonian hordes and their Median allies poured into the doomed city. What is there here to suggest the strange and forced interpretation often put upon so plain a passage? Were it not so common a view, who could believe that sober men would attempt to see in words like these references to railroads, electric cars, and automobiles! Yet sermons have been preached and books written in which such mechanical devices are declared to be the fulfilment of this portion of Nahum's prophecy.* It is an instance of the careless way in which men read Scripture; for, clearly, "the day of his preparation" was the day of Nineveh's destruction; and the "chariots with flaming torches," running "like the lightnings," were the war-carriages of the victorious Babylonians.

Against such a terrific onslaught the king of Nineveh tried in vain to rally his worthies. Drunken, as a result of their unholy feasts, they stumbled in their walk as they hastened to the wall, only to find it was too late now to attempt a defence (ver. 5). The rise of the river opened the already weakened sluice-gates; the floods crumbled the foundations of the palace, and made hope of resistance vain (ver. 6).

Diodorus Siculus describes the end of the siege in the following language: "There was an old prophecy that Nineveh should not be taken till the river became an enemy to the city. And in the third year of the siege, the river being swollen with continual rains, overflowed every part of the city, and broke down the wall for twenty furlongs; then the king, thinking that the oracle was fulfilled, and the river become an enemy to the city, built a large funeral pile in the palace,

* I have even known prophetic lecturers to wax eloquent over "The valiant men are in scarlet;" applying the verse to the red-jerseyed soldiers of the Salvation Army!

and collecting together all his wealth and his concubines and eunuchs, burnt himself and the palace with them all; and the enemy entered at the breach that the waters had made and took the city."

Thus with violence was Nineveh's pride abased and "Huzzab" ("the established") led away captive. She had proudly thought herself established to abide forever, but her end had come because she exalted herself against the Lord (ver. 7).

Vers. 8 to 13 are too plain to require comment. In language unmistakable they describe the desolation following the complete overthrow of what had been the world's most glorious city. So exactly were the words fulfilled, that for ages the very site of Nineveh was lost, till, in the last century, Layard and Rawlinson made excavations and discoveries that brought to light the ruins of a metropolis so vast that none could longer doubt the declarations of Jonah and Nahum in regard to its splendor and magnificence, and its destruction when in the very zenith of its glory.

It may be well to remark that the lion of vers. 11, 12 is the king; and the lions and lionesses his household who perished with him amid the flames of his palace.

CHAPTER III

BEYOND HEALING

OF Nineveh's doom we have been reading. The last chapter continues the subject, and tells us that doom is irretrievable. But it does more. Its first four verses give us Jehovah's terrible indictment, and show us why unsparing judgment had to fall upon it.

A city of blood, full of lies and robbery! Such is the divine description. All its glory was stained by the iniquity of its people (ver. 1). In cruel warfare and sanguinary carnage its haughty inhabitants delighted. The sight of armies rushing together in battle was their joy.* Therefore others should exult over them when they fell beneath the power of their victorious enemies (vers. 2, 3). Uncleanness abounded; the filthiness of the flesh and spirit, prostitution and sorcery, were openly carried on, and linked with the worship of their demon-gods (ver. 4). Therefore was Jehovah's face against them, and He had determined to make them a gazing-stock and

---

* Nineveh seems to have been inbred with the spirit of its founder, Nimrod, the Cushite, "a mighty hunter before the Lord" (Gen. 10: 8, 9), taking pleasure in the wanton chase of nations for prey.—[Ed.

a warning to all who should follow their pernicious ways (vers. 5, 6).

It was but a little before that their great king, Sargon, is reputed to have destoryed No Amon (called in the A. V. "populous No"), and carried her people into captivity. But Nineveh was equally guilty, and must herself become a prey. In that day the surrounding nations would take up a taunt against her, crying, "Nineveh is laid waste: who will bemoan her?" Her course had left her friendless and alone in the day of the Lord's anger. Imperious and vindictive, she sought only her own agrandizement, and in no sense the welfare of subject cities and provinces. So she must learn that "righteousness [alone] exalteth a nation: but sin is a reproach to any people" (Prov. 14:34). No human power can long exist that persistently practises and encourages corruption and violence. The Most High rules in the kingdoms of men whether they own Him or not; and He puts down one people and exalts another at His own pleasure, taking into account all of their ways (vers. 7-10).

The 11th verse seems again to refer to the last drunken orgy, to which, history tells us, the whole city was given up on the night of its awful fall.

Unable in anywise to resist the invading hordes, the very strongholds poured forth their inebriated hosts for destruction like a fig tree casting her first ripe figs into the eater's mouth when shaken (vers. 12, 13). Thus her ruin was complete in the day when the fire devoured her palaces (vers. 14, 15).

Eaten up as green leaves are destroyed by the locusts, so was Nineveh's splendor to have an end. And if any might apply the locust-figure to the Assyrians themselves, they had become but as an insect host benumbed by cold, unable to pursue their prey, and who, when warmed by the rays of the sun, flee away, "and their place is not known where they are" (vers. 16, 17).

So should perish Saracus, grandson of the famous Esar-haddon, Assyria's last king, together with all his nobles and his people; for the God whom he knew not, nor cared to know, had solemnly declared, "There is no healing of thy bruise; thy wound is grievous: all that hear the bruit (or, report) of these shall clap the hands over thee: for upon whom hath not thy wickedness passed continually?" (vers. 18, 19).

Nineveh has fallen to rise no more forever. Her mighty men have passed off the scene, together with all their guilt and sins, never more to be numbered among the living till that day

> "When the sun is old, and the stars are cold,
> And the leaves of the judgment-book unfold."

But in the crisis of the last days a fierce and unholy power will occupy the land once dominated by Huzzab on the Tigris (chap. 2:7), who will have the traits and bitter hatred of God and His people once characteristic of Assyria, and, appearing in Asshur's spirit and power, will be emphatically denominated "*The* Assyrian," or "the king of the north," whose final doom is prefigured in Nahum's prophecy of the fall of Nineveh of old.

Thus this book has for us a double value; letting us know how completely inspired prophecy has been fulfilled in the past, and in this way assuring our hearts as to the literal carrying out of all God has caused to be spoken by His divinely-inspired seers. May it be ours to "eat the book" till our whole being is pervaded with its truth, that thus we may walk as strangers and pilgrims through a scene over which the Most High has written the awful word TEKEL! (Dan. 5:27).

Notes on the

PROPHECY OF HABAKKUK

INTRODUCTION

ONE of the shortest books of Scripture—the prophecy of Habakkuk—contains important truth which no reverent student of the Word of God can afford to overlook. Brief as it is, it is directly referred to, or quotations made from it, a number of times in the New Testament.

The great apostle to the Gentiles is particularly partial to it, finding in it the inspired authority for the fundamental doctrine of justification by faith, and the certainty of judgment to come upon all who reject the testimony of the Holy Ghost as to the Lord Jesus Christ. Compare Acts 13:40, 41 with Hab. 1:5; and Rom. 1:17; Gal. 3:11; Heb. 10:38 with Hab. 2:4. There is evidently, likewise, very close connection between Hab. 3:17, 18 and the 4th chapter of the Epistle to the Philippians. As it is purposed to look carefully at these passages in the course of our study, they can be passed over now.

Of Habakkuk personally very little is known. Like John the Baptist, he is "the voice of One," himself hidden; though the exercises of his soul are vividly portrayed in his vigorous and soul-stirring prophetic poem. Jewish tradition asserts that he was of the tribe of Simeon, and he is commonly supposed to have been contemporary with Jeremiah during the latter part of "the weeping prophet's" ministry. His book would seem to evidence this, as it was written in view of the Chaldean invasion. Of his birth or death we have no record. He is said to have remained in the land when the mass of the people were carried away by the triumphant armies of Nebuchadnezzar.

The form of the book is that of a dialogue, and the structure is exceedingly simple. Habakkuk, oppressed by a sense of the prevalence of iniquity, unburdens his heart to Jehovah, who in grace answers the cry of His servant. The true divisions are easily found. Chap. 1:1-4 gives the prophet's complaint. Vers. 5-11 are the Lord's answer. From ver. 12 to ver. 17 we have Habakkuk's remonstrance. Ver. 1 of ch. 2 stands by itself. There is no immediate reply to the cry with which the previous chapter was concluded. In vers. 2 to 4 the Lord goes far beyond the prophet's thoughts, and predicts the final bringing in of blessing through Messiah: meantime "the just shall live by his faith." The actual response to the remonstrance of chap. 1 is given in vers. 5 to 8. The balance of the chapter would seem to be prophetic ministry. Having been made to know the end of the Lord, His servant delivers His word to four classes who walk not in His ways. A woe is pronounced upon each of them: the covetous, vers. 9-11; the unrighteous, vers. 12-14; the intemperate and shameless, vers. 15-17; and the idolatrous, vers. 18-20. Chap. 3 concludes with the prayer of Habakkuk, and is one of the most precious and sublime portions of Old Testament Scripture.

While having its primary application to Israel and Babylon in the dark days following the cutting-off of Josiah (the same period covered by the major portion of Jeremiah), this book contains solemn and important principles applicable to all the Lord's people, and to all seasons. "Written for our learning," we may well ponder its searching chapters listening like the prophet himself, "to see what He will say unto us, and what we shall answer when we are reproved."

That God should thus deign to meet the longing cry of His servant's heart, is for our encouragement and cheer. He regardeth the cry of the humble, but "the proud He knoweth afar off." "The meek will He guide in judgment; the meek will He teach His way." Unquestionably, the paramount reason why we get, as a rule, so little out of God's word, is because of the appalling lack of self-judgment and brokenness before its Author, so prevalent on every hand. Pride, haughtiness, and self-sufficiency, resulting in headiness and wordy strife, abound on all sides, coupled with grave moral laxity and inability to try the things that differ. True-hearted subjection to God and His Word is very little known or regarded.

In great measure it has been forgotten that there must be a right moral state to enter into the things of God, for "spiritual things are spiritually discerned." Consequently, carnal, self-complacent Christians, walking as men, are often found seeking to make up for lack of genuine, Spirit-given ministry by receiving or listening to empty platitudes or expressions (true and precious enough in themselves) learned by rote, and given out in a mechanical, parrot-like manner, instead of waiting upon God until His voice is heard in the soul, exercising the conscience of hearer and speaker alike.

In a day like the present, when "of the making of many books there is no end," it is very easy for any person of average intelligence to acquire a fair mental acquaintance with the truths of Scripture, and to pose, in the presence of less instructed or unspiritual persons, as an oracle of divine wisdom, when in reality the holy eye of God sees nothing but vain conceit and self-sufficiency in it all.

Truth learned by others in deep exercise in the school of God, is often retailed out to admiring crowds of worldly Christians and Christless professors, incapable of true, godly discernment, by men who themselves have known little or nothing of its power in their own souls, or of that subduedness before God consistent with the teachings they set forth.

Especially will this be found to be the case in regard to the teaching of Scripture as to the Church. How many today talk glibly of the one Body and the unity of the Spirit, who do not appear to have a particle of real concern because of their practical denial of that truth by identification with unscriptural and sectarian systems, where the Head of the Church is in practice disowned, and the Holy Spirit is refused His true place; while a human system of clergy and laity takes the place of the divine order laid down in the book of God!

Many doubtless know Jesus as Saviour, and the Holy Ghost as the earnest of their inheritance, who have never learned to truly own Christ as the Church's one Head, and the Holy Spirit as the controlling power in the assembly. With large numbers this is unquestionably the result of ignorance, and the Great Shepherd of the sheep will take into account the lack of instruction and the faulty teaching in that day of manifestation, now so near at hand, when "we must all appear before the judgment-seat of Christ." But, alas, by how many among us can this be pleaded? Knowledge is even boasted of when there is no corresponding concern as to the existing conditions in the house of God, and latitudinarianism and independency are the order of the day. It is godly exercise that is so sadly lacking, which accounts for the indifference to Christ and the truth everywhere evident.

In Habakkuk we see the very opposite of all this. He is a man deeply exercised both as to the state of his people—yea, his own state and the ways of God in government. Nor can he rest in quietness until he has the mind of the Lord as to it all. His book, therefore, is of special value in our degenerate and Laodicean times, characterized by what another has designated as "high truth and low walk." It strikingly portrays the working of spiritual sensibilities, and the divine answer to the same, in a man of like passions with ourselves, as each chapter will make manifest.

CHAPTER I

THE PROPHET'S PERPLEXITY

THE opening verses of the first chapter set before us the deep exercises of the prophet's soul on account of the fallen estate of the nation of Judah, dear to his heart, not only because they were his people, but because he knew them to be Jehovah's peculiar treasure; now, alas, so defiled and marred by sin.

"The burden which Habakkuk the prophet did see. O Lord, how long shall I cry, and Thou wilt not hear! even cry unto Thee of violence, and Thou wilt not save! Why dost Thou show me iniquity, and cause me to behold grievance? for spoiling and violence are before me: and there are that raise up strife and contention. Therefore the law is slacked, and judgment doth never go forth: for the wicked doth compass about the righteous; therefore wrong judgment proceedeth" (vers. 1-4). In a few graphic touches he depicts, as by a master hand, the various evils afflicting the unhappy nation. He takes no delight in thus portraying the sins of those so tenderly loved. It is into the ear of God, not of man, that he pours his complaint. For long he has been crying to Him; and now, overwhelmed with a sense of the hopelessness of recovery, he appeals to Jehovah in accents fraught with deepest anguish and concern. Could it be that his prayer was to go unheeded? If not, how long must he supplicate ere the Lord gave evidence that He had heard and was about to interfere?

He felt, as many another has done, that it were better not to see the evil than to see it only to be burdened thereby, finding no remedy for the state that so distressed his sensitive soul.

There is grave danger, in the present disordered condition of Christendom, that one who is able to see things in the light of the word of God may be similarly affected. Some there are who, quite conscious of the lapsed state of the Church, and aware of the unholy influences at work, can yet be supremely indifferent to it all; manifesting thereby their lack of real heart for what so intimately concerns the glory of God and the welfare of His saints. Others, whose eyes have been anointed and whose consciences have been exercised by the Holy Spirit, are in danger of being unduly oppressed and disheartened by the rising power of the mystery of iniquity. Quick to see dishonor done to Christ and departure from the truth on the right hand and on the left, they are oppressed in spirit by the seemingly irremediable and distressing conditions prevailing.

Needless to say, both are wrong. Indifferent, no truly exercised soul could or should be. But disheartened none need be; for all has been long since foreseen and provided for. It was so with Israel: it is so with the Church. No failure on the part of man can avail to thwart the purposes of God.

In regard to Judah, the greatest danger was from the spirit of strife and contention prevailing among the people, giving rise to spoiling and violence. As a result, the law was ignored, and judgment miscarried. The wicked were in high places, and perverted statutes proceeded from them.

It was surely enough to bow the soul before God, not as one competent to pass sentence upon others, but as one who was a part of that which had so grievously failed. This is where Habakkuk is found. He was one of them that sighed and cried for the abominations done in what had once been the holy city.

Nor does Jehovah ignore His servant's cry; but He answers him, telling of the chastisement He had prepared for the instruction of His disobedient and rebellous people. "Behold ye among the heathen, and regard, and wonder marvelously, for I will work a work in your days, which ye will not believe, though it be told you" (ver. 5). This is the verse quoted by Paul at Antioch of Pisidia, when warning the Jews of the danger to which they were exposed if they neglected the gospel of Christ (Acts 13:40, 41). There, the work so wondrous, in which none would believe though it be told them, was the work of grace wrought out on Calvary's cross. In the Lord's reply to Habakkuk's entreaty, it was His strange work of judgment. Though it seem to be unbelievable, He was raising up the Chaldeans —"that bitter and hasty nation"—to "march through the breadth of the land, to possess the dwelling-places that were not theirs." Terrible and dreadful, carrying out what they thought were but the purposes of their own hearts, they should come up with their vast and irresistible armies against Jerusalem, like the eagle hastening to its prey! They should be permitted to override all the power and dignity of Judah; as a result of which they would be lifted up in pride, imputing their power unto their false gods. In such manner Jehovah was about to deal with His wayward people (vers. 6-11).

Is there not for us a weighty lesson in all this? Of old, in regard to the Egyptians, we are told that God "turned their heart to hate His people" (Ps. 105:25). In our short-sightedness we might only have seen the energy of Satan's power; but it was the Lord that used even Satan to chasten His people. So here: He it is who brings the armies of Nebuchadnezzar to the gates of Zion!

And has He not dealt in a similar manner with the Assembly? It is customary to bewail the divisions and the distressing state of Christendom, and particularly of those who have learned the truth as to the Church. But are not these very things the evidences of the Lord's discipline? He loves His people too well to allow them to prosper and remain a united company when pride and worldliness have usurped the place of humility and the pilgrim character. So He permits the power of Satan to work, and the result is dispersion and scattering. How this should call for confession and brokenness on our part!

In Habakkuk's case, he was amazed that God should so deal with the sheep of His pasture as to give them into the power of the wild beast of the nations. Discipline and chastening he knew were deserved, but he is astounded when he learns who the agent of their punishment is to be. But at once he turns again to the Lord, pouring out his prayer into His ear. "Art Thou not from everlasting, O Lord my God, my Holy One? We shall not die. O Lord, Thou hast ordained them for judgment; and, O mighty God, Thou hast established them for correction" (ver. 12). His faith is very simple, and very beautiful. They were in covenant-relation with the everlasting One, who "will not call back His words." Therefore, however sorely they might be afflicted, it could never be that they should utterly be cut off. Corrected in measure they must be, but cast off forever they could never be without violating the sure mercies of David.

But that so evil a nation should be the instrument in the Lord's hand for the punishment of His wayward people, passes the prophet's comprehension. "Thou art of purer eyes than to behold evil, and canst not look on iniquity," he rightly declares; but then asks, in perplexity, "Wherefore lookest Thou upon them that deal treacherously, and holdest Thy tongue when the wicked devoureth the man that is more righteous than he?" (ver. 13). He goes on to recite the cruelties and iniquities practised by the Chaldeans; their inhumanity, and their gross idolatry; for of the latter Babylon was the mother. If permitted to take Judah in their net, will they not give the glory to their own prowess, and to their false and revengeful deities? How can so perverse a people be Jehovah's agency? It is what has perplexed more than Habakkuk—the toleration and use of the wicked to further the counsels of God.

The chapter closes without an answer; but in the next a reply is given that is altogether worthy of God, far transcending the prophet's highest thoughts, and leading to abasement of soul in His holy presence.

CHAPTER II

ON THE WATCH-TOWER

THERE is nothing harder for man to do than to wait on God. The restlessness and activity of the flesh will not brook delay, but counts time spent in waiting and watching as so much time lost. It is blessedly otherwise with Habakkuk. As no reply is at once given to his eager, anxious questionings, he takes the attitude of the patient learner who remains silent till the Master is ready to make known His mind.

"I will stand upon my watch," he says, "and set me upon the tower, and will watch to see what He will say unto me, and what I shall answer when I am reproved" (ver. 1).

His words bespeak a very right and proper condition of soul. Perplexed and confused by the seeming enigma of God's ways, he owns he may require reproof, and takes his stand upon the watch-tower, above the mists of earth, and beyond the thoughts and doings of men, where he can quietly wait upon God, and look out to see what He will say unto him.

Such an attitude ensures an answer. God will not leave His servant without instruction if there be a willing mind and an exercised conscience.

As he maintains his lonely watch, Jehovah answers, bidding him, "Write the vision, and make it plain upon tables, that he may run that readeth it" (ver. 2). The oracle about to be revealed is not for the prophet alone, but through him for all men. It is a principle of vast importance, far-reaching in its application. Therefore let him take his stylus and set it forth plainly upon a writing-table, that he who reads it may run and proclaim the message far and near.

"For the vision is yet for an appointed time, but at the end it shall speak, and not lie: though it tarry, wait for it; because it will surely come, it will not tarry" (ver. 3). What is to be declared is not for then-present alone. It shall have fuller, wider application in a time of the Lord's appointment, which was then in the future. Forward to this day of blessing is the prophet directed to look.

We know from Heb. 10: 37 that it is really Messiah's reign to which he is pointed. When the verse is quoted there, the pronouns are no longer in the neuter, but they become intensely personal. To Christ alone do they refer. "For yet a little while, and He that shall come will come, and will not tarry." When the apostle wrote, He had already come the first time, only to be rejected and crucified. But He is coming back again, coming in a "very, very little while," as the words might be rendered. When He returns He will put down all unrighteousness, and bring forth judgment unto victory. Then shall that for which the prophet yearned have come to pass. The mystery of God's long toleration of evil shall be finished, and the reign of righteousness shall have come in. To this period of blessing Habakkuk is to look forward; and meantime, though of the man of self-will it can be said, "Behold, his soul which is lifted up is not upright in him," yet, however wickedness may triumph, the man of God is given to know that "the just shall live by his faith" (ver. 4).

This is the oracle which Habakkuk had been bidden to write so plainly. This is the word that the reader should run to declare.

Such a reader, and such a runner, was the apostle Paul. This verse is the key-note of his instruction to both saint and sinner. Having read the prophet's words with eyes anointed by the Holy Ghost, he runs the rest of his days to make them known to others.

Three times they occur in his epistles, and in each place they are used with a different object in view.

When, in the letter to the Romans, he is expounding the glorious doctrine of the righteousness of God as revealed in the gospel (chap. 1: 16, 17), he finds in these words the inspired answer to the question raised ages ago in the book of Job, "How then can man be justified with God?" (chap. 9:2; 25:4). Triumphantly he points to the revelation of the watch-tower, and exclaims, "*The just* shall live by faith!"

When Judaizing teachers sought to corrupt the assemblies of Galatia by turning them away from the simplicity that is in Christ, implying that while it is by faith we are saved, yet the law becomes the rule of life afterwards, he indignantly repudiates the false assertion by declaring that not only is faith the principle upon which they first begin with God, but "the just *shall live* by faith" (Gal. 3: 11). Immediately he proceeds to show that "the law is not of faith," and therefore cannot be the Christian's standard. Christ, and Christ alone is that. In Him we are a new creation. "And as many as walk according to *this rule,* peace be on them, and mercy, and upon the Israel of God" (chap. 6: 16).

Again, when, in the treatise to the Hebrews, he is tracing out the pilgrim's path through this world, from the cross to the glory, he shows most blessedly that only the entering into the power of the unseen can sustain the believer through a life of trial and conflict; and so once more he declares, "The just shall live *by faith*" (Heb. 10: 38). He adds, "But if any man draw back, my soul shall have no pleasure in him," which is the first half of the verse in the Septuagint rendering.

Thus the secret made known to Habakkuk so long ago becomes the watchword of Christianity, as at the Reformation it most properly became the battle-cry of Luther and his colleagues.

It was all-important that the lonely prophet look beyond and above what his natural eyes beheld, and thus would he endure "as seeing Him who is invisible."

So today. Much there is to dishearten and discourage. But dark though the times may be, the man of God turns in faith to the Holy Scriptures, there to find the mind of the Lord. He acts on what is written, let others do as they may. His path may be a lonely one, and his heart be ofttimes sad; but with eager, glad anticipation he looks on to the day of manifestation, and seeks to walk *now* in the light of *then.*

Thus his eyes are opened to behold everything clearly, and he is able to estimate the pretensions of ungodly and spiritual men at their true value. The Chaldean proudly boasted of being helped by his gods to overthrow the people of Jehovah. Habakkuk is shown that he is but an instrument used for present chastening, but soon to be recompensed double for all his sins. "Yea also, because he transgresseth by wine, he is a proud man, neither keepeth at home, who enlargeth his desire as hell (sheol), and is as death, and cannot be satisfied, but gathereth unto him all nations, and heapeth unto him all people" (ver. 5). Inflated, and self-important, like the false world-church of the day, Babylon would gather all into its fold, and stifle everything that is really of God. But the hour of doom is coming, when he shall be the sport of the people, and they shall tauntingly cry, "Woe to him that increaseth that which is not his!" Suddenly his enemies shall arise, and he shall be spoiled because of his blood-guiltiness and his blasphemy against Jehovah (vers. 6-8).

Meantime, though the times be difficult, and waters out of a full cup be wrung out to the little flock who seek to walk in obedience to God, the trusting soul looks up in holy confidence, knowing that the triumphing of the wicked is short. Thus "the just shall live by his faith."

In every age, when declension came in, those who would live for God have found themselves in a position similar to that of Habakkuk. Jeremiah, his companion-prophet, felt it most keenly: but grace sustained him through all. And it is well if, in our day, when the word of God is in large measure given up, and human expedients take the place of divine precepts, that we be found walking humbly in the path of faith, able to say, "All my springs are in Thee!"

The woes that follow have their application not only to the king of Babylon, and his cruel, relentless armies, but they declare the mind of God regarding any who are in the same unholy ways.

"Woe to him that coveteth... !" The sentence,

uncompleted, causes the special sin to which attention is drawn to stand out all the clearer. It was covetousness that drew the hordes of Chaldea to the gates of Jerusalem. Nebuchadnezzar would add "an evil gain to his house" (literal rendering), that he might magnify himself and "set his nest on high." But though he might build a costly and magnificent palace by means of the spoil he should take, the very stones would cry out of the wall, and the beam of the timber would answer, exclaiming, "Woe unto him that buildeth a town with blood, and stablisheth a city by iniquity" (vers. 9-12). Unrighteousness springs out of covetousness, even as we read, "The love of money is a root of all evil." That is, lust for wealth is a suited root for every kind of iniquity to spring from.

Covetousness is unquestionably the crying sin of the present day. Insidiously it creeps in and lays hold of the people of God as well as of men of the world. Yet it is a sin against which the word of God warns with fearful solemnity. It has proven the undoing of many an otherwise valiant man, and has destroyed the pilgrim character of thousands.

What, then, is covetousness? And how is it to be distinguished from honorable thrift and a proper use of opportunities whereby to provide things honest in the sight of all men? In our English Bibles four words are used to express the one sin—"covetousness," "concupiscence," "lust," "desire." Believers are exhorted to be "content with such things as ye have" (Heb. 13: 5); we also read, "Having food and raiment, let us be therewith content" (1 Tim. 6: 8). Covetousness is the very opposite of this. It is the unsatisfied craving of the heart for more than God has been pleased to give. "Covetousness," we are told, "is idolatry!" Then it is plain that the covetous man is the one who puts gain between his soul and God. Anything that turns us from heart-occupation with Him is an idol. By this we may readily test ourselves as to where we stand.

The sluggard and the shiftless are not commended by the word of God, but rigorously condemned, and exhorted to thrift and energy. But to run to the other extreme, and to set the heart upon business and the accumulation of wealth, is equally fatal to spirituality. The happy medium is that laid down by the Holy Ghost, who bids us be "not remiss in zeal, fervent in spirit, serving the Lord." When *He* is served, all else will fall into place. I shall then use this world "not disposing of it as my own," but shall hold all committed to me as His steward.

One cannot but feel that, had we a single eye as to this, we should hear less of pilgrims embarking in doubtful (not to say shady) business schemes and speculations, because of possible large profits; the failure of which oftentimes brings grave dishonor on that holy name by which we are called. It may be laid down as an axiom, that no saint should be in any way connected with any business, however profitable, that could not bear the searching inspection of Him "whose eyes are as a flame of fire."

If it be otherwise, there may seem to be present success and assured prosperity, but it shall turn out at last as Habakkuk has written, "Behold, is it not of the Lord of Hosts that the people shall labor in the very fire, and the people shall weary themselves for very vanity?" (ver. 13). Another passage says, "Behold, all ye that kindle a fire, that compass yourselves about with sparks: walk in the light of your fire, and in the sparks that ye have kindled. This shall ye have of My hand; ye shall lie down in sorrow" (Isa. 50:11). How many, alas, have had to prove this to the full! Laboring in the very fire, they have wearied themselves in the search for vanity; kindling their own fire, and walking in the light of its sparks, they have had to lie down in sorrow, because of their neglect of the word of the Lord.

But however great the apparent triumph of sin in the present time, the outlook is all bright for the man of faith. When the present evil age is passed away, "the earth shall be filled with the knowledge of the glory of the Lord, as the waters cover the sea" (ver. 14). Who that has part in the coming day of glory but would gladly surrender all present gain, were it his to live once more a life of faith during the rejection of his Lord and Redeemer! But it will then be too late to be faithful. For all self-seeking we shall "suffer loss" in the time when those who have held all here in view of the coming of the Lord shall have an entrance ministered unto them abundantly into His everlasting kingdom.

The next woe is pronounced upon him that giveth his neighbor drink in order to encompass his destruction and manifest his shame. It is that wretched hypocrisy that speaks fair, while hatred fills the heart; that unholy dissimulation which leads one to proffer a soothing but brain-intoxicating draught to another in order to accomplish his ruin (vers. 15-17). Terrible shall be the recompense of Jehovah when He makes inquisition for blood! To put an occasion of stumbling in the way of another is to draw down judgment on one's own head. He who causes one of Christ's little ones to fall, might better have had a millstone tied to his neck, and be thrown into the depths of the sea!

The final woe is against idolatry, the making and worshipping of the idols in which Babylon boasted. But the idol and its worshiper shall perish together in the hour of Jehovah's fury (vers. 18, 19). He alone is God over all, blessed forever, now manifested in flesh in our Lord Jesus Christ.

"The Lord is in His holy temple: let all the earth keep silence before Him" (ver. 20). When He speaks, it is for man to hear, and to bow in subjection to His Word. Thus has Habakkuk heard His voice, and his anxious questionings vanish. His heart is at rest, and his soul awed before the majesty of Jehovah's glory. May we too be of the same chastened and humbled spirit!

CHAPTER III

THE PRAYER OF HABAKKUK

THE proper object of divine ministry is to abase the soul in the presence of God, and to draw out the heart to Him in worship and adoration. It was so in the case of Habakkuk. He had been admitted into the secret counsels of Jehovah. His word had been brought home in power to his soul. The result is that he prostrates himself before Him in the attitude of prayer and worship. His prayer-poem is one of the sublimest portions of the Old Testament. While he is, as it were, overpowered by the sense of the majesty and omnipotence of God so that he trembles before Him, nevertheless he looks up with confidence to the only One who can bring revival and blessing to His chastened people, so rightfully under His rod because of their sins.

The term "Shigionoth" in the introductory line indicates that it was set to music. Blessed is it when all our prayers and supplications are thus made to partake of the character of praise! "Be careful for nothing," we are told, "but in everything by prayer and supplication, *with thanksgiving,* let your requests be made known unto God: and the peace of God, which passeth all understanding, shall keep your hearts and minds through Christ Jesus" (Phil. 4: 6, 7). Praise well befits the lips of sinners saved by sovereign grace, however trying and perplexing their circumstances at times may be. David could compose a psalm to the same measure when in deep affliction. Psalm 7 is described as "Shiggaion of David, which he sang unto the Lord, concerning the words of Cush the Benjamite." Cush is generally supposed to be another name for Shimei, who cursed him as he fled from Absalom his son. Shiggaion is the singular of Shigionoth. The actual meaning is not known with certainty; it is supposed to be, "A wandering ode." In this measure, the prophet pours out his heart to the all-glorious One, who from of old had been the deliverer and the support of His redeemed people.

"O Jehovah, I have heard Thy speech," he says, "and I was afraid.
O Jehovah, revive Thy work in the midst of the years,
In the midst of the years make known;
In wrath remember mercy" (ver. 2).

The word of the Lord filled him with fear as he realized something of the depravity of his own heart and the state of his people. Like Isaiah, he could cry, "Woe is me! for I am undone; because I am a man of unclean lips, and I dwell in the midst of a people of unclean lips." On the ground of merit he has nothing to plead. But as he remembers who it is with whom he has to do, he can supplicate with confidence and assurance for revival and blessing.

Because a people are under the hand of God for their failure to carry out His revealed will is no reason to sink down in despair, and conclude that the candlestick has been removed and all corporate testimony is gone. It is unbelief, not godly subjection, that leads saints to take ground like this. In so writing, one thinks of that movement which in these last days resulted from the recovery of much precious truth which had been treated as a dead letter for centuries. In the practical carrying out of that truth there has been undoubted failure of the most humiliating kind. As a result, God has permitted division and strife to take the place of happy unity and holy fellowship. All this is cause for brokenness and humiliation on our part, but not for utter discouragement. Whatever failure may have ensued, God and His truth abide. "That which was from the beginning" is still with us, that we may order our ways thereby. To make failure a reason for further unfaithfulness is to walk in self-will, and to lose the force of the very lesson that our God would have us learn. Like Habakkuk, we have reason to take a very low place indeed; but, like him too, we can count upon God to be with us in that low place.

For revival he pleads—revival, which we know God was pleased to grant when the chastisement had exercised His people. The remnant, delivered from Babylon, own the grace of the Lord in giving "a little reviving" in their bondage (Ezra 9:8). So, may we be assured, will our God delight to give revival now, though the hour be late, if He discerns among us that same spirit of lowly subjection to His will that we see here.

The wondrous way in which Jehovah of old had led Jacob like a flock through the wilderness, when He came from Teman and shined forth from mount Paran, when His glory covered the heavens and the earth was full of His praise, is what the prophet contemplates as he pleads for present mercy. Vividly does he describe the march of the Mighty One of Israel through the desert, spreading terror and consternation among the heathen and filling His redeemed with exultation and rejoicing (vers. 3-6). He who had thus cared for His people before, would care for them still, however the enemy might rage.

Like a glorious panorama, the marvelous scene is unfolded before his eyes. He sees the fiery pillar going before to drive out the hostile nations and to find out a path for the armies of the Lord. He beholds the floods rolling back to permit His chosen to pass through their beds. He notes the mystic river springing from the smitten rock. He takes up the song of the book of Jasher as the sun and the moon obey the word of a man and stand still in their habitation. He hears the shout of the victor and the wail of the vanquished. And as he realizes that the Shepherd of Israel still abideth faithful, though so dreadfully dishonored, his inward parts tremble and his lips quiver at the voice of the Majesty. Rottenness enters into his bones, all self-confidence is gone, and he trembles in himself, that he may quietly rest in the day of trouble that is so soon to come upon the land; yea, that has already begun, for the invader had even then come up with his troops (vers. 7-16).

All this is but the proof that in Habakkuk's soul at least revival had already taken place. Oh, to enter more fully into the same spirit!

The last three verses are the expression of a truly revived man who has learned to find all his springs in God. The apostle speaks in a similar strain in the 4th chapter of Philippians. In fact, so closely are his words allied to what we have here, that, as noted in the introduction, it would seem that he had this very scripture in mind when writing his epistle.

"Although the fig tree shall not blossom,
Neither shall fruit be in the vines;
The labor of the olive shall fail,
And the fields shall yield no meat;
The flock shall be cut off from the fold,
And there shall be no herd in the stalls:
Yet I will rejoice in the Lord, I will joy in the
God of my salvation.
The Lord God is my strength,
And He will make my feet like hinds' feet,

And He will make me to walk upon my high
places.
Unto the chief singer, on my stringed instruments."

How great the difference in the opening and the closing of the burden of Habakkuk! He begins as a man bewildered and confused, who is filled with questions and perplexities; he closes as one who has found the answer to all his questions, and the satisfying portion of his soul in God Himself. This is most blessed. As we thus are permitted to enter into the varied experiences that this man of like passions with ourselves passed through till the Lord alone filled the vision of his soul and satisfied his every longing, likewise resolving all his doubts and difficulties, we get some little sense of what may be the sustaining portion of our own hearts if He be but permitted to have His own way with us in all things. Crops might fail, flocks might be destroyed, fields might be barren, and cattle be cut off; but God would abide, and in Him was abundant supply to meet every need. He is the God of our salvation. He is the strength of our hearts. What more can we crave?

Happy in this glorious consciousness, Habakkuk, and we too, can walk, in faith, on our high places, far above the mists and snares of earth. Like the goats of the 104th psalm (ver. 18), we will be enabled to mount up to the top of the rocks and dwell in the high hills. Surely if a child of God in the twilight of a past dispensation could so exult and triumph over all circumstances, we who live in the full blaze of the day of grace, may well be stirred up to a holy jealousy, that, continually dwelling "in the heavenlies," we may daily be found overcoming through the power of faith!

The closing line is the dedication, and is unspeakably precious. The Chief Singer on the stringed instruments is, for us, none other than our Lord Jesus Christ, who as the risen One now leads the praises of His redeemed. As His hand sweeps the wonderful strings of the hearts of His people, what strains of heavenly melody greet the ear of our God and Father, and salute angelic hosts unnumbered who are learning through the Church the manifold wisdom of God. "In the midst of the assembly will I sing praise unto Thee," He has said, as His Spirit spake through the prophet-poet in the 22d psalm. Whenever His people are gathered unto His peerless name, He is in their midst as the Director of their worship, as well as the Object of their adoration.

Alas, that so many of our hearts are so often out of tune! Only by constant self-judgment and careful walking in the Spirit shall we be maintained in suited condition to add to the sweetness of the great orchestra of the Chief Singer!

Notes on the
PROPHECY OF ZEPHANIAH

CHAPTER I

THE DAY OF THE LORD

OF the prophet Zephaniah practically nothing is known beyond what he himself tells us in the first verse. His pedigree is traced back through four generations, and the date of his ministry is given as "in the days of Josiah the son of Amon, king of Judah." Those were days of blessing and revival for a remnant; but the mass of the people, though outwardly reformed, were in the sad state described in this book and in the early chapters of Jeremiah. The object of the Spirit in Zephaniah was, therefore, to warn the formalists of coming judgment, and to comfort the hearts of the godly residue who had a little strength, and had not denied His name. In fact, the prophecy of Zephaniah has much in common with the New Testament letter to the Philadelphian assembly, contemplating a condition of things answering in large measure to what we see at the present time—a day when many vaunt themselves in Laodicean pride while walking in utter indifference to the written Word of God and despising a feeble remnant who cling to that Word and seek to honor Him who gave it. Such may be like Zephaniah himself, whose very name means, "Hidden of Jehovah;" but though unknown to men, they are well known to Him who speaks of an hour coming when the haughty opposers of the truth shall "come and worship before thy feet, and know that I have loved thee" (Rev. 3: 7-13).

The very fact that a remnant are at any time distinguished from the mass implies that the latter are ripe for judgment; for when all goes as it should, there is no occasion for the faithful to be thus distinguished. Therefore this prophecy has much to say about the coming of the Lord when everything will be dealt with in the light of His revealed will. Zephaniah speaks of judgment about to fall, first on Judah and Jerusalem, yea, the whole land (though the ten tribes had been carried into Assyria nearly a century ere his time); then, on all the surrounding nations. For, if God begins with His people, He will not stop there, but all must know the power of His anger when He makes inquisition in regard to their ways.

The three chapters may be considered as three divisions. Chapter 1 presents the general truth as to the day of the Lord which is coming upon Judah. Chapter 2 gives the judgment of the nations. Chapter 3 is the indictment of Jerusalem, with the customary promise of restoration, to be made good after the purging of the period of tribulation.

Zephaniah was contemporary with Jeremiah for at least a part of the latter's ministry, but he probably passed off the scene before the predicted destruction of Jerusalem was fulfilled.

Coming to a somewhat careful notice of this first chapter, we find in verses 2 to 6 the solemn announcement of the stretching out of Jehovah's hand in judgment against the people of His choice. He was about to consume all things from off the land. Man and beast, fowls and fishes, all alike must feel the stroke. It speaks of utter desolation—the result of the fearful ravages of bloody warfare. Judah and Jerusalem were to be given up to the woes of which they had been warned for so long. They had turned away from Him, who would have been their Saviour, to follow Baal, the demon of the heathen. God would not cease His strange work until He had cut off the last vestige of Baal-worship from the land. The idolatrous priests who had been the instruments used to deceive the people were to be cut off too till the very name of the Chemarim would cease. The worshipers of the heavenly bodies, together with those who professed to follow the Lord, but whose profession was unreal, as also those who swore by Malcham,* the "great king" —all must be included in the coming doom.

The host appointed to death is divided into two classes in the sixth verse: "Them that are turned back from the Lord; and those that have not sought the Lord, nor inquired for Him." There were some who had at first heeded Josiah's call to repentance, and who had sought for a time to obey the voice of the Lord; but, putting their hand to the plow, they looked back and relapsed into their old idolatrous ways. There were others who had never known, nor cared to know, the mind of God. All must perish in the common destruction that was coming.

Beginning with verse 7, we have a more detailed account of the manner in which the awful threatenings were to be carried out. It will be noticed that while the prophet himself had before his mind, beyond any doubt, the Babylonian conquest, the Holy Spirit who empowered him to speak and write had something far more serious before Him. The day of the Lord was at hand, a day which will only be known in its fulness when man's day has come to a close. In that day the Lord will prepare a great sacri-

---

* Malcham is generally identified with Milcom, or Molech, whose abominable worship, with its human sacrifices, the Israelites were warned against when they first entered the land, but whose vile service many were early led to adopt.

ficial feast. Already "He hath bid His guests." The language reminds us of the supper of the great God, or, as it should be rendered, the great supper of God, in Rev. 19: 17, 18. In that day He will visit the iniquities of the princes and the king's household upon them, as also all of foreign birth who are gathered together in the land of Palestine. Violence and deceit shall meet their just desert, and evil be everywhere abased (vers. 7-9).

From gate to gate the cry of anguish will be heard. The merchants and great ones who have lived in pleasure on the earth shall in no wise escape the day of His wrath. James 5: 1 seems to be intimately connected with verse 11 of this chapter. Both have to do with the collapse of the great commercial system which in our own day has assumed such gigantic proportions.

It is a matter of solemn moment, the place given in Scripture to the mad rush for silver and gold in the last days. The world today presents an amazing spectacle if viewed from this standpoint. Commerce is the Baal of the hour. In the accumulation of great wealth, conscience and Christianity are pressed to the wall. Gold is king and god. For gold men will sacrifice every principle, human and divine. Covetousness is the ruling passion of the age. All else must go down before it. And Scripture warrants us to expect this, and emphasizes the fact that it is a sign of the near approach of the end. Happy are those saints who are preserved from this unholy spirit of the times, and who, having food and raiment, seek to be therewith content!

With a lighted lamp the Lord will search Jerusalem in that day; not, as now, to find the lost piece that typifies the poor sinner lying in dust (Luke 15: 8-10), but to ferret out every man who has been indifferent to His truth and has sought to make God a nonentity in His own creation, saying, "The Lord will not do good, neither will He do evil" (ver. 12). This is likewise characteristic of the present times. Men no longer believe in a particular providence. Even the so-called clergy often ridicule he idea of divine intervention in the affairs of men. Law, hard and inexorable, is supposed to control all things; so that human responsibility and a prayer-hearing God are alike practically denied. But the hour of awakening is nearing, when, too late, men will be made to know the reality of God's government and the truth of His Word. Their goods shall become a prey and their abodes a desolation when they are snatched away by the fierce anger of the Lord, whose power and hatred against sin they have disdainfully ignored (ver. 13).

In fervid rhythm the prophet winds up the first section of his book with a stirring description of the day so long expected—the day of the Lord. It is near, and hasteth greatly; the day wherein the mighty man shall cry bitterly when he sinks beneath the weight of divine wrath. It shall be "a day of trouble and distress, a day of wasteness and desolation, a day of darkness and gloominess, a day of clouds and thick darkness, a day of the trumpet and alarm!" No refuge will then avail, no high tower protect from the avenging hand of Him whom men have insulted to His face for so long. Like the blind who stumble in the daytime, they shall grope in their distress, only to fall into the pit prepared, "because they have sinned against the Lord." The riches for which they have labored will be useless to save them. "Neither their silver nor their gold shall be able to deliver them in the day of the Lord's wrath." He will not cease until He has made "a speedy riddance" of all who have defiled His land. The fire must burn till all the chaff be consumed (vers. 14-18).

To this, men are fast hastening on. For this, the Jews are even now returning in unbelief to their ancient home. For this, men are sacrificing every right and noble instinct, building, as has been well said, for the fire!

What sobriety and other-worldliness* becomes

---

* I have purposely written, "other-worldliness." Mere unworldliness is not enough. To walk apart from this world might make a nun or a monk. To walk in the power of another world will make a true ambassador for Christ.

the Christian in view of the end toward which everything is now hastening so rapidly! The day of the Lord is near. The Morning Star will soon shine forth. Be it ours then to live and act as men who wait for their Lord!

CHAPTER II

THE JUDGMENTS OF THE NATIONS

IT is a principle over and over again emphasized in the Scriptures that while God will overlook nothing in His people's ways that merit its rebuke, He will, on the other hand, visit severest judgment on all who lift their hands against them. Philistia, Moab, Ethiopia, or Assyria, might be used of Him to chastise Israel; but they should not delight in such service, and glory over them. Because of their unholy hatred and vindictive spirit, their own punishment would be all the more severe.

This is all a picture of the time of the end. Judah then will be much in the position she occupied in Zephaniah's day—in the land, surrounded by enemies, a feeble remnant, crying, "How long, O Lord?" the mass, apostate and swayed by Antichrist—and all this because of their rejection of Messiah when He came in grace. Therefore they must drink the cup of retribution to the dregs; but that cup emptied, the Lord will arise in His might as their Deliverer, and their enemies who have gloried over their helplessness shall become the objects of His avenging wrath, preparatory to the ushering in of the world-kingdom of our God and His Christ.

The three opening verses are a call to Judah with a view to the distinguishing of the remnant. The nation as such is not desired; they are no more lovely in His eyes. Polluted by sin and bearing the brand-marks of apostasy, Judah has become as a vessel wherein is no pleasure. But, ere the day of the Lord's anger arrives, there is a summons for the faithful to gather together. As in Malachi's day, they will speak often one to another, and will be drawn to their own company by a common tie and common interests. They are bidden to seek the Lord, to seek righteousness and meekness. Indeed, they are distinctively called, "Ye meek of the earth, which have wrought His judgment" (ver. 3).

Pretension is never becoming in fallen creatures, much less in a remnant in days of apostasy. Nor power nor great things are they to seek, but Jehovah Himself is to be their object, and therefore, necessarily, righteousness coupled with lowliness. It is the only suited state to such a company at such a time. No matter what the ruin that has come in throughout each succeeding dispensation, God has always had a remnant who have sought grace to walk in His truth. But there is ever danger of pride destroying such a testimony, and thus they who begin in weakness, owning their nothingness, become occupied with their fancied remnant place and character, in this way getting out of the very position they at first took in meekness.*

The true remnant will not be occupied with their remnant character, but with Him to whom they are separated. Such will not talk of being "the testimony," or "Philadelphia," but will be here to testify of Christ, and will seek to manifest Philadelphia ("brotherly love") in their ways, while holding fast Christ's word and not denying His name. Thus will they have His approbation in *that* day, if content to be unapproved of men in *this*. Satisfied to let the Lord act for them, they will be concerned about acting for Him. In His own time He will show what was truly of Himself, even as, in connection with Judah, the hour was about to strike when He would deal with the surrounding nations and the apostate mass, bringing to light the hidden things of darkness and making manifest the counsels of the heart.

Philistia must be one of the first powers destroyed, answering largely to corrupt Christendom; for the Philistines, of Egyptian origin, were

---

* Only lately I heard of one self-complacently locating the special company of Christians to which he was particularly attached as follows: God had called out a remnant in these last days. Certain meetings formed the remnant. Divisions had come in. A few remained on "divine ground," and "alone had the Lord's table." It was like a biscuit: pieces had been broken off here and there, "but *we* remain the middle of the biscuit!" Could anything be more wretchedly pretentious in such a day?

dwellers in Canaan, who sought to hold all for themselves apart from divine title, and vauntingly gave their name, Palestine, to the whole land. It is religious pretension seeking to control all that stands for God, yet only an imitation like that false, corrupt church that for centuries dominated Christendom, and still claims, while but a fragment of the professing body, to be alone catholic and apostolic. Verses 4 to 7 relate to Philistia's judgment and the deliverance of the despised Jewish remnant, picturing for us the overthrow of prelatic domination and the setting free of a Thyatiran residue (Rev. 2:24) at the coming of the Lord. For Judah and Philistia there has already been a carrying out of this prediction literally. A more complete fulfilment will take place in the last days.

Moab and Ammon (vers. 8-11) are, as often in the past, linked together, both being illegitimately descended from fallen Lot (Gen. 19:33-38). They too will be judged nationally in the last days, when the remnant of Jehovah's people shall possess them. "This shall they have for their pride, because they have reproached and magnified themselves against the people of the Lord of hosts" (ver. 10). For centuries they have been under God's hand. They shall be fully dealt with at the time of the end. For us they speak of those who, having a name to live, are dead: who, professing to be of the family of God, were never truly born again, but are "strange children," in whom is no faith. We see them all about us in the so-called "church," saying, "I am rich, and increased with goods, and have need of nothing," while in God's sight they are "wretched, and miserable, and poor, and blind, and naked." It is the proud, Christless professors of the day who look with contempt and pity on any who seek to be guided only by the Word of God, and press the need of new birth giving life eternal.

Ethiopia and Assyria are appropriately joined together, Nineveh being the chief city of the latter (vers. 12-15). Man in the darkness of nature—the Ethiopian unable to change his skin—and man in his pride and haughtiness, having no sense of need whatever—of these do the two nations speak: on all, such desolation is soon to fall. We get a full description of Nineveh's doom in Nahum's prophecy. She shall never rise again. For Ethiopia there is yet hope, when she shall stretch out her hands unto God (Ps. 68:31).

The true significance of Nineveh is given in verse 15: "This is the rejoicing city that dwelt carelessly, that said in her heart, I am, and there is none beside me." It is man all-sufficient in himself, utterly indifferent to God, living in pleasure on the earth, and nourishing his heart as in a day of slaughter. But the hour of his doom is about to strike, when he will learn that power belongs to God alone.

CHAPTER III

THE REMNANT AND THE LORD IN THE MIDST

THE remark made in the notes on chapter 1, that we have here what answers largely to Philadelphia, is fully sustained in this last section. Here the mass are viewed in utter rejection of the truth, but the remnant are seen in weakness, yet holding fast the Word and the Name, while the Lord Himself is found "in the midst," as He in the days of His flesh declared He ever would be where two or three were gathered together unto His name (Matt. 18:20).

It is Jerusalem, the most highly privileged of all cities, which is described in verse 1 as filthy and polluted. A fourfold indictment is drawn up in verse 2: "She obeyed not the voice; she received not correction; she trusted not in the Lord; she drew not near to her God!" Intensely solemn are these statements. Well may we search ourselves before Him who is called "He that is holy, He that is true," that we may detect in our ways any departure answering to what is here charged against Jerusalem. Have we obeyed the voice? Have we received correction from the Word of God? Do we truly confide in the Lord, and *draw near* to our God? Serious questions are all these. May we answer in the fear of the Lord!

Verse 2 is collective. In verses 3 and 4 the various classes who should have been the leaders in the things of God are mentioned, and individually indicted. The princes were roaring lions, seeking only for prey; *i. e.,* they sought their own profit, not the blessing of the flocks they should have shepherded. The judges were even worse—evening wolves, secretly devouring all they could obtain, while professing to administer justice. The prophets were triflers with holy things, handling the Word of God deceitfully, traitors to their trust. The priests, who should have been holy and undefiled, had polluted the very sanctuary itself with their uncleanness, and done violence to the law.

Thus, all had failed that God had established in responsibility. What then remained? Only this: "The just Lord is *in the midst* thereof; He will not do iniquity." He remained "the faithful and true witness." He, the Amen, was still the resource of every faithful heart, and in Him the heart of God could rest.

It is the manifestation of the Man of God's pleasure when all else has been, humanly speaking, a disappointment. In the Millennium this will be seen in its fulness. It is to that time of blessing the passage applies. It is then that the words will be fulfilled: "Morning by morning doth He bring His judgment to light, He faileth not; but the unjust knoweth no shame" (ver. 5).

Never will wickedness have risen to such a height as at the very time when the Lord descends to take the kingdom; but righteousness will then be firmly established, and morning by morning the wicked will be cut off. For centuries men have been warned of this, but then it will be actually carried into effect (vers. 6-8).

Then shall the confusion of Babel be undone, and the Lord will give to all peoples "a pure language, that they may all call upon the name of Jehovah, to serve Him with one consent" (ver. 9). From all the lands of their scattering He will bring His redeemed earthly people home to Zion, purging out pride and haughtiness, and making them willing in the day of His power (vers. 10, 11).

The apostate portion of the nation of Judah will be destroyed in the time of Jacob's trouble, and at the appearing of the Son of Man; but He says, "I will also leave in the midst of thee an afflicted and poor people, and they shall trust in the name of the Lord. The remnant of Israel shall not do iniquity, nor speak lies; neither shall a deceitful tongue be found in their mouth: for they shall feed and lie down, and none shall make them afraid" (vers. 12, 13). Thus are the faithful found in weakness and dependence, owned of the Lord, preserved in the midst of all the surrounding corruption, and made the nucleus of the kingdom when Gentile dominion and Jewish and

Christian apostasy have alike been overthrown forever. It is the preserved virgin-company of Rev. 14:1-5, standing with the Lamb on Mount Zion when the glory is about to be displayed.

In the present time it is part of God's ways to preserve likewise an afflicted and poor people who trust in His name. Such will be characterized by loving devotedness to Christ, by brotherly kindness, by integrity of heart, by the endeavor to maintain a conscience void of offence toward God and man, by holding fast the faithful Word, by not denying the name of the Lord, by consistent testimony to the world and the world-church for the absent One now rejected, by separation from evil, by following "righteousness, faith, love, peace, with them that call on the Lord out of a pure (or single) heart." This is the "original ground of gathering." This is Philadelphian position. This alone constitutes a true remnant company. Such a path can only be maintained in the energy of faith. Nature can form a confederacy of assemblies based on mutual acceptance of certain guiding principles, or the bowing to assembly-judgments; but this is not faith, and only results in the formation of a system as rigid and unscriptural as any of the sects of men. It does away with the individual exercise of conscience, and substitutes the voice of the church for the voice of God in His Word.

In the last part of our chapter the book comes

to a fitting close (vers. 14-20) by setting forth the day of display, when the hitherto despised remnant will be enjoying the unalloyed favor of the Lord for whose name they had borne reproach in restored Jerusalem, with Himself in their midst. For us, faith appropriates this now, and enters into the enjoyment of it in spirit.

Zion is called upon to sing; Israel, to shout. The day of gladness and rejoicing has arrived for Jerusalem; for the Lord will then have taken away her judgments and cast out her enemy. He Himself, the glorious King of Israel (once crucified outside the gate, on a felon's cross, beneath the title, "This is Jesus of Nazareth, the King of the Jews"), will then dwell *in the midst* of the restored city and people, and they shall not see evil any more.

This will be their joy and blessing throughout the Millennium. To Jerusalem it shall be said, "Fear thou not;" and to Zion, "Let not thy hands be slack." Loving service will follow full deliverance from all her foes. Again it is stated, "The Lord thy God *in the midst* of thee is mighty." To Him salvation is ascribed. He will rejoice over them with joy and rest in His love, joying over them with singing. It will be "the time of the singing" spoken of in the Canticles (2: 12), when all redeemed creation, heavenly and earthly, will resound with songs of praise and exultation.

Once more Israel will keep her solemn assemblies, and her griefs will be changed to gladness. All who have afflicted her will be undone, and she who was driven away in weakness will be regathered in power. In every land where the people of the wandering foot had been put to shame, they will become objects of praise and fame when the Lord Himself shall make them "a name and a praise among all people of the earth, when I turn back your captivity before your eyes, saith the Lord" (ver. 20).

Thus are we brought again to the end of the ways of God with Israel on the earth; who, whatever their failures, are beloved for the fathers' sakes.

Their portion is earthly. Ours is heavenly. But both alike are to contribute to the glory of our Lord Jesus Christ, and both alike shall be vessels for the display of the matchless grace of our God throughout all the ages to come.

Notes on the

PROPHECY OF HAGGAI

INTRODUCTION

THERE are six books of the Old Testament which may be read together most profitably. I refer to Ezra, Nehemiah, and Esther, of the historical part of the Bible, coupled with the prophetic messages of Haggai, Zechariah, and Malachi. To these a seventh might be added, *viz.*, the book of Daniel, showing the exercises of soul which led up to the restoration.

The book of Ezra opens with the people of the Lord in captivity to the Persian, dwelling in the provinces once controlled by the kings of Babylon. God's centre, Jerusalem, where He had set His name, was a blackened ruin. The walls of the Holy City had been thrown down, and the very stones buried beneath piles of rubbish. All this may well be looked upon as a picture of the subjection of the Church of God to human systems of error and superstition. For long centuries the truth as to simply gathering to the name of the Lord Jesus had been lost. The place of the name, we may say, was at Jerusalem destroyed by her enemies. The walls, speaking of that godly separation from the world that should have kept the Church as "a garden enclosed," had been completely demolished, and ecclesiastical rubbish of all descriptions had so buried the truth that it seemed as though it was lost beyond all recovery. Separation from evil, then, is ever God's principle for His people.

However, God was watching over all, and in His grace raised up a testimony to these precious and important teachings, which had lain dormant, as it were, in His Word for so long. Then the result was a movement very much like that detailed in the record made by Ezra. From the confusion of human theologies and man-made sects and parties, there was a returning on the part of some whose hearts God had touched to the simplicity of early days. In much weakness, yet in much freshness too, and with a deep sense of the ruin of the Church, as a testimony for God in the world, and fully owning their own sad part in it all, a remnant returned to the Lord, finding in His name their centre of gathering, and abjuring everything for which they could not find a "Thus saith the Lord." This is all foreshadowed, one might say, or at any rate a similar movement is pictured, in the book of Ezra. There is a separation of the clean from the unclean, a taking forth of the precious from the vile, and a setting up of the altar, called by Malachi "The

Table of the Lord" (Mal. 1:7), round which gather the recovered remnant—great in nothing but the faith that led them thus to put Jehovah's claims before all else: for, be it remembered, their circumstances were such under the rule of the Persian that they might well have dwelt more comfortably in the land of their captivity than in the land of Israel.

Nehemiah emphasizes the need of complete separation from all that is contrary to the mind of God. He comes up later than Ezra, but his special work is to restore and build Jerusalem. Led on by this faithful servant, the remnant engage in the building of the wall that was to shut them in to God; and that angered their neighbors by its, in their eyes, sinister exclusiveness. Bit by bit the rubbish of years was cleared away, and one by one the stones of the wall were brought to light and fitted into their appointed places. Surely to all this there has been something analogous among those who at first gathered in feebleness and with little light around the table of the Lord. Gradually, yet in such a manner as to make it manifestly the testimony of the Holy Ghost, the thoughts of men were put to one side, the rubbish of traditionalism was cleared away, and the stones of divine truth were recovered and built up—shall I say?—into a wall of separation, which angered the "societies," who could not bear to think of a work of God carried on apart from their organized control. But unmoved by mockery, undeterred by threats, and unseduced by proffers of help from those who had neither part nor lot in the matter, the work went on till the wall was finished. The truth as to the individual believer's standing and state; the unfolding of the great mystery of Christ and the Church; the cluster of precious truths connected with the Coming and Day of the Lord, with their sanctifying effect on heart and life,—one by one, and often at the cost of deepest exercise and soul-travail, coupled with severe conflicts with the enemy within and without, were these stones of the separating wall recovered, and thus God was glorified and His people blessed.

In the book of Esther we have set forth His gracious care over those who, while equally His, yet chose to remain where they were, rather than return to God's centre: but as I have treated of this at length elsewhere, I need not follow it out here.*

Happy would it have been if what has been traced above from the records of Ezra and Nehemiah were the only things necessary to notice. But, alas, it is far otherwise. It was not long till almost all the evils which had at one time been on the *outside*, appeared *within* the wall. Pride, dissension, covetousness, worldliness in its various

* See "Notes on the Book of Esther" (clo.,75c.; pa.,30c.).

forms, self-seeking, and kindred unholy things which no walls could shut out (because they dwelt in the heart and were allowed to exist unjudged), soon marred the lovely scene. And oh, who with eyes to see and a heart to understand and mourn, can fail to observe how in all this likewise we have a picture of what has been so sadly true among those whose happy boast it has been that Christ alone is their Centre, and His Name their tower of strength?

But, blessed be the God of all grace, He left not His people without needed conscience-stirring ministry; but among the returned remnant He raised up prophets whose messages led to self-judgment and abasement of soul in His presence. Haggai and Zechariah come in here, as polished shafts from the quiver of the Lord, whose mission it was to recall the hearts of those so privileged to Himself. The province of the latter was especially to unfold the glories to come, that they might be stirred up to live then in the light of that coming day. He is emphatically "the prophet of the glory." To Haggai it was given, on the other hand, to press home upon the conscience the actual conditions existing, and with trumpet voice to recall them to ways of practical holiness, with signal blessing resultant.

That Malachi follows, in a generation later, bewailing the complete breakdown of the people, is pregnant with warning, and may well cause *us* to search and try our ways, who today seek to answer to what I have been considering. Truth alone will not preserve if there be not corresponding exercise as to living in its power, and being controlled thereby.

Nothing is more wretched than to see unspiritual, carnal men debating questions involving nice discriminations as to the relative bearing of particular lines of truth, whose unholy ways are a reproach to Him whose truth it is.

It is important to remember that God teaches through the conscience, not merely through the head; therefore the spectacle often presented of brilliant, gifted men floundering where humble, godly men walk securely! Blessed it is when gift and godliness go together; unhappy indeed when they are divorced!

Of Haggai himself little is recorded in Scripture. Even his father's name is not given, nor his tribe in Israel. He appears suddenly on the page of inspiration in Ezra 5: 1, in all the dignity of a heaven-appointed messenger, with no credentials but that the word of the Lord was on his lips and the power of the Lord was manifested in his ways. And these are surely credentials enough. God had fitted him to be, as he himself puts it, "the Lord's messenger in the Lord's message." There is something very fine in this. It brings before us the divine character of prophetic ministry—a ministry much needed in our day, and for which, in measure, we often have cause to give thanks. "He that prophesieth speaketh unto men to edification, and exhortation, and comfort" (1 Cor. 14: 3). Such ministry is Spirit-given, and sure to result in blessing; for what God Himself gives shall never return unto Him void. What that ministry was in the special case before us we shall now proceed to notice.

CHAPTER I

CONSIDER YOUR WAYS

THE date given in verse 1 is in harmony with the statement recorded in Ezra 4:24. There we learn that, owing to the opposition of the adversaries of Judah and Benjamin, the work of rebuilding the house of the Lord ceased "unto the second year of Darius, king of Persia." As the letter which resulted in a prohibition to continue was written in the reign of Artaxerxes, several years had elapsed in which nothing had been accomplished. A period of lethargy had set in, which only came to an end when a God-appointed ministry was given to stir up the consciences of the people.

In the year above referred to, on the first day of the sixth month, Haggai addressed himself to the rulers, Zerubbabel the governor, who was of David's line, and Joshua the high priest, saying, "Thus speaketh the Lord of hosts, saying, This people say, The time is not come, the time that the Lord's house should be built" (vers. 1, 2). It is evident from this that they were only too ready to refrain from the work, and that had there been the energy of faith, the decree of Artaxerxes, apparently contradicting that of Cyprus, would have been no real hindrance. The unalterable character of Persian decrees rendered the second one invalid had it really repealed the first. But already self-seeking, and consequent listlessness as to the things of God, had come in. Hence they could build their own houses while neglecting the house of the Lord. But Artaxerxes' decree, rightly read, contained no direct prohibition against building the temple, but rather was directed against restoring and fortifying the city.

When the conscience is not active people readily interpret circumstances to suit themselves; and at such times it is often amazing the amount of energy that will be expended on that which ministers to one's own comfort, whereas utter indifference characterizes that which is connected with the Lord's glory.

Thus saints have time and means for much that does not profit, who find it difficult to get a few hours for a meeting, or to spare of their means for the furtherance of the gospel. Once let the conscience be in exercise, and all will be in place.

"Is it time for you, O ye, to dwell in your ceiled houses, and this house lie waste?" is the Lord's challenge through His prophet. No Persian decree hindered their providing warm and even expensive houses for themselves; but it was readily made the excuse for indifference to what should have had the first place in their thoughts (vers. 3, 4).

"Now therefore thus saith the Lord of hosts: Consider your ways. Ye have sown much, and bring in little; ye eat, but ye have not enough; ye drink, but ye are not filled with drink; ye clothe you, but there is none warm; and he that earneth wages, earneth wages to put it into a bag with holes" (vers. 5, 6). This is all intensely solemn. May reader and writer weigh it well. Undoubtedly it gives the secret of many failures and disappointments among Christians today, as well as among the Jews of old. God cannot bless self-seeking. He calls on each one to *"Consider your ways."* The Hebrew reads, "Set your heart on your ways." It is a summons to self-judgment; for the ways manifest the state of soul.

We may look at it as entering into every ramification of the life. Consider your ways, ye who have to do with the commercial world in its present conditions. How much is often tolerated among us that would not bear the all-searching eyes of Him who seeth not as man seeth! The covetous spirit of the age is eating the very life out of many companies of the Lord's people. The grasping avariciousness everywhere prevalent in the world is making dreadful inroads among Christians. Alas, how much is sacrificed for money! Christian fellowship, the joys of gathering at the table of the Lord, gospel work, and privileges of mutual edification and instruction in divine things—all are parted with often simply because the opportunity arises of adding a few paltry dollars to the monthly income and savings. Brethren with families even will leave a town or city where the spiritual support and fellowship of their brethren is found, and where their children have the privileges of the gospel meeting and the Sunday-school, simply because they see, or fancy they see, an opportunity to better their earthly circumstances. Alas, in many instances they miss all they had hoped for, and lose spiritually what is never regained!

Consider your ways in the home life. What place do you give the things of God there? Is the Bible habitually neglected, and the knee seldom bowed in prayer before the children? What wonder then if they grow up to think lightly of what you seem to place so slight a valuation upon! Do you discuss servants of Christ, and the people of God in a cold, hard, critical manner before these same children? Then do not be surprised if they learn to despise all ministers of the Word, and lightly esteem all those that bear the name of Christ.

Consider your ways in connection with the service of the Lord and the assembling of His people. Do trifles keep you from the assemblies of God's people for the remembrance of our Lord in His sufferings for us? Or do you neglect the preaching of the Word on the plea that "it is only the gospel?" Are you generally missed at the prayer-meeting, and seldom found at the Bible-reading? Is it months, or years, since you handed out a tract, or spoke to others of Christ? How then can you expect God's blessing to be on you and your plans while you are so indifferent to Him and His purposes ?

"Thus saith the Lord of hosts: CONSIDER YOUR WAYS. Go up to the mountain, and bring wood, and build the house; and I will take pleasure in it, and I will be glorified, saith the Lord" (vers. 7, 8). Aroused from the deadening effects of self-seeking, judge yourself and your past loose ways in God's presence; then "Put first things first," as one has said, and give the Lord the supreme place in heart and life. Because of the lack of this purpose of heart to cleave to Him, He could not bless as He otherwise would; hence "Ye looked for much, and, lo, it came to little; and when ye brought it home," God blew upon it, and it fled away. Did you wonder why failure succeeded failure, and plan after plan did not result as you hoped? Because God was not given His place, His house is neglected, "Therefore the heaven over you is stayed from dew, and the earth is stayed from her fruit," and drought and barrenness prevail in place of blessing and refreshment (vers. 9-11).

The effect of Haggai's words was at once manifest. Oh that this rehearsal of them may also be used to the arousing of those of us who are sleeping among the dead!

Both leaders and people forthwith "obeyed the voice of the Lord their God," and the neglected work was at once resumed (ver. 12).

"Then spake Haggai, the Lord's messenger in the Lord's message unto the people, saying, I am with you, saith the Lord" (ver. 13). It was a word of cheer and encouragement, and the way it is introduced is very fine—"the Lord's messenger in the Lord's message!" It is quite possible to be truly the Lord's messenger, and yet to miss the Lord's mind. To give His message, one must be in touch with Himself. Such was Haggai's happy state.

Aroused by the stirring call to consider their ways, and comforted by the knowledge of the Lord's presence with them, the remnant went willingly to work, so that the actual labor on the house of God was resumed in twenty-four days (vers. 14, 15). The next chapter gives further ministry as the work proceeded.

CHAPTER II

BE STRONG

THE work of building the long-neglected house of the Lord had been going on less than a month when the word of Jehovah came a second time through the prophet Haggai. On this occasion it was a message, not of rebuke, but of cheer and encouragement to both rulers and people alike (vers. 1, 2). It is thus that God delights to comfort and sustain the hearts of those who, however poor and feeble, yet seek to honor Him.

Three questions are asked: "Who is left among you that saw this house in her first glory? and how do ye see it now? is it not in your eyes in comparison of it as nothing?" (ver. 3). We know from Ezra 3:12 that there were among the restored remnant "ancient men who had seen the first house," and who wept bitterly when they contrasted its former glory with the smallness of the present house among the ruins, and that the gladness of the younger ones (who had just been delivered from Babylon, and whose whole past lives had been in the midst of idolatry and oppression) was almost drowned in the noise of the weeping.

Now God assures them that the future has

brighter things in store than the past had ever known; and He makes this hope the ground of a word of encouragement. "Yet now be strong," is His message, "for I am with you. . . My Spirit remaineth among you: fear ye not" (vers. 4, 5).

Ruin and desolation may have come in; division and scattering may have taken place; but those who are gathered back around Jehovah's centre have the joy of knowing, on the authority of His own Word, that He is in the midst, and His Spirit remaineth among them. Well may they be strong and fear not.

In like manner is the assurance given to Philadelphia, in the last solemn book of the Bible. The saints may have only "a little strength;" but His Word and His Name abide, and He, the holy and the true, is in their midst. Division and strife cannot alter this; nor can any particular company of believers claim it to the exclusion of others, as though they alone composed "the remnant." "For where two or three are gathered together in (or unto) My Name, there am I in the midst of them." By this may every little company of saints be comforted, who morally occupy the ground of the remnant in Haggai's day.

Not only had they the Lord's presence, in Spirit, among them, but His coming in person was to be their hope, that thus their hearts might be lifted above their lowly circumstances as they waited for the coming glory. In "a little while" the heavens and earth, the sea and the dry land, together with all the nations, would be shaken by the power of Jehovah, and then "the Desire of all nations shall come: and I will fill this house with glory, saith the Lord of hosts" (vers. 6, 7). The long-desired One is none other than our Lord Jesus Christ. He came once in grace only to be rejected. He is coming again to bring in the glory long foreseen by the prophets of old. To that house (albeit refurbished and enlarged by the Idumean Herod) He came, only to be unrecognized and cast out. To that house, rebuilt in the last days, He will come again to take the kingdom and reign in righteousness.

The remnant might be too poor to embellish the rebuilt temple, but His are the silver and the gold. Nothing shall hinder the manifestation of the glory when the set time has come. "The latter glory of this house shall be greater than the former, saith the Lord of hosts: and in this place will I give peace, saith the Lord of hosts" (vers. 8, 9). The rendering of the A. V.—"the glory of this latter house" — is misleading, and has been generally taken by commentators to mean that the rebuilt temple, being hallowed by the personal presence of the Son of God was thus far greater than that of Solomon, despite the grandeur of the one and the paucity of the other. Some have supposed that the architectural beauty of the temple after Herod's embellishments even surpassed that of the "house, exceeding magnifical," built by the wise king. But this was by no means the case.

To the first interpretation there could be no real objection. It is beautiful and true in itself, but does not seem to be what is really meant to be conveyed here. "The latter glory of this house" refers undoubtedly to the millennial splendor of the temple depicted prophetically in Ezekiel 40 to 48. Men may speak of temples or houses of God, He speaks but of *the* temple, or *the* house. Whether the building erected by Solomon, Zerubbabel, or Herod, be contemplated; or whether that to be rebuilt by unbelieving Judah in the coming tribulation, or the millennial temple succeeding—all are denominated "the house" and "the temple" of God. It is one in His eyes. In that temple of old every whit of it uttered His glory. To that temple He came in grace only to be rejected. In that temple the Man of Sin shall yet sit. Cleansed, that temple shall be the centre of earth's worship and thanksgiving for the Millennium. At present, in this interval of "the dispensation of the mystery," God owns no material building as His abode. Believers in the aggregate, through the whole church period, are growing into a holy temple in the Lord. All saints on earth at a given time form the house of God, composed of living stones, who have come to *the* Living Stone.

Prophecy is not occupied with this spiritual building. It has to do with the *earth,* and earthly things.

In verses 10 to 14 another line of truth is brought in. The transition from what we have been considering seems most abrupt, but doubtless the state of the people demanded it. In reply to a question by Haggai, the priests aver that if one "bear holy flesh in the skirt of his garment, and with his skirt do touch" articles of common food, the latter are not sanctified thereby and rendered holy. On the other hand, they bear testimony to the solemn fact that one who is unclean by the dead defiles everything he touches, making it unclean likewise. Such was the condition of the people. They were all defiled, and all they did was unclean before God. But this only gave occasion for grace to act; and so, despite their uncleanness, the Lord had taken them up in blessing. But He would have them remember that all has come from His own heart, apart from their deserts. Though defiled, yet when they turned to God and bowed in subjection to Him, He could manifest Himself strong on their behalf.

So in verses 15 to 19 He contrasts their condition when apathetic in regard to His house, and now, that they are working in accordance with His word. Before, poverty, blasting and mildew were their portion. Now, He has, "from the day the foundation of the Lord's temple was laid," given increase and plenty, even as He had declared long before that "they that honor Me, I will honor; and they that despise Me, shall be lightly esteemed."

We may be sure none will ever be the loser who puts the claims of God first. "From this day will I bless you" is a promise for all who judge what is evil and seek to walk in the truth.

The chapter concludes with another message given the same day. It is addressed alone to Zerubbabel, the uncrowned son of David, who had been appointed governor of Judah. To him the Lord announces the shaking of the heavens and the earth, and the final overthrow of all the kingdoms of the Gentiles, but assures him that he shall abide as a signet before Him, "for I have chosen thee, saith the Lord of hosts."

From Zerubbabel's loins shall spring "the prince," who would seem to be the earthly representative of "great David's greater Son" (who likewise came in direct descent from this lowly-minded scion of king David), in the day when all nations acclaim the splendors of "the latter glory of this house."

Notes on the

PROPHECY OF ZECHARIAH

INTRODUCTION

ZECHARIAH, like Haggai and Malachi, was a post-captivity prophet. He was one of those who came up from Babylon with Zerubbabel (having been born in the land of the stranger) and gave the word of the Lord to the returned remnant. It was Haggai's mission to arouse to action when they had been overcome by sloth and self-seeking. Zechariah followed with messages of cheer and encouragement designed to bring the souls of the people into the power of the coming glory. He is therefore largely occupied with the appearing of Messiah and His reign of righteousness. There is blessing in thus having heart and mind transported to the days of heaven upon earth. It is then that one is able to estimate aright the transitory glories of this present evil age. The hope of the Lord's coming has a purifying effect upon the lives of those held by it. "Every man that hath this hope in Him purifieth himself, even as He is pure" (1 John 3: 3).

The Church has lost much, therefore, by neglecting the study of prophecy. It should be borne in mind that while the prophets of the Old Testament do not speak of the assembly of the present dispensation, nevertheless those who compose the Body of Christ and the Bride of the Lamb may learn much that is for edification and blessing through Jehovah's word to Israel. Then too it should be enough for the devoted soul to know that Christ is to be the center of all that glory which is soon to be revealed. If He is concerned in it, all who love Him will find spiritual delight in tracing the steps leading up to His exaltation and the establishment of His kingdom.

This is what is characteristic in Zechariah. He marks out the various stages leading to the appearing of Messiah, thus opening up, in large measure, "the sufferings of Christ and the glories to follow."

His book falls readily into two main parts. The first six chapters relate the visions of the prophet. The last eight are devoted to instruction based upon these visions. There are numerous subdivisions which we shall notice as we go on.

It would seem as though Zechariah, like many of his predecessors, died a violent death, and that at the hands of the Jews returned from Babylon, when decline had again set in. At least our Lord Jesus speaks of "the blood of Zacharias son of Barachias, whom ye slew between the temple and the altar," and which was to be required of the men of that generation, who had filled up the iniquity of their fathers (Matt. 23:35).

It is barely possible, though not probable, that our Lord was referring to the martyrdom of Zechariah the son of Jehoiada, who was stoned to death in the court of the temple (2 Chron. 24: 20, 21); but in that case we have to suppose a Berechiah in the genealogy of Jehoiada, or else a copyist's error in transcribing the Greek text. In the absence of proof to the contrary, it seems safer to assume that Zacharias the son of Barachias is none other than the prophet to whose writings we are about to turn for instruction and warning.

The Jews have a tradition that he perished in the manner described. J. N. Darby, in his "Irrationalism of Infidelity," says that "the Jewish Targum states that Zechariah the son of Iddo, a prophet and priest, was slain in the sanctuary."*

As the rabbis could have no possible reason for seeking to confirm the words of the Lord Jesus, it would seem as though their testimony were conclusive.

---

* The whole question is pretty thoroughly examined in the work referred to, pp. 150-159, a volume which I am glad to take this opportunity of commending to any troubled with doubts as to the full inspiration of Holy Scripture. (It may be had from my Publishers.)

CHAPTER I

ISRAEL AND THE DIVINE GOVERNMENT

BY comparing verse 1 with the opening words of Haggai's prophecy, it will be observed that an interval of two months, approximately, occurred between the beginning of the recorded ministry of the two prophets. Conscience was aroused, and the work of building the house of the Lord begun, as a result of Haggai's stirring message. In the seventh month he sought to encourage the now awakened people by directing their attention to the future day of Messiah's glory. Then in the month following, the eighth of Darius' second year, Zechariah was bidden to speak to them, first in a rousing call to self-judgment, followed later on by a remarkable unfolding of what Haggai had so briefly outlined in chapter 2: 6-9.

Others have long since noticed the striking significance of the names in this first verse: "Zechariah the son of Berechiah, the son of Iddo." Zechariah means *Jehovah remembers*; Berechiah is *Jehovah blesses;* and Iddo, *The appointed time.* So read, we would have: "Jehovah remembers, Jehovah blesses at the appointed time." Thus, when the set time to favor Zion has come, all the promises of the Lord will be fulfilled, and carried out in blessing. If any think such an interpretation fanciful, let them remember how the apostle, by the inspiration of the Holy Ghost, dwells on the meaning of names, and their order, in the case of Melchizedek, King of Salem, in Hebrews 7:2. There is surely more than a hint in that remarkable passage that there are vast stores of instruction in the names of men and places used throughout the Scriptures that many of us have little dreamed of.

Verses 2 to 6 comprise Zechariah's first message, and are a suited introduction to the book. In view of the return from captivity and the rebuilding of the temple, the people are warned not to repeat the errors of their fathers—a warning, alas, soon forgotten and quite unheeded.

With their ancestors the Lord had been grievously displeased, and because of their sins had given them into the hand of the Gentile foe. Now let the children of those who had failed so repeatedly turn to Him with all their hearts, and He would turn unto them, openly acting for them as Jehovah of hosts. Let them not refuse to hearken as their fathers refused to obey the messages of the prophets that had given them the word of the Lord prior to the long-predicted captivities of Assyria and Babylon. To them He had cried, "Turn ye now from your evil ways, and from your evil doings!" but His words had been despised. Where were they now who had thus dared to refuse obedience to the Word of the living God? They had been made to know the power of His displeasure, and had at last been obliged to own that His word was infallible. In the land of the enemy they sadly confessed, "Like as the Lord of hosts thought to do unto us, according to our ways, and according to our doings, so hath He dealt with us" (ver. 6). Thus had He been glorified even in their abasement and discomfiture. In all this how serious and important the lesson for us!

In verse 7 Zechariah begins to relate a series of eight visions, all intimately connected; all of which seem to have been given him on the four and twentieth day of the eleventh month, in the same year as that of verse 1. The first vision and its partial explanation occupies verses 7 to 17. For convenience we shall call it, The Man among the Myrtle Trees.

The prophet beheld a man riding upon a red horse, in a deep valley, among a grove of myrtle trees, "and behind him red horses, speckled, and white." In reply to his surprised inquiry, "O my lord, what are these?" an angel replied, "I will show thee what these be."

Upon this the rider on the red horse, twice called a man, but in verse 11 identified as the angel of Jehovah, said, "These are they whom the Lord hath sent to walk to and fro through the earth."

Then, as though summoned to give account, the

hitherto unmentioned riders* on the attending horses answered the angel of the Lord, and said, "We have walked to and fro through the earth, and, behold all the earth sitteth still, and is at rest."

The rider on the first horse would seem to be the Covenant-Angel, standing for the people of Jehovah's choice. The other horses speak of the providential agencies, possibly angelically-directed, working among the Gentile nations. Observe, the Lord had sent them. The powers that be are ordained of God. They had lately been used for the chastisement of offending Israel. Now all the world was at peace, and the nations utterly indifferent to the low estate of the seed of Abraham.

Hence the cry of the Angel of Jehovah, "O Lord of hosts, how long wilt Thou not have mercy on Jerusalem and on the cities of Judah, against which Thou hast had indignation these threescore and ten years?" (ver. 12). The Babylonian captivity had come to a end. Cyrus had given permission for the Jews to return to Jerusalem; but though a remnant had gone back, there was utter indifference on the part of the great powers as to any recognition nationally of the people who

---

* Some suppose the other horses to be riderless, and see in this a significant picture of the restless energy of Gentile dominion; but this involves speaking horses, a figure, it seems to me, grotesque and unimplied here.

were destined to be the chief of the nations. Hence the angel's question, which Jehovah answered with good words and comfortable words.

It is a little difficult here to distinguish between the Angel of Jehovah riding on the horse among the myrtles (who really speaks of Messiah Himself as the Angel-intercessor on behalf of Israel, as in Rev. 8: 1-4), and the interpreting-angel who explained the visions to Zechariah. The latter it is, in verse 14, who gives the seer a prophetic message telling him to, "Cry thou, saying, Thus saith the Lord of hosts: I am jealous for Jerusalem and for Zion with a great jealousy. And I am very sore displeased with the heathen that are at ease: for I was but a little displeased, and they helped forward the affliction."

Proud and self-sufficient, the Gentile powers seek only their own, and regard His chosen with indifference and scorn; but He is looking on, and they are thereby but adding to the cup of their iniquity.

In His own set time, as intimated already in connection with the prophetic character of the three names in verse 1, Jehovah will arise on behalf of His people, and return to Jerusalem, so long trodden under foot of the nations, with great mercies, bringing in all the blessings of the new covenant for the long-despised nation. His house shall be built in the land once more, on a more magnificent scale than ever, as set forth in the last eight chapters of Ezekiel. Jerusalem itself shall arise from its ruins, a glorious city, unequaled in splendor by any of the cities of the nations, in the day when "the Lord shall yet comfort Zion, and shall yet choose Jerusalem" (vers. 16, 17).

It is of importance throughout to distinguish between vision and interpretation. Verses 8 to 13 give the vision. Verses 14 to 17 are the divine explanation. Judah and Jerusalem form the subject. There is no reference to the Church of the present dispensation whatever. Spiritualizers have always been fond of so applying it, but to do so is to violently wrest the passage.

The second vision, of the four horns and the four carpenters, or four smiths, is given in verses 18 to 21. The four Gentile world-empires, made familiar to us in Daniel's prophecy, are exemplified by the horns (symbols of power), viz., Babylon, Medo-Persia, Greece, and Rome.

But for every horn there is a carpenter; and like as they have agreed together to oppress and destroy Israel and Judah, so shall God use these carpenters to destroy them. Israel's enemies are God's enemies, and must be frayed and broken when their appointed course is run, with a view to the full deliverance of the remnant of the people of His choice.

In the Hebrew text this vision belongs to the next chapter, as chapter 1 ends with verse 17. It requires no further comment. For the saint of any dispensation it ministers blessed truth, reminding him that God worketh all things after the counsel of His own will; and evil is only permitted in so far as it will serve in the carrying out of His wondrous purposes of blessing.

CHAPTER II

JERUSALEM'S RESTORATION

THIS chapter contains but one vision—that of the man with a measuring-line in his hand. Upon beholding him, Zechariah asked, "Whither goest thou?" The man replied, "To measure Jerusalem, to see what is the breadth thereof, and what is the length thereof."

Upon this, the interpreting angel left the prophet's side, and advanced to meet another angel who was coming toward him. The latter cried, "Run, speak to this young man,* saying, Jerusalem shall be inhabited as towns without walls for the multitude of men and cattle therein; for I, saith

---

* I suppose most are aware of the foolish Mormon conceit which makes this young man to be Joseph Smith, the pseudo-prophet, and the angel to be Moroni, who reveals to him the golden plates of the book of Mormon!

The most casual reading of the passage will make clear that it has no reference to a Zion in America, but is intimately connected with what has gone before, and follows after, as to Jerusalem in the land of Palestine.

the Lord, will be unto her a wall of fire round about, and will be the glory in the midst of her." See Zeph. 3 : 5, 14-20.

The young man is Zechariah himself, who is to be informed of Jehovah's purposes as to Jerusalem in order that he may write it for future generations. The city that he knew was mean and paltry indeed in comparison with the Jerusalem that was yet to be. In the day of its glory and splendor there would be no need of a wall of masonry. The Lord Himself would be her wall of fire, protecting from every assailant, and dwelling in her midst in the glory of the Shekinah.

Verses 6 to 9 form the summons to the remnant to return to their land, in the day when all that God has promised is about to be fulfilled. Morally, they will still be dwelling with the daughter of Babylon, for Gentile dominion was established in Nebuchadnezzar, and the powers that have succeeded him are all of his spirit and character. For over two millenniums they have been the persecutors and haters of the Jew; and though in our day the position of the Hebrew is much more tolerable than ever before since their dispersion, there are still angry mutterings of anti-Semitism in many parts of Europe, which are destined to start a conflagration of unequaled fierceness in the time of Jacob's trouble which follows the translation of the Church to heaven. But when apparently friendless and helpless, the

Lord will send His angel to gather together His elect from the four winds of heaven, and to re-establish them in peace in their long-promised inheritance, the land of their fathers.

The exact time when this is to take place is given in verse 8: "*After the glory* hath He sent me unto the nations which spoiled you: for he that toucheth you, toucheth the apple of His eye." The expression, "after the glory," refers to the period immediately following the revelation, or apocalyptic appearing of Christ from heaven, when He descends in power and great glory to take the kingdom and assert His rights, as in the 2d psalm. Then the world shall know that Israel are the people of His choice, and the sheep of His pasture. As in Esther's time, the Jews will have light and joy, gladness and a good day, while their enemies will be humbled in the dust before them, and made to know that in oppressing the seed of Jacob they have been fighting against the living God.

Verses 10 to 13 form a fitting close to such a prophecy. The daughter of Zion, who has hung her harp on the willow for so long, as she wept by the rivers of Babylon, is called upon to sing and rejoice: for her glorious Lord will Himself dwell in her midst, and they shall all know Him, "from the least to the greatest."

Then shall many nations be joined to Jehovah and become His people, being brought into the same blessed knowledge vouchsafed to Israel. This is far different from the call of the Gentiles in the present dispensation. Now God is taking out from among the nations a people for His name, and uniting Jew and Gentile into one body. Then Israel will be supreme in the earth, and all the nations shall find their blessing through her, when "the Lord shall inherit Judah His portion in the holy land, and shall choose Jerusalem again" (ver. 12).

So shall the years of her mourning be ended, and Israel's long warfare be accomplished. In that day the portion of the Church will be in the heavenly glory, while the earthly people will find their blessing in the land promised to Abraham, Isaac and Jacob as an inalienable inheritance, from which their seed shall never be expelled.

The last verse expresses the attitude of all the world in the day when the Lord shall do this: "Be silent, O all flesh, before the Lord: for He is raised up out of His holy habitation."

Sweet it is to know that the rising tide of evil will soon be checked; sin and rebellion shall in every shape be eliminated from the earth; all the spared of the nations will own the benignant yet righteous sway of the now-rejected Saviour, and Jehovah of hosts be everywhere worshipped and obeyed.

CHAPTER III

A BRAND PLUCKED OUT OF THE FIRE

THE fourth vision may be looked at in two ways. Primarily it sets forth Israel's cleansing, judicially and morally, in the last days. It is also a lovely gospel picture, which the soul delights to dwell upon.

Joshua the high priest, the associate of Zerubbabel, the uncrowned heir of David's line, is seen standing before the angel of Jehovah, as if for judgment. At his right hand appears Satan, the adversary, ever the accuser of the people of God. But he is not permitted to raise any question, or to bring any charge, though Joshua is clothed in filthy garments; for the Lord Himself speaks, saying, "Jehovah rebuke thee, O Satan; even Jehovah that hath chosen Jerusalem rebuke thee; is not this a brand plucked out of the fire?" (vers. 1-3).

It is strikingly solemn, and yet a lovely scene. Joshua represents the entire remnant company; for as priest he went in to God on their behalf. But he is clothed, not in the unsullied robes prescribed by the law, but in filthy garments—setting forth the moral pollution of the whole nation. Isaiah's description well accords with this significant picture, "Why should ye be stricken any more? Ye will revolt more and more: the whole head is sick, and the whole heart faint. From the sole of the foot even unto the head there is no soundness in it; but wounds, and bruises, and putrifying sores: they have not been closed, neither bound up, neither mollified with ointment" (Isa. 1:5, 6).

Constitutionally corrupt, the filth of Judah's pollution defiled all her garments, and made them filthy and vile in God's sight. Who would have supposed any people so unclean could have been accepted of Jehovah? Surely the adversary would find ready ear when he sought to prefer his charges before the throne of infinite holiness! But God had taken into account all Israel's failures when He first took them up in grace, so He will listen to no charge against them. He rebukes the devil with the declaration that He has chosen Jerusalem, and that Joshua, as the people's representative, is a brand plucked out of the fire. This is matchless lovingkindness surely, but just what we should expect here; for "the gifts and calling of God are without repentance." He will chasten and discipline his failing people, but He will not allow Satan to prefer a single charge against them, for provision has been made for their moral fitness for His presence. Zechariah then hears Jehovah's voice saying to those who stood before Him, "Take away the filthy garments from him." While to Joshua himself the word is given, "Behold, I have caused thine iniquity to pass from thee, and I will clothe thee with change of raiment."

At this the prophet's soul was stirred to its depths, and, entering into the spirit of the occasion, he cried out, "Let them set a fair mitre upon his head!"

Immediately it is done as he requested, and as God had commanded. So Joshua appears no longer as a type, or symbolic character, of Judah, polluted by her failures and sins, but of the remnant which shall be regenerated in the day of Jehovah's power, when she shall be cleansed from all her pollutions and He will be pacified toward her for all that she has done (Ezek. 16: 60-62).

No more beautiful gospel picture is found within the Bible covers than this. As aptly as Joshua stands for Judah, so does he represent the poor sinner coming into God's holy presence with all his guilt upon him. It is thus every soul must meet Him for the first time. None can put away his iniquity and thereby fit himself to face that righteous throne. But clad in his filthy garments, owning fully all his dreadful guilt, every repentant soul may approach God with the conscious knowledge that for such as he there is mercy and cleansing.

The adversary will be there to hinder if he can; but Jehovah will not listen to him, for He has His eye on the work of the Lord Jesus Christ, accomplished on Calvary's cross, when "He bare the sin of many, and made intercession for the transgressors" (Isa. 53:12). Against that mighty intercession no Satanic charges can avail. Too loudly cries the blood in God's ear that speaketh better things than that of Abel. Therefore of every believing sinner He delights to say, "Is not this a brand plucked out of the fire?"

Nor is it merely judicial clearance, but there will be moral fitness too; for those whom God justifies He likewise cleanses, purifying their hearts by faith, when they are born of the water of the Word and by the Spirit of holiness.

To Joshua, after he has been vindicated, cleansed, clothed, and crowned, the angel of the Lord protests, bidding him hear the word of Jehovah of hosts, that he may walk in His ways, and keep His charge, assuring him that if there be faithfulness and devotedness, he will judge God's house and keep His courts, having "places to walk among these that stand by:" that is, being associated with those seraphic beings whose joy it is to obey the slightest behest of the all-glorious and thrice-holy One (ver. 7).

Thus are God's redeemed ones called to serve Him whose grace has plucked them as brands from eternal fire. And so, in the coming age, will restored and purged Israel delight to obey the voice of Him who shall have made them willing in the day of His power.

In verse 8 Joshua and his fellows are said to

be "men wondered at," or, more correctly, "men of signification;" making clear that we have been correct in seeing in the high priest, and his companions likewise, symbolic personages.

Only in Christ shall all these prophetic pictures be made good; so at once we are told, "I will bring forth My Servant the Branch." The title is not a new one as applied to the Lord Jesus. Again and again had the older prophets so designated Him. Isaiah more than once foretold the day when "the Branch of the Lord" should be for beauty and for glory (Isa. 4:2; 11:1); and Jeremiah twice spoke of David's righteous Branch, who was to be called Jehovah Tsidkenu (Jer. 23:5, 6 and 33:15, 16). So Zechariah but amplifies here and in chapter 6:12 what God had long before made known.

The Branch of verse 2 is identified with the Stone of verse 9, which is to be engraved as with the engraving of a signet, with the sign of perfect intelligence, namely, seven eyes. This is the Stone of salvation which was once a rock of offence, and, as such, was rejected by the builders. Soon it shall fall from heaven, in accordance with Nebuchadnezzar's vision (Dan. 2), grinding to powder the enemies of the Lord, but removing the iniquity of the land of Palestine in one day. Then shall the blessings of Messiah's reign be entered into by the spared remnant, who shall call every man neighbor, under their own vine and fig tree.

It is an apparently abrupt conclusion to so marvelous a chapter, but it accords with the general character of Zechariah, where sudden terminations and quick transitions abound throughout.

CHAPTER IV

THE TWO ANOINTED ONES

THE striking vision next recorded, being the fifth in the series, is of prime importance to any reverent student of the word of God. Not only does it set forth precious and important truth relative to Israel, as God's light-bearer in the world, but it is the only instance where the typical meaning of oil is distinctly explained. It gives us therefore an unerring key whereby to unlock many of the treasures of symbolic teaching throughout the Old Testament.

The prophet seems to have fallen into a slumber after the interpretation of the previous vision; for we are told that the angel who had been speaking with him came again, and waked him, as a man is waked out of his sleep, saying, "What seest thou?" (vers. 1, 2). Zechariah looked, and beheld a sight of great beauty and splendor. A golden lamp-stand, evidently somewhat similar in construction to that which is described in Exod.

25:31-37, appeared before his eyes. But in one marked respect it differed from that whose lamps the priest had to carefully fill daily lest they should be extinguished. Here no human hand provided the oil, nor was responsible to maintain the light of testimony. The stand and its lamps were of one piece, and the latter were continually supplied in a most remarkable manner. Upon the top of the central shaft was a golden bowl, or fountain. From this radiated seven pipes, which connected with the seven lamps. On either side of the stand an olive tree was growing, the branches of which were represented as bending over the receiver-fountain, and pouring their oil into it in a continual stream. Thus the light was ever maintained in its beauty and power (vers. 2, 3).

In response to Zechariah's request for enlightenment as to the meaning of this, the angel said, "This is the word of the Lord unto Zerubbabel, saying, Not by might, nor by power, but by My Spirit, saith the Lord of hosts. Who art thou, O great mountain? Before Zerubbabel thou shalt become a plain: and he shall bring forth the headstone thereof with shoutings, crying, Grace, grace unto it."

Here was no meaningless oracle, such as those of heathen sybils, but a plain declaration that just as the oil pouring into the golden bowl fed the lamps, so the Holy Spirit would confirm and unfailingly furnish Israel to be Jehovah's testimony-bearer in the earth. He who had brought up a remnant from Babylon under Zerubbabel, the prince of David's line, would infallibly fulfil every promise made through His holy prophets. Human power and might could neither hinder nor help. The Holy Spirit alone could sustain and maintain them as His light in the world. Thus we know what oil typifies. It speaks ever of the Spirit of God, whether as anointer or earnest. In His divine power alone can any testimony be carried on for God at any time. During the present dispensation of Israel's scattering, the Church is the light-bearer, even as her Lord was while here upon the earth. By and by, when Israel shall be restored in the saved remnant, she will once more become God's witness. But whether with the blessed Lord Himself, the Church His Body, or Israel His people, all true testimony is in the energy of the Holy Spirit.

Endued by power divine, who need fear the face of man? Before Zerubbabel and the feeble remnant in the land, Gentile authority might seem like a great mountain, hindering all progress in the special work committed to them. Only unbelief could so count it. Faith would say to the mount of difficulty, "Become a plain," and so it should be. No weapon formed against them should prosper, no arm should be strong enough to hinder, till the temple was completed to the glory of Jehovah, and Zerubbabel should bring forth the capstone amid the shoutings of a rejoicing people, crying, "Grace, grace unto it?" (vers. 4-7).

Even so shall every promise made in the word of God be fulfilled to the letter. In this case he who had begun the house should finish it (see Ezra 3: 10-15 and 6: 14-18); thus proving that a prophet had been among them. It was a day of weakness, a day of small things; but they should not despise it, for it was the day of Jehovah's energy. The nations of the earth might be utterly indifferent to what was transpiring at the insignificant place where the Lord had set His Name; but there He was, working in mighty power, nevertheless. There the plummet of truth was in the hands of Zerubbabel, and the people wrought according as they found it written. There too the eyes of the Lord rested with complacency, after running to and fro through the whole earth (vers. 9, 10).

In God's sight it was "a great work" that was going on in Jerusalem, for it was the carrying out of His own word, with a view to the coming of His Son into the scene.

On one other point Zechariah desired enlightenment. He had been contemplating the two olive trees, wondering what they might signify; so he inquired boldly of the angel, asking for information regarding them. It would seem as though there was slowness of apprehension on his part;

for he not only had to put his question twice over, but the angel did not immediately reply, but questioned him, as in verse 5, where it seemed as though spiritual intuition ought to have made all clear, saying, "Knowest thou not what these be?" Confessing his ignorance, Zechariah is told that, "These are the two anointed ones, that stand by the Lord of the whole earth."

To him the two anointed ones could be no other than Zerubbabel, the prince, and Joshua the high priest. So in kingly and priestly power the testimony of God was to be maintained. These were the agencies through which Jehovah would work.

In Rev. 11:4 the two witnesses are said to be "the two olive trees, and the two candlesticks standing before the God of the earth." The reference is clearly to Zechariah's vision; yet there is a marked difference. There we have two candlesticks; here, but one. The reason is plainly this: the two witnesses come on the scene before Israel is established as God's lamp-stand nationally. With them it is individual testimony. Therefore in place of one seven-branched lamp-stand, setting forth completeness of testimony we have two witnesses described as two lamp-stands. And they are also said to be the two olive trees; for they stand before God as His anointed sons of oil in the day when His name is denied and His word despised. Coming in the spirit and power of Moses and Elijah, they prophesy in the energy of the Spirit till put to death by the Beast and his adherents. Thus, for the moment, all testimony for God will seem to have been blotted out; but the word of the Lord shall not fail, for the seven-branched lamp-stand shall be set up when the Lord descends and delivers His people Israel out of the hands of all who oppress them.

CHAPTER V

THE FLYING ROLL AND THE EPHAH

THE visions of glory which we have been contemplating in the last two chapters are succeeded by others of very diverse kind. If Judah and Jerusalem are to be blessed, it must be on the ground of sovereign grace alone. Merit there was none, but the very opposite. It is this the "flying roll" makes manifest. It speaks of unsparing judgment "according to their works," which must fall on all who refuse to judge themselves according to the word of the living God. But it lets us know likewise that He, the Holy One, so grievously sinned against, has found a way to save in a righteous manner all who turn to Him and call upon His name; otherwise all should of very necessity be cut off.

There is no word or apparent hint of anything

but wrath to the uttermost; yet, read in the light of the preceding symbols, our hearts are lifted up in holy exultation to the praise of the grace that saves.

We are told, "Then I turned and lifted up mine eyes, and looked, and behold a flying roll. And he said unto me, What seest thou? And I answered, I see a flying roll: the length thereof is twenty cubits, and the breadth thereof ten cubits. Then said he unto me, This is the curse that goeth forth over the face of the whole earth (or, land, R. V.; *i. e.,* Palestine): for every one that stealeth shall be cut off as on this side according to it; and every one that sweareth shall be cut off as on that side according to it. I will bring it forth, saith the Lord of hosts, and it shall enter into the house of the thief and into the house of him that sweareth falsely by My name: and it shall remain in the midst of his house, and shall consume it, with the timber thereof and the stones thereof" (vers. 1-4).

I have quoted the account of both the vision and its interpretation in full; for it is of a most solemn character, and may well speak loudly to every heart, both of the sinners of the Gentiles and of the people of Israel. Primarily it refers distinctively to Judah. They will be restored to the land in unbelief when it has its fulfilment. Note well that the Revised reading, "land," in verse 3, here, as generally in the Prophets, is much to be preferred to the more general "earth" of the A.V. In studying the seventeen books that make up the last part of the Old Testament, it is of prime importance to remember that throughout God has Israel as a people and Palestine as their land before His eyes. That apparently insignificant strip of country is, for Him, the centre of the earth, and of all His ways with men on the earth. He gave it by inviolable covenant to Abraham and his descendants. There His blessed Son was born, and lived and died. Thence He ascended to heaven. To that same land He shall descend in person to usher in the kingdom long foretold.

For centuries that land has been trodden ignominiously beneath the foot of the haughty Gentile conqueror, while its rightful inhabitants have, for their sins, been dispersed among the nations. But thither they shall return; yea, even now are returning in large numbers, though as yet in darkness of soul and unbelief. There, God will pass them through a trial of unequaled fierceness, called "the time of Jacob's trouble," or "the great tribulation," separating thereby the precious from the vile; destroying the sinners and transgressors from among them, and saving the repentant subjects of His grace, who shall form the nucleus for the kingdom in the day of His power.

Of this preparatory judgment the vision now claiming our attention speaks. Zechariah beheld in the heavens a vast scroll in majestic yet hurried notion, moving swiftly through the air, over all the land of Canaan. Closely observing, he saw that it was written on both sides with curses and judgments. On the one side was God's word against those who wronged their neighbor, in accordance with the second table of the law (first mentioned, for man can best appreciate the wickedness of sin against his fellow); on the other side, the doom pronounced on those guilty of impiety, according to the first table.

That law, in itself "holy, and just, and good," becomes their condemnation; for "as many as are of the works of the law are under the curse: for it is written, Cursed is every one that continueth not in all things which are written in the book of the law to do them" (Gal. 3:10). The Jew makes his boast in that law; yet it speaks only for his condemnation.

The flying roll is the answer to the foolhardiness of the people who cried at Sinai, "All that the Lord hath spoken will we do." After a trial lasting through long centuries and millenniums, it is the witness against them, making manifest the solemn fact that they have failed at every point, so must be cut off in judgment.

Into every house where the thief or the false swearer is found the curse enters, bringing utter destruction in its wake. This is all *the law* can do for any sinner. It can only condemn and curse the violator of it.

And who has not violated it? Wherever it has been promulgated, it has found many to promise, but none to perform. No honest man can claim to have kept it; therefore on that ground, as righteousness he has not, salvation there cannot be.

But, blessed be God, He has found a ransom for men and women who have forfeited all title to His favor. "Christ hath redeemed us from the curse of the law, being made a curse for us: for it is written, Cursed is every one that hangeth on a tree" (Gal. 3: 13). On the ground of an accomplished redemption, grace flows out now to every transgressor who owns his lost condition and trusts the sinner's Saviour. On the same ground will the flying roll be turned aside from the houses of all the remnant of Judah in the last days, who turn to God in repentance, and, like their fathers on the passover night in Egypt, find shelter beneath the blood of atonement. This the wondrous vision of chapter three has already set forth.

Beginning with verse 5, we have another and a stranger symbol. Zechariah, evidently musing with downcast eyes on the awful portent we have been considering, was aroused by the interpreting angel, and called upon to observe the next remarkable vision. He saw a great ephah, a vessel for measuring merchandise, with a weighty piece of base metal, akin to lead, upon the top of it. This being lifted, he beheld a woman who was cast into the ephah, which was again covered with the lead. Two other women then appeared, with wings like those of a stork, who lifted up the measure between them and flew with it to the north. In reply to the seer's question, "Whither do these bear the ephah?" the angel said, "To build it a house in the land of Shinar: and it shall be established, and set there upon her own base" (vers. 5-11).

Such was the strange portent beheld by the prophet. What is the meaning to be gathered from it?

It is noticeable that, as we go on with the series, there is less and less given in the way of interpretation. It is as though the Lord would give enough in regard to the earlier visions to lay a solid foundation for the understanding of the later ones. Thus the need of carefully comparing what we have here with what has already come before us.

Various interpretations have been suggested, many of which seem to be extremely fanciful. One of the most common is this: The ephah is a symbol of commercialism, setting forth the great characteristic mark of the Jewish race, who are a nation of keen bargainers. The woman sets forth iniquity in business, now come to the full. The carrying of the woman in the ephah to the land of Shinar indicates the revival of the ancient city of Babylon in great splendor as the commercial centre of the coming day. Interpreters of this stamp point to certain negotiations now going on for the opening up of Mesopotamia and the extension of railroad enterprise in that direction as sure indications that they are on the right track. But to our mind all this is pure speculation, and absolutely unsupported by Scripture. Both Jeremiah and Isaiah make it clear, in my judgment, that Babylon has fallen to rise no more.* It has been literally burned with fire and utterly destroyed, and God Himself has solemnly declared that for that wicked city there shall be no healing nor revival.

Nor is there any solid reason for supposing that the ephah is in itself, of necessity, a symbol of great commercial enterprise. Is it not rather the recognized symbol of measurement, telling us that God shall weigh and measure Judah's sin, and the sin of the whole house of Israel, with unerring accuracy. When their iniquity has come to the full, in wondrous grace He will separate the wickedness from the preserved remnant, dealing with it in connection with the place of its origin, the land of Shinar. For the woman in the ephah sets forth unmistakably, I judge, wicked-

---

* I do not enter into this in detail here, as I have already done so in commenting on Jeremiah, chapters fifty and fifty-one. The interested reader may consult "The Weeping Prophet: Notes on Jeremiah and the Lamentations." Same author and publishers.

ness of a religious character, as in the parallel cases of the woman hiding the leaven of evil teaching in the food of the people of God (Matt. 13), and the woman Jezebel corrupting the assembly at Thyatira, issuing in the awful impiety of the scarlet woman of Rev. 17.

Now, Israel's great religious sin was idolatry. They had been separated from the nations to be Jehovah's witnesses to the unity of the Godhead. Instead of maintaining the place of testimony thus given them, they turned to the practices of the heathen, provoking their Rock and causing Him to fall upon them in indignation. Babylon was the mother of idolatry. It was the home of all that is false in a religious way. In the time of the end this spirit of wickedness will be separated from Judah and carried by stork-winged women (symbol surely of the unclean energy of the human mind, femininely lovely, but propelled by the energy of the prince of the power of the air) to the land of Shinar, where its house will be built. That is, there its habitation will be, and there will it be judged.

It is a moral continuity. In mystical Babylon literal Babylon finds her identity continued and her sin fully dealt with. With her sorcery have all nations been deceived, and in her shall be "found the blood of prophets, and of saints, and of all that were slain upon the earth" (Rev. 18: 24).

Thus shall Israel be purified and idolatry of every form meet its just and final doom, preparatory to the establishment of the world-kingdom of our God and His Christ.

CHAPTER VI

THE FOUR CHARIOTS, AND THE CROWNING DAY

THIS chapter concludes the first division of the prophecy, and is itself divided into two parts. Verses 1 to 8 give us Zechariah's final vision. Verses 9 to 15 set forth the glorious climax of all prophetic instruction, in figure; the crowning of Joshua the high priest representing the coronation of our Lord Jesus Christ when He shall be manifested to Israel as "a Priest forever, after the order of Melchizedek," who combined in himself the kingly and priestly offices.

The vision is simple, yet comforting, and requires but little explanation. Zechariah saw four chariots, drawn respectively by red, black, white and speckled bay horses. No mention is made of drivers. It would seem as though the horses were directed by unseen agency, which is fully in keeping with the explanation given afterward.

The chariots and their horses were seen coming out from between two mountains of brass. The prophet inquired as to the identity of the symbols, and was answered by the angel, who said, "These are the four spirits of the heavens, which go forth from standing before the Lord of all the earth. The black horses which are therein go forth into the north country; and the white go forth after them; and the grizzled go forth toward the south country. And the bay* went forth, and sought to go that they might walk to and fro through the earth." Then the angel addressed the restless steeds directly, bidding them, "Get you hence, walk to and fro through the earth."

At once they started on their mission, whereupon the angel turned again to Zechariah, and said, "Behold, these that go toward the north country have quieted my spirit in the north country" (vers. 1-8).

The vision evidently sets forth God's control of all destructive agencies used by Him in the punishment of the nations that have deserved His wrath. It was intended to give repose of heart and confidence of mind to the remnant, making known to them the fact that the God of Israel was the Lord of all the earth. "All things serve His might." In His own way and time, therefore, He would send the chariots of His government against the nations that had made a prey of and spoiled His people. "Mountains of brass" speaks

---

* Some read, "the red;" see R.V., margin. Others translate this word, "the strong."

of power in righteous judgment. From between two such mountains the chariots go forth.

God's providential agencies may seem, to unbelief, like restless, uncurbed horses rushing here and there according to blind chance or their own uncontrolled energy. But the man of faith, though he cannot always see the Hand that guides the reins, yet knows that divine wisdom orders all according to righteousness.

The special prophetic application of what Zechariah had beheld was at that moment connected with the kingdom of Babylon on the north and Egypt on the south. Between these two powers God would sustain His feeble flock, checkmating every effort to destroy them till Messiah should Himself appear. Alas, that when He came they knew Him not! therefore they have been driven from their ancestral home and scattered among the Gentiles. But in the last days they will again be found in a similar, though more serious, state than that in which they once failed so grievously. Then the lesson of this vision will be for their comfort and cheer, bidding them look up in confidence to Him who controls all agencies that would seek their overthrow. Compare Rev. 7: 1-3, where four angels are seen holding the winds, or spirits of destruction, in check till the sealing of the remnant who are to be preserved for the kingdom soon to be established.

We have thus gone over the apocalypse of

Zechariah, seeking to understand his visions in their prophetic and moral bearing. They harmonize perfectly with those of Daniel and the Revelation, as also with the unfolding of the ways of God in Hosea.

We are now to notice a symbolic action on the part of the prophet, which sets forth the bringing in of the glory, or the crowning day—the coronation of the once-rejected Jesus as Priest-King over all the earth.

Zechariah was bidden to go to some of the returned captivity, and to take from them gifts of silver and gold to make crowns. One he was directed to set upon the head of Joshua the son of Josedech, the high priest; but even as he did so, he was to speak of a greater than Joshua, saying, "Behold the Man whose name is The BRANCH; and He shall grow up out of His place, and He shall build the temple of the Lord: even He shall build the temple of the Lord; and He shall bear the glory, and shall sit and rule upon His throne; and He shall be a priest upon His throne: and the counsel of peace shall be between them both" (vers. 12, 13).

Upon the brows of the associates of Joshua crowns were also placed, as setting forth the dignity of restored Israel when they shall all be a kingdom of priests. This was done "for a memorial in the temple of the Lord" (ver. 14). Then followed a declaration that "they that are far off shall come and build in the temple of the Lord, and ye shall know that the Lord of hosts hath sent me unto you. And this shall come to pass, if ye will diligently obey the voice of the Lord your God" (ver. 15).

Those directly addressed by Zechariah did not diligently obey Jehovah's voice, and so forfeited the promised blessing. But in a future day an obedient remnant will be found who shall be born again, and in whose hearts and minds will be written the law of God so that they shall delight in His testimonies. Then shall the Branch of Jehovah be glorious throughout the whole earth, and the crown be placed upon that brow that was once pierced with the mock crown of thorns, when Pilate led Him forth, uttering unconsciously the very words of the prophet, "Behold the Man!" There he stopped, for the hour had not yet come when that lowly Man was to be invested with His regal glories. But when God brings His First-begotten into the world again, He will call upon all created intelligences, human and angelic, to do Him homage. Then shall the promise of the 110th psalm be fulfilled, and His Melchizedek priesthood, in relation to Israel and the earth, be ushered in.

The words, "He shall build the temple of the Lord," together with the prophecy of verse 15, make it clear that another and more glorious temple than that of Zerubbabel was contemplated. That house, "exceeding magnifical," is fully described, together with its surroundings and order, in the last eight chapters of Ezekiel. It is to be built when the long-looked-for King has come, and in His Person the two offices of Priest and Ruler combine.

"The counsel of peace shall be between them both," we are told. That is, the new covenant will rest, not on an agreement entered into by man and God, but it will be established forever on the ground of "the counsel of peace" made between Jehovah of hosts and the Man whose name is "The Branch." He, the Man of God's purpose, settled every question as to sin when He died upon the tree; and now, "having made peace through the blood of His cross," He is the agent through whom the reconciliation of all things in heaven and earth will be effected (Col. 1:20).

Thus have we been carried in spirit from the days of Judah's first restoration to her final blessing in the land, when "this Man shall be the peace," and "in His own times He shall show, who is that blessed and only potentate, King of kings, and Lord of lords."

This is the ultimate goal of prophecy, and closes the first division of our book.

CHAPTER VII

THE NEED OF REALITY

THE opening date for the second division of the prophecy of Zechariah is a little more than two years later than what we have been considering. In the meantime royal permission had been given for the completion of the temple, and the work went on with some degree of energy. See Ezra, 5th chapter. Already there had been some effort made to revive the ancient feasts, and likewise to keep the more modern fasts. Concerning one of the latter, a deputation of Jews came to consult Zechariah and the elders, both of the priests and prophets. Their Chaldean names tell that they had been born in captivity. As representatives of the people, "Sherezer and Regem-melech, and their men," came "to pray before the Lord, and to speak unto the priests which were in the house of the Lord of hosts, and to the prophets, saying, Should I weep in the fifth month, separating myself, as I have done these so many years?" (vers. 2, 3).

There seems to have been propriety in the question. For the fast of the fifth month, as also for the fasts of the fourth, seventh and tenth months (chap. 8:19), there was no direct authority in the word of God, and the returned remnant had been learning to inquire, "What saith the Scriptures?" as to both command and teaching.

During their Babylonian sojourn they had kept the four fasts mentioned, commemorating various events in their past sad history, all connected with their punishment for their sins. None need doubt the piety that prompted the observance of these special seasons of humiliation before God.

The only trouble was, that formality so readily took the place of reality and genuine self-humbling in the presence of the Lord. On the tenth day of the fifth month Nebuzar-adan burnt the temple and the city of Jerusalem. On the yearly anniversary of that solemn event they fasted and wept, beseeching the Lord to have mercy, and restore the house and the city.

Naturally, now that they were again in the midst of Jerusalem's ruins, and their prayer seemed answered in measure before their eyes as the house of God neared completion, the question of the righteousness of continuing the self-appointed fast of the fifth month came before them.

The word of the Lord of hosts came through Zechariah in reply. But there was no legislation regarding the fast at all: He neither forbade nor enjoined it. In itself, such a fast was without positive scriptural authority. On the other hand, it was in full keeping with the general tenor of the Word. It was extra-scriptural, rather than un-scriptural. If the people met in true self-judgment and brokenness of spirit before God on that day, or any day, it would have been acceptable. If they met simply as legally observing a fast which, after all, He had never appointed, it was a weariness of the flesh, and worthless in His sight. Therefore Zechariah presses home the need of reality. What had been their object and condition of soul as they kept the fasts in the past? When they commemorated the burning of the temple in the fifth month (2 Kings 25: 8; Jer. 52: 12), and the death of the faithful Gedaliah in the seventh month (2 Kings 25: 25; Jer. 41: 1, 2),* did they at all fast unto Jehovah all the years of the captivity?

When, on the other hand, they kept the appointed feasts, in place of the fasts, was it His glory they sought? Or did they simply come together for social enjoyment, eating and drinking, without one thought of honoring Him whose power and grace they were supposed to be remembering? (vers. 6, 7).

---

* I have thought that possibly commentators in general are wrong in applying "the fast of the seventh month" to the lesser fast commemorating the murder of Gedaliah, and that it really refers to the great fast of the day of atonement. In that case the prophet would be showing that whether directly appointed by God in His Word, or added by pious consent, no observance was acceptable apart from *reality*. But as the Jews themselves apply the passage as in the text, I have left it at that.

Surely, if all before had been unreal and hollow, now, with such marked evidences both of divine grace and government before them, they should turn to God with all their hearts, remembering the words which He had cried by the former prophets, who had testified to their fathers before Jerusalem was destroyed, and when they dwelt therein in peace, and prosperity was in the land (ver. 7).

This is all the answer that was given for the moment. It was left to them to decide whether they should keep the fast or not. And this is most significant, and has a voice for us whose lot is cast in a similar day, if we will hear it, emphasizing the fact that mere formality will never do for God. He must see a true turning to Himself if He would find delight in the gathering together of His people. There may not always be chapter and verse for every practice, but God will graciously accept all that springs from true self-judgment, and that is not opposed to the plain letter of His Word. It has become the fashion in some places to ask, "Where is the scripture for a Bible-reading, or where the direct verse for gathering the young together to teach them the knowledge of the Bible, and thus to lead them to Christ?" We need not be troubled by such cold-hearted queries as these. Rather let the Sunday-school worker ask himself, or herself, "Why do I thus labor among the children? Is it with me but a weariness of the flesh, and a matter of form? Has it become simply legal drudgery, which I carry on because such work is now customary? Or do I seek thus to glorify the Lord Jesus Christ? Is my purpose so to minister Him to those young in years that their tender hearts may be drawn to Himself ere they become hardened by the deceitfulness of sin?" If this be the case, let there be no further question, but go on joyfully with your service, doing it heartily, as unto the Lord.

The same principle applies to the meeting appointed for the study of the Word, among believers. There is no direct scripture that such meetings are to be held at stated intervals; but there is plenty in the way of scripture warrant and example to make it clear that when such meetings are convened by earnest, loyal-hearted saints, who come together hungering for the precious truth of God, and ever letting it sit in judgment on them and on their ways, it is truly pleasing in His sight. Otherwise it is but a work of the flesh—religious flesh, no doubt, but flesh still, for all that.

And what has been said is equally true of the assembly-meeting of 1 Cor. 14 and the meeting for the breaking of bread of 1 Cor. 11 and Acts 20:7. It is quite possible to sit down at the Lord's table, where the bread and wine speak of His body given and blood shed for us, and yet not eat the Lord's Supper at all, because the mind is so fully occupied with other things that there is no true remembrance of Christ. One may go from the meeting-room eased in conscience because he has not neglected the table of the Lord, and superciliously regarding himself as superior to Christians whose light and privileges seem of a lower order, when all the time there has been nothing for God in it all, but the whole thing was a perfunctory and empty ceremony, detestable in His eyes, if indeed there has not been an actual eating and drinking of judgment to oneself.

But if there is to be reality when saints are gathered together, there must be righteousness in their daily lives. So Zechariah again speaks the word of the Lord, saying, "Execute true judgment, and show mercy and compassions every man to his brother: and oppress not the widow, nor the fatherless, the stranger, nor the poor; and let none of you imagine evil against his brother in your heart" (vers. 9, 10). Solemn words are these! Would that they had been oftener called to mind by the people of God in all ages! He has said, "Woe unto them that decree unrighteous decrees!" (Isa. 10: 1), yet how frequently has ecclesiastical authority been invoked to enforce the most palpably cruel and unholy decisions! Oh, the crimes that have been committed in the name of the Lord and His truth! The cruelties of those who have vaunted the exclusive mind of the Lord will make a terrible and a humiliating record at the judgment-seat of Christ. When will saints learn that nothing is of God which is unholy; that nothing is right which is not righteous; that nothing is bound, or ratified, by the Just One which in itself is unjust! Neither is anything to be owned as having divine sanction which outrages the mercy and compassions of Christ.

Because Israel forgot all this, and "made their hearts as an adamant stone," the former prophets had been sent to warn them, and they would not hear; therefore great wrath came upon them. As they were indifferent to the cry of the distressed, and calloused as to the sorrows of the needy, God gave them over to learn in bitterness of soul what distress and need really meant. In the day of their anguished cry, He refused to hearken, even as they had refused to hear His voice of entreaty and warning. So they had been scattered with a whirlwind among all the nations (vers. 11-14). Would their children learn from the sad experiences of the past, or must they too be broken and driven forth because of indifference to the claims of the Holy and the True?

To Christians of the present day the same questions may well be put. May God give us grace to profit by the failures of the past, and to walk softly and in charity, according to truth, in the little while ere the Lord Jesus comes again!

CHAPTER VIII

THE LIGHT OF THE FUTURE SHINING ON THE PRESENT PATH

THE value of the study of future prophecy is strikingly displayed in this chapter, where we find God, through His servant, drawing back the veil that hides the coming glory, in order that His people may comprehend in some measure their hope, that their present path may be in accordance therewith.

It would perhaps have been better had there been no break between this portion and that which we have just had before us, as it all seems to be part of Jehovah's answer to the inquirers regarding the propriety of observing the fast-day of the fifth month.

Verses 1 to 8 form a lovely millennial picture, describing the conditions which will prevail when "Jerusalem shall be called, A city of truth, and the mountain of the Lord of hosts, The holy mountain." Because of their idolatrous ways the Lord had been "jealous for Zion with a great jealousy," and with great wrath had delivered Judah into the hands of their enemies, that they might learn in the strangers' land the folly of trusting in graven images and sacrificing to the demons behind the symbols (ver. 2). Their sojourn in Babylon had cured them of this for the time, though our Lord Jesus showed that they were but as a house empty, swept and garnished, to which the unclean spirit who had gone out will yet return, bringing with him seven demons worse than himself. This will be fulfilled when idolatry of a worse kind than ever before is established among them—even the abomination of desolation standing in the holy place.

But all this is passed over here, for it is God's purpose that is before us, not the people's failure. Nothing is plainer than that the latter half of verse 3 never could have been properly applied to Jerusalem and Mount Zion since the return from Babylon. Yet it is there intimately connected with the first part, "I am returned unto Zion, and will dwell in the midst of Jerusalem." All the succeeding failure, even to the rejection of Messiah Himself and their consequent dispersion, is passed over in silence, and the future glorious estate of Jerusalem is linked up with the remnant then in the land. Only when the Lord has been manifested in power will the words that follow be fulfilled. Then shall there be old men and aged women dwelling in the restored city, while "the streets of the city shall be full of boys and girls playing in the streets thereof" (vers. 4, 5). The street is now the place of danger. Then the children can play therein with perfect safety. It is a sweet and touching thing thus to see how the Eternal God concerns Himself even about the innocent pastimes of the little ones. It might be well if some parents who are prone to a more than Puritanic legality pondered this 5th verse; for I fear that the boys and girls are often made to feel that their simple pleasures are, if not displeasing to Him, at least unprofitable and vain.

The accomplishment of what has here been outlined must be marvelous indeed in the eyes of puny man; but it is but a small thing with Him who hurled worlds into space, and directs the movements of the minutest of His creatures. His omnipotent Hand shall surely perform what His mouth has spoken. But that a future return from among the nations was before His mind is evidenced by what follows: "Behold, I will save My people from the east country, and from the west country; and I will bring them, and they shall dwell in the midst of Jerusalem: and they shall be My people, and I will be their God, in truth and in righteousness" (vers. 7, 8). This is the universal testimony of the prophets. The restoration from Babylon was but temporary, in order that what had been written concerning Messiah might be fulfilled. He having been cut off, they who refused Him were driven forth into all the ends of the earth. From thence, in God's appointed time, they shall return again to that country, which is still to them "the land of promise," where all that the prophets have spoken shall come to pass.

In verse 9 the practical application is pressed home. In view of the glory that is coming, the hands may well be strong. What need to be downcast and discouraged with such a portion assured us in Christ? So the people were urged to labor and hope, cheered by the promises of rich reward. God was caring for their interests. He would have them in earnest as to His. When Haggai was first raised up to speak to them, famine threatened, and disappointment clouded all their sky. But when they willingly and cheerfully gave themselves to the work of building His house, He had declared, "From this day will I bless you" (Haggai 1:9-11; 2:18, 19). He had been as good as His word, and would still watch over them for blessing, giving prosperity and increase while they "put first things first," making His glory their object (vers. 10-12).

But in all these promises it is plain that God has something more before Him than the little company then returned. He was looking on to fulness of blessing in the Millennium. Hence He declares that Israel, once a curse among the nations, shall be saved and made a blessing, according to His oath to Abraham. This was not true in any large measure, nor for long, of the actual company, or their descendants, to whom Zechariah spoke; for in less than six hundred years later we hear the Holy Spirit declaring that through them the name of God was blasphemed among the Gentiles (Rom. 2:24). And so it has been ever since. But God's Word abides nevertheless, and in a future remnant every promise shall be made good (ver. 13).

The Lord had no delight in afflicting His people; but their fathers had provoked Him to wrath. Let their children take heed to their ways therefore, and obey His voice, and all would be well. "These are the things that ye shall do: Speak ye every man the truth to his neighbor; execute the judgment of truth and peace in your gates: and let none of you imagine evil in your hearts against his neighbor; and love no false oath: for all these are things that I hate, saith the Lord" (vers. 16, 17).

Practical righteousness and true morality are the same in all dispensations. Christians may well challenge their hearts as we read these verses and note what is abhorrent in God's sight. Truth, and judgment according to truth: in these He delights. Evil surmisings (a most fruitful source of trouble in all ages) and false oaths: these He hates. May we have grace given to cleave to the former and refuse the latter!

The question as to the fasts (chap. 7:3) is again reverted to in verses 18, 19. Those of the fifth and seventh months we have already noticed. That of the fourth month commemorated the taking of Jerusalem, while that of the tenth called to mind the beginning of its siege. If the restored residue sought to walk with God, truly judging the past, these fasts would be transformed into cheerful feasts. "Therefore love the truth and peace," they were told. Notice that truth comes first, then peace; as in 2 Tim. 2:22 believers are called upon in a day of confusion and distraction to follow righteousness first of all. Then faith, love and peace would rightly follow.

The chapter concludes by portraying the happy spiritual conditions which will prevail in the day that Messiah's kingdom is established. It shall be no matter of hardship or cold, formal obedience to come together in a solemn assembly before Jehovah when Israel shall be a regenerated and sanctified people. Each city shall then vie with the other in "provoking unto love and to good works," saying one to another, "Let us go speedily to pray before the Lord, and to seek the Lord of hosts: I will go also" (vers. 20, 21). His service will then be their joy and delight. The 122d Psalm will be fulfilled, and the voices of the restored remnant will sing with exultation, "I was glad when they said unto me, Let us go into the house of the Lord." It is ever thus when Christ Himself is before the soul. The gatherings of the children of God become in very deed as foretastes of heaven when He is to His own the altogether lovely. There are no dry, listless meetings then; but every heart thrills with a joy not earthly as He fills the vision of the enraptured soul. If right with God, there would ever be this holy freshness and fervent longing for His presence. But when permitted sin has been allowed to do its deadly work unjudged, the Holy Spirit is grieved, Christ is hidden, and what would have been a delight becomes a weariness of the flesh.

When the saints of God are enjoying Christ, others are attracted to Him and to them. So, when Israel shall be gathered round Himself, dwelling under His shadow, and happy in His love, there will be a great stirring of heart among the spared of the nations who will not have been destroyed when the stone falls from heaven—"Many people and strong nations shall come to seek the Lord of hosts in Jerusalem, and to pray before the Lord." The Jew, so long despised and hated, will be looked upon as the ambassador of the Lord, and ten men of all languages shall cleave to one who is of Judah, saying, "We will go with you: for we have heard that God is with you" (vers. 22, 23). It is impossible, by any principle of honest interpretation, to make these words fit any revival of the past or present. They apply only to the day when Jerusalem shall be the spiritual metropolis of the whole earth, and when the name of Jew, so often used in contempt and derision, will proclaim one who is truly a son of praise,* joyfully worshiping the Lord of hosts as he stands upon redemption ground. Then indeed shall all the nations know that "salvation is of the Jews."

But that there is a spiritual application, I have already pointed out. When the people of God, in any age, are going on in happy fellowship with their Lord and Saviour, the unsaved will be attracted to Him, and will be found seeking out His disciples, saying, "We would see Jesus."

---

* Jew is but a contraction of Judah, which means "praise." Note how the apostle interprets the name in Rom. 2: 28, 29.

CHAPTER IX

THE COMING KING

WE have already pointed out that this book divides into two parts. The second division embraces chapters 7 to 14. Our study has shown us that, of these, chapters 7 and 8 stand together. A second section, or subdivision, begins with chapter 9, and goes on to the end of chapter 11, giving in a most instructive way the coming of Messiah, and His rejection by Judah. Chapters 12 to 14 follow with the inspired account of His second coming and His acceptance by the repentant remnant.

The refusal of Christ when He came in grace is morally connected with the state into which the people had fallen long before. The cross was but the culmination of a course of wilful hardening that had been going on from the days of the wilderness. Because of this were the various captivities and the many afflictions which had come upon them. When these resulted in exercise and repentance, the peaceable fruit of righteousness and repentance followed. To this the remnant had been called in chapters 7 and 8. Now the prophet points them on to the coming Saviour-King, that there might be heart-preparation for His reception. But the 11th chapter closes with the solemn prediction of the selling of the true Shepherd for thirty pieces of silver, and the consequent acceptance of the Idol-shepherd, the Antichrist.

The opening verses, 1 to 8, are occupied with the destruction of the Syrian power in "the land of Hadrach," together with all Israel's enemies bordering on the land of Palestine, preparatory to the extension of the promised kingdom; and evidently have a double application, setting forth, as they do, the past overthrow of the kingdoms ere the first coming of the Lord (which would have been final had He been received and owned as the Anointed of Jehovah), as well as the future doom of the powers which will be in those lands when comes the final triumph of the King of kings. In that day He will "encamp about His house," becoming as a wall of fire for the protection of His own, and every foe shall be destroyed, so that "no oppressor shall pass through them any more."

Through all these lands the victorious armies of Alexander passed, overthrowing all of the cities mentioned, in strict accordance with the prophetic Word. Damascus, Hamath, Tyre and Zidon, and the strongholds of the Philistines, were all alike subjugated, and some utterly ruined, to rise no more. Yet Judah and Jerusalem were spared, as if by direct divine intervention, and the Grecian armies became the protectors, in place of the destroyers, of the seed of Abraham.

The temple and city were preserved that in them might be carried out all that the prophets had spoken concerning the coming of the Just One, who was to suffer and to die there.

So in verse 9 we have recorded the words which Matt. 21: 4, 5 and John 12: 14, 15 tell us were directly fulfilled when the Lord Jesus Christ rode into Jerusalem amid the welcoming cries of the disciples, the children, and of the people. "Rejoice greatly, O daughter of Zion; shout, O daughter of Jerusalem: behold, thy King cometh unto thee: He is just, and having salvation: lowly, and riding upon an ass, and upon a colt the foal of an ass." Thus He came as the Prince of Peace, only to be eventually despised and set at naught. When He comes the second time, it will be as the Warrior-King on the white horse of victorious judgment (Rev. 19).

Between verse 9 and verse 10 this entire dispensation of grace comes in; for it is evident that the latter part of the chapter has never yet had its fulfilment. The King came, but was refused. His cross becomes the sign of salvation for all who trust Him; while He Himself has taken His seat on the Father's throne in the heavens. Never for one hour has He occupied the throne of David which is yet to be His. That throne He will take when He descends from the heavens with power and great glory. Then He will cut off all the enemies of Jerusalem, and

"He shall speak peace unto the heathen: and His dominion shall be from sea to sea, and from the river to the ends of the earth" (ver. 10). Only when He appears in person will these words come to pass. There can be no Millennium without Christ.

At His glorious revelation He will deliver Judah's prisoners out of the pit wherein is no water, through the blood of the covenant confirmed in His death, bringing salvation to these prisoners of hope, who will find in Him a stronghold and a defence from all their enemies—after He has rendered to Israel double for all their iniquities (Isa. 40:2; 61:7). Then shall Judah be as a strong bow in His hand, and Ephraim as a polished shaft, before whom the nations shall bow, owning the excellency of the God of Jacob (vers. 11-13).

Again we have to notice a secondary application of a part of this prophecy. Verses 13 to 16 seem to refer in measure to the Maccabean contest with Antiochus Epiphanes, type of the Antichrist of the last days. Then Jehovah raised up the sons of Zion against the sons of Greece, and made the army of Judah "as the sword of a mighty man." But undoubtedly the fuller interpretation is that which refers these words to the conflicts of the great tribulation, when, in their darkest hour of trial, "the Lord shall be seen over them, and His arrow shall go forth as the lightning," when He shall blow the trumpet for the defence of those who in their distress shall turn to Him with all their hearts.

He will "save them in that day as the flock of His people," when they shall become the jewels of His crown, brilliantly shining upon Immanuel's land (ver. 16). What a day of glory for the people so long hated and oppressed! They who have been accounted by many as the very off-scouring of the earth shall shine in unequaled brilliancy in the diadem of the Crucified, when they cry, "Blessed is He that cometh in the name of the Lord!" No longer will He be to them "without form or comeliness," and bereft of all beauty that would cause them to desire Him. On the contrary, as they gaze astonished upon His head once crowned with thorns and His visage once marred more than any man, they will cry, with rapturous amazement, "How great is His goodness, and how great is His beauty!" Then shall He feed them with bountiful hand, providing them with every needful blessing, so that "corn shall make the young men cheerful, and new wine the maids" (ver. 17). Fasting and sorrow will have ceased forever. The joy of an unending feast in the banqueting house will have begun with the banner of love waving over all.

CHAPTER X

THE GATHERING

THE chapter pursues the same general subject, detailing the glory which might long since have been enjoyed by Israel had they owned Messiah's claims, but which, consequent on their rejection of Him, has been in abeyance during the present period of the calling out of the Church, and will only be made good to the earthly people when they own Him, whom they once spurned, as the Anointed of Jehovah.

It will be noticed that all Israel are included, however (vers. 6, 7)—not merely Judah. At the appointed time a remnant from all of the twelve tribes will be brought into blessing and settled in the land of their fathers, never more to be uprooted by an enemy's hand.

Without the latter rain (see Joel 2:23 and notes) Palestine becomes little better than a wilderness, though in our day conservation of the waters and irrigation are made somewhat to answer in its place. But under natural conditions the former and the latter rains are required to ensure plenty and prosperity. Therefore we need not be surprised to find the prophets using the rains in a figurative sense. Spiritually, Israel has had her former rain, but a long season of drought has since come in. Now they are bidden to look up in hope, and ask of the Lord "rain in the time of the latter rain;" in response to which He pledges Himself to give showers of blessing. This is undoubtedly the outpouring of the Spirit predicted by Joel, which will surely take place at the time of the end.

Till then spiritual famine necessarily prevails. In their idols no comfort was to be found, so at the captivity they put them away; but they have been since like an unshepherded flock, taking their own course, and wandering in a dry, desolate land. The undershepherds and the leaders of the people, "the goats," have caused them to stray, thus incurring the Lord's anger, who is about to visit His flock (limited here to the house of Judah, for it was *they* who crucified the Lord of glory); and, bringing them once more under His control, they shall become "as His goodly horse in the battle" (vers. 1-3).

Out of him, that is, Judah, came forth the Corner-stone and the Nail. Both of these names I take to refer to Christ. He is the Head of the corner, and "it is evident that our Lord sprang out of Judah." He is also the Nail upon whom Jehovah will hang all the glory of His Father's house. (See Isa. 22: 22-24.)

But the Battle-bow and every exactor, or ruler, together shall likewise spring from Judah. The Battle-bow seems also to be used symbolically of the Lord when He rides forth in His might to overthrow all His enemies. With Him will be associated the rulers of Judah when the first dominion shall have returned to the royal tribe.

Victorious over all who have sought their destruction, the once feeble remnant shall become as mighty men treading down their enemies when led to certain triumph by the Lion out of Judah (ver. 5).

Every enemy at last overthrown, Jehovah will strengthen the house of Judah, and save the house of Joseph, bringing them again in mercy to their land, and making them one people, restoring them to His favor as though He had never cast them off (ver. 6), thus repealing the Lo-ammi sentence of Hos. 1: 9. The Jews, first brought back to their land in unbelief, will pass through the sorrows of the great tribulation, by means of which the remnant will be separated from the apostate mass. The ten tribes will be gathered later, and added to Judah and Benjamin, when Messiah Himself has appeared in glory. They had no direct part in the crucifixion of God's Son, so the special hour of trial is not for them.

The restoration will be far more than a political or national event giving them back to Palestine, their ancestral home. There will be a divine work in the souls of the people so long blinded, so that the veil of unbelief having been taken away, they shall rejoice in the Lord, and be glad in His presence. It will be the fulfilment of the type of the feast of tabernacles, the happiest season of all the year (ver. 7). Joying in conscious redemption, fruitfulness will again be theirs, and they shall increase as in the days of old.

The manner of their ancient deliverance (vers. 9-12) is used as a figure of this future one. They are to be gathered from all the lands of their captivity, to the land of promise, thus set in the midst of the nations, in accordance with the word of the Lord as to Jezreel, the seed of God (Hos. 2:22, 23—see the notes.) Passing in triumph through the sea of affliction* and the river of sorrow, they shall find in the Lord their God strength and victory, and shall walk at liberty in His name.

This is the universal testimony of Scripture as to the future glory of the nation now scattered and despised. Their blindness is to pass away; and, with the eyes of their heart enlightened, they will behold the beauty of Him who was once abhorred and crucified.

Thus shall their whole history become a lovely illustration of the precious words of Psalm 76: 10, "Surely the wrath of man shall praise Thee: the remainder of wrath shalt Thou restrain;" God will only permit so much evil as will ultimately glorify Him. Anything beyond that He will hold

---

* In verse 11 read, "He shall pass through the sea of affliction," as in R. V.,—not "with affliction," as the A. V. has it.

in check. How consolatory is this for the tried saint in any dispensation! How often is the spirit overwhelmed and the soul cast down! But faith can look up in the hour when all seems hopeless, and darkness overspreads the scene, knowing that,

> "God sits as Sovereign on His throne,
> And ruleth all things well."

He can make a way for His redeemed through the sea. His power can dry up the rivers, and make His people to pass over dry-shod. What will be true for Israel nationally, it is for every child of God to enjoy personally.

Zech. 10: 9-12 coalesces with Isa. 43: 1-7. "But now thus saith the Lord that created thee, O Jacob, and He that formed thee, O Israel, Fear not: for I have redeemed thee, I have called thee by thy name; thou art Mine. When thou passest through the waters, I will be with thee; and through the rivers, they shall not overflow thee: when thou walkest through the fire, thou shalt not be burned; neither shall the flame kindle upon thee. For I am the Lord thy God, the Holy One of Israel, thy Saviour: I gave Egypt for thy ransom, Ethiopia and Seba for thee. Since thou wast precious in My sight, thou hast been honorable, and I have loved thee: therefore will I give men for thee, and people for thy life. Fear not; for I am with thee: I will bring thy seed from the east, and gather thee from the west: I will say to the north, Give up; and to the south, Keep not back: bring My sons from far, and My daughters from the ends of the earth; even every one that is called by My name: for I have created him for My glory, I have formed him; yea, I have made him."

What human words could compare with this divine declaration of God's unchangeable purpose in regard to His earthly people! And by what perverse system of interpretation can such words be made to find their fulfilment in the present work of grace going on among the Gentiles? It is an instance of that high-mindedness which the apostle rebukes in Rom. 11, that such passages are wrested altogether from their true connection by unspiritual spiritualizers, and applied to the Church, whose heavenly calling is lost sight of, while Israel's hope is denied.

Only as one learns to rightly divide the word of truth do its various lines fall into order and its happy distinctions become plain to the anointed eye. The confusion will then be seen to exist, not in God's perfect Word, but in man's bewildered mind, controlled by tradition, and often clouded by self-sufficiency. Truth is learned in the conscience. If that be in exercise, the Holy Spirit, who is the Spirit of Truth, can be depended on to make plain the mind of the Lord to the simplest.

CHAPTER XI

"THIRTY PIECES OF SILVER"

SURPASSINGLY lovely have been the scenes briefly depicted in the preceding chapters. But the glory there promised is in abeyance during the present interval because of the rejection of the One upon whom it all depends. So we now have a sorrowful account of the scornful refusal of the Good Shepherd and the acceptance instead of the Anti-shepherd, who seeks only his own exaltation and cares not for the ruin and scattering of Jehovah's flock.

The two opening verses sound an alarm, and speak of woe and disaster. "Open thy doors, O Lebanon, that the fire may devour thy cedars. Howl, O fir tree; for the cedar is fallen; because the goodly ones are laid waste: howl, O ye oaks of Bashan; for the strong forest is come down" (R.V.). It is the solemn announcement of wrath upon the land and people because of the tragedy of the cross. Fire, in Scripture, speaks of God's holiness exerted in the judgment of what is opposed thereto. Against Judah it has been fiercely burning for centuries since the day when they cried, as to the Lord Jesus, "His blood be on us, and on our children." He had come in grace as the Shepherd of Israel to gather together and feed the poor of the flock; but though He came unto His own, His own received Him not; so desolation and dispersion ensued. The under-shepherds might well cry out in dismay, for they themselves had led the revolt against Him whose love would have been as a rod and staff in the hour of need. Their glory is spoiled, and the pride of Jordan likewise. No barrier any longer hindered the coming in of the lions of the wilderness, seeking to prey upon the flock of slaughter (ver. 3).

Zechariah is directed to act the part of the shepherd. He is to feed the flock whose buyers slay them and hold themselves guiltless. Unpitied by their own shepherds, they were appointed to death; but a remnant are distinguished, even the poor of the flock aforementioned (vers. 4-7).

In obedience to the command given, the prophet took two symbolic staves, and fed the flock. One staff was called Beauty; the other, Bands, or, Concord. They spoke of the pastoral care Israel is yet to know, when, with the beauty of the Lord her God upon her, she shall dwell in unity and concord as one nation in the land covenanted to Abraham. Then she will sing with joy, "Jehovah is my Shepherd; I shall not want. He causeth me to lie down in pastures of tender grass: by waters of rest He leadeth me."

All this they might now be in the happy enjoyment of had there been but ears to hear and a heart to understand when He who spake as never man spake cried, yearningly, "Come unto Me, all ye that labor and are heavy laden, and I will give you rest." But they turned a deaf ear and hardened their hearts to the voice of loving entreaty; so they must know to the full the bitterness of forsaking the only One who could meet their need, both nationally and spiritually. So Zechariah (in vision, I take it) cuts off the hireling shepherds, who loathed him, and whom he loathed, because of their unprincipled conduct. Three in one month are judged. But there is no recognition, on the part of the flock, of his tender care; so he gives them up too, that desolation and cutting-off, both by their enemies and internecine strife, may be their portion (vers. 7-9).

As signifying the breaking of Jehovah's covenant, which was forfeited by their sin, he destroyed the staff called Beauty—for all their loveliness was gone and they were unclean in His sight. But still a feeble remnant is distinguished, for God has ever preserved an election of grace; and so we read, "The poor of the flock that waited upon me knew that it was the word of the Lord" (vers. 10, 11).

Then, impersonating Messiah in a manner most striking, he said to them, "If ye think good, give me my price; and if not, forbear." They need no time to consider. All is settled in their minds. His rejection is fully determined upon before he speaks. At once they weigh for his price "thirty pieces of silver"; the very sum for which Judas afterwards sold the true Shepherd of Israel (ver. 12).

Observe, it was not merely the prophet who was estimated at this sum; but Jehovah speaks, saying, "Cast it unto the potter: a goodly price that *I* was prized at of them." By reference to Exod. 21:32 the irony of this expression, "a goodly price," becomes clearly manifest. Thirty pieces of silver was the value the law set on a slave who had been gored and slain by an ox. Such was the value man put upon Him who had been acquired as a bondman from His youth, See chap. **13:5, 6,** and notes.

The money was cast to the potter in the house of the Lord; and the other staff, Unity, or Concord, was broken, that it might display the breach between Judah and Israel (vers. 13, 14).

All this we see fulfilled to the letter in the case of the Lord Jesus. Sold for thirty pieces of silver, the wretched betrayer cast down the money in the house of the Lord; but, in blind obedience to the Word, which they seemed too dull to comprehend the import of, the chief priests gave it to the potter as the purchase-price of a field to bury strangers in. Such a potter's field, an Aceldama of wrath, has Palestine been ever since.*

---

* I do not consider it needful to go into the question of the reference to Jeremy the prophet in Matt. 27:9. Many theories have been suggested. The day will declare it.

But ere His rejection, our Lord said to the Jews, "I am come in My Father's name, and ye receive Me not: if another shall come in his own name, him ye will receive" (John 5: 43). He spoke, undoubtedly, of the wilful king, the personal Antichrist of the last days, who will be received by the Jews as the Messiah when he comes with all power and signs and lying wonders. This dreadful person, Zechariah is next called upon to set forth. He is directed by the Lord to take the instruments of a foolish shepherd and impersonate one who is to be raised up in the land, in whom Judah will vainly hope for deliverance. Unmarked by compassion for the flock, he will seek only his own ends, and "he shall eat the flesh of the fat, and tear their hoofs in pieces." Upon this impious wretch the judgment of indignant heaven is to descend; so we read, "Woe to the idol shepherd that leaveth the flock! the sword shall be upon his arm, and upon his right eye: his arm shall be clean dried up, and his right eye shall be utterly darkened" (vers. 15-17). His final doom is given in Rev. 19, where we see the false prophet cast alive into the lake of fire.

In our days of great achievement and marvelous advancement on all lines, we hear much of the *coming man*, the fully-developed, cultivated man of the twentieth century, upon which we have so recently entered. The expression refers, of course, to the vaunted progress of the race, not to any solitary individual; but it may well remind us of the two coming men spoken of in this chapter, and elsewhere in the book of God, though both are alike forgotten by people generally. God has *His* coming Man—the Man Christ Jesus. In speaking so of Him, the dignity of His Person should not be lost sight of. He is indeed declared to be "God over all, blessed forever" (Rom. 9: 5). Long before this century has run its course, He will perhaps have returned in glory to this world, which, having slain Him when He was here before, turned, Cain-like, to building cities, and making advancement in the arts and sciences, quite forgetful of the blood shed on Calvary's cross, which cries still unto God from the ground. (Compare Gen. 4: 8-22). It is not as often insisted on as it should be that there are *two* aspects in which the death of Christ is brought before us in the Bible, with widely different results. Viewed as His offering Himself a sacrifice to God for sin and sins, and suffering at the hand of God for guilt not His own, the result is free salvation and complete justification for all who believe in Him. On the other hand, viewed as the One rejected of earth, and suffering from the hands of wicked men, the result is dire and unmixed judgment on the ordered system of things called the world, that cast Him out. (These two aspects and results are especially presented to us in Psalms 22 and 69).

When He returns the second time, it will be

"without sin unto salvation" (Heb. 9:28), for all who have trusted Him as their Saviour, who will be "in the twinkling of an eye" changed and caught up together in the clouds to meet Him in the air (1 Cor. 15:51, 52; 1 Thess. 4:16, 17); but He will shortly after be revealed from heaven in flaming fire, to take vengeance on all who have rejected His grace (2 Thess. 1:7-10).

He is to be judge of both living and dead (2 Tim. 4: 1; 1 Pet. 4: 5). The living who have spurned His proffered mercy He will judge at His appearing to institute the kingdom long promised by the prophets (Rev. 20: 1-6; Isa. 32, 63, etc.). This is the judgment of the "sheep and goats" depicted in Matt. 25, and is premillennial. The wicked dead will be judged by Him when He sits on the Great White Throne, at the close of the ages of time.

Of the day or hour of His return no man knows, or can know. Computations are useless. "In such an hour *as ye think not* the Son of Man cometh." It behooves all, then, to be ready to meet the Coming Man, and not be ashamed before Him.

There is only *one* way by which any one born in sin and a transgressor by practice can be ready to face Him, the Holy and the True. All who trust Him are instantly cleansed from every sin by His precious blood. His work, finished when He was here before, is of such infinite value, and so thoroughly met all the claims of God's holiness, that all who believe are "made meet to be partakers of the inheritance of the saints in light" (Col. 1:12). If the reader has rested his soul upon Him as his Saviour, he will be ready to meet Him, and will be rapt away to be forever with Himself, if spared till He comes.

But Satan also has his "coming man," of whom our Lord spoke, as we have seen, in John 5:43. In the interval between the rapture of the Church and the appearing in glory of the Saviour, this monster of infamy, in himself a very incarnation of the devil, will arise to dazzle the eyes of the world by his unhallowed brilliancy and power. He will be Satan's masterpiece of deception, the false Christ, who will have sway over the minds and consciences of those who reject the love of the truth.

He is called "the son of perdition," linking him in character with that awful apostate who sold his Master for "thirty pieces of silver."

Think of men, men of greatest culture and erudition, bowing down before this vile creature, and owning him as their Lord! He is well called a "beast" in Rev. 13:11, though in appearance he is the counterfeit of the Lamb of God; but his speech is that of the dragon, "that old serpent, which is the devil, and Satan."

This is the coming man of the earth, as the Lord Jesus is the Coming Man from heaven.

Which, dear reader, will have your heart and

your allegiance? If you are left behind unsaved at the Lord's coming, you will worship Antichrist, for *God* will *send them strong delusion,* to those who obeyed not the truth, that they may believe the lie of "the man of sin," to their eternal condemnation (2 Thess. 2: 8-12).

May it be yours then, if still out of Christ, to "turn to God from idols to serve the living and true God, and to wait for His Son from heaven." Then your portion will be with that blessed Man in glory forever. If you turn from Him, awful must be your doom, with "the man of the earth," yea, and all the lost, in the lake of fire for eternity.

CHAPTER XII

THE TRUE DAY OF ATONEMENT FOR JUDAH

THE last three chapters relate almost entirely to the period denominated the great tribulation, or the time of Jacob's trouble, with the establishment of the kingdom following. To that short but solemn season our attention has already been directed in what we have been noticing as to the Antichrist. It is the moral result of the rejection of the Lord Jesus, and will be the final governmental display of Jehovah's wrath because of that colossal error on Judah's part.

He speaks of Himself in the first verse as the One which stretcheth forth the heavens, and layeth the foundation of the earth, and formeth the spirit of man within him.

This latter clause deserves our careful attention. God forms man's spirit within him. The spirit then is an entity existing distinct from the body. It is not to be confounded with the breath, nor is it merely the same as the mind. Mind is one of the functions of the spirit, for it is the seat of the intelligence. "What man knoweth the things of a man, save the spirit of man which is in him? Even so the things of God knoweth no man, but the Spirit of God" (1 Cor. 2: 11). It is impossible logically to deny the personality of man's spirit and not likewise deny the personality of the Spirit of God. The spirit is the real man, who inhabits the body during life, and at death puts off the tabernacle of flesh and goes out unclothed into the unseen world, called by the Jews *Sheol,* by the Greeks *Hades.* This is not the grave, but the condition of departed spirits, whether saved or lost. The spirit of the believer is "absent from the body and present with the Lord." That of the unsaved is "in torment," but awaiting the final judgment, when "death and Hades will be emptied into the lake of fire" (Rev. 20:15).

Sadducees of every stripe deny the true personality of the spirit, as an unseen something formed within the man our eyes behold. God links this special creation with that of the heavens and the earth. "Thus saith God the Lord, He that created the heavens, and stretched them out; He that spread forth the earth, and that which cometh out of it; He that giveth breath unto the people upon it, and spirit to them that walk therein" (Isa. 42:5). Here breath and spirit are clearly distinguished. The one is fleeting, the other exists forever. True, it is but incidentally, as we would say, this statement as to the spirit of man is here introduced; but it is all-important nevertheless, and a distinct guard againt Sadduceeism, if carefully considered.

In verse 2 Jerusalem, the centre of all God's ways as to the earth, is introduced, and a siege spoken of, which is evidently that of the last days. Jersualem is then to be a cup of trembling, or reeling—that is, an intoxicating draught—unto all nations. Possessed with an almost insane desire to control the ancient city which is recognized by all as the key of the East, they will make desperate attempts to obtain suzerainty over it. But it shall prove to be then, as it has been down through the centuries, a burdensome stone. Every nation burdening itself with it shall be destroyed, even though a coalition were effected for this purpose between all the people of the prophetic earth (ver. 3).

There will be a number of powers, however, each acting for itself, in the time of the tribulation. The Roman empire will be revived in the form of ten kingdoms voluntarily associated together, and giving their support to that impious character denominated the Beast in the first part of Rev. 13, whose seat will be in Rome, proudly called the Eternal City. In Jerusalem itself the Antichrist will reign, having made a league, offensive and defensive, with the Beast. He is the second Beast of Rev. 13, who simulates the Lamb of God, but whose dragonic speech betrays his real character.

Against him, as prophesied in Dan. 11, two rival powers will set themselves, endeavoring to obtain Jerusalem and destroy him and each other, namely, the kings of the north and of the south. That is, an Egyptian power will attain some prominence and aspire to Palestine in that time of trouble, but will be opposed by a northern power inhabiting the territory now called Turkey in Asia. This is identical with the Assyrian so frequently mentioned.

Farther north will be the great empire of Gog, the last enemy to come against Jerusalem, which is undoubtedly Russia, ever the inveterate enemy of the Jews, and grasping eagerly after their land. The end of this power is foretold in Ezek. 38 and 39.

Another confederacy is mentioned in Revelation as "the kings of the east," or, "the sun-rising;" but it would seem as though the hordes of these nations barely reach the land ere the judgment falls. It is significant that Japan is called the kingdom of the rising sun. Who can say that the German emperor's fear of "the yellow peril" is not based on something more substantial than a political nightmare?

In the time of the end, mighty armies will be gathered from all quarters against Jerusalem just before the appearing of Messiah in glory. They will clash together in the great battle of Armageddon, long since predicted by the prophets, and briefly depicted in verses 4 and 5, but more fully described in chapter 14 and in Rev. 19.

Following upon the utter discomfiture of all Israel's foes, government will be established firmly in Judah, and Jerusalem shall be rebuilt in unequaled splendor, and inhabited by a redeemed and happy people (ver. 6).

The ten tribes will be regathered after the kingdom is set up. The tents of Judah are to be saved first, then the house of David distinguished from them, and one taken therefrom, who shall act as prince-regent on earth for the true Son of David who will reign from heaven. Afterwards, as we learn from various scriptures, the ten tribes will ask the way to Zion, and will return from all the countries whither they have been driven.

Thus will that ideal state have been reached, so long anticipated by inspired seers, when the Lord Himself shall be the defence of His people, and the weakest among them shall be as David, the heroic defender of the liberties of Israel, whose house shall be in direct communication with heaven, thus establishing a pure theocracy on earth, when every enemy shall be destroyed and peace and good will everywhere prevail (vers. 7, 8).

All this the chosen people might long since have been in the enjoyment of, had they but obeyed the Spirit's call to repentance as given in the 2d of Acts. It was a summons to self-judgment and humiliation in Jehovah's presence because of their national crime, the crucifixion of the Messiah. All their blessings wait for this, which will mark their entering into the truth of the atoning value of the work of the Lord Jesus. Only then will they in spirit have reached the great feast of the seventh month, the true day of atonement.

There is important instruction as to this in the 23rd chapter of Leviticus. There we have the yearly calendar of the seven great feasts. The sabbath is introduced as the symbol of the rest which is to follow all the dispensations when the course of time has come to a close, as declared in Heb. 3:10—4:11.

The passover prefigures the Cross, even as we are told that "Christ our passover was sacrificed for us." This is immediately followed by the feast of unleavened bread; so the passage referred to goes on to say, "Therefore let us keep the feast, not with old leaven, neither with the leaven of malice and wickedness, but with the unleavened bread of sincerity and truth" (1 Cor. 5:7,8). This sets forth the call to repentance, now extended to Jew and Gentile alike, who, resting beneath the sheltering blood of the slain Lamb, are to be found in holy separation from all evil, waiting the hour of their full redemption.

But this does not necessarily imply the heavenly calling; so we next get the day of Pentecost, or the feast of weeks, when a new meal-offering was presented before Jehovah, setting forth the present truth of the mystery never made known till the final rejection of the testimony of the Lord and His apostles by Israel as a nation. Observe that this was in the third month.

Then there is a long break, until the seventh month. Now, as it is clear that Pentecost includes the calling out of a people for the name of the Lord from among the nations, it is evident that all the feasts of the seventh month have reference particularly to Israel when the fulness of the Gentiles shall have come in, and the trumpet of recall will once more summon God's earthly people to gather around Himself in the land of their fathers. That trumpet will blow when the Church has been caught up to heaven. This the feast of trumpets beautifully pictures. It is the awakening of Israel when the veil shall begin to be taken away. (See Rom. 11, *et al.*). Then will come the call to self-abasement and contrition of heart for their fearful sin, which was manifested in the cross, and consummated in the rejection of the Holy Ghost. This is, for them, the great day of atonement. Long centuries have elapsed since the Victim bled, but they have never yet kept the day of fasting and affliction of soul that God joined with the offering up of the sacrifice to make atonement for their souls.

To this they will come in the hour of their deep distress, just prior to the appearing of the Crucified in the glory of His Father, and all His holy ones with Him. This, therefore, is the mourning referred to in Rev. 1: 7, and here, in verses 10 to 14. In the Apocalyptic passage we read, "Behold, He cometh with clouds; and every eye shall see

Him . . . and *all tribes of the land shall mourn over Him.*" It is not wailing in terror that is contemplated, but the anguished mourning of the awakened remnant when they realize the dreadful impiety of which their fathers were guilty in crucifying the Lord of glory.

God Himself will pour upon the house of David and the inhabitants of Jerusalem the spirit of grace and supplications, and "they shall look upon Me whom they have pierced, and they shall mourn for Him, as one mourneth for his only son, and shall be in bitterness for Him, as one that is in bitterness for his first-born" (ver. 10). The word "look" might be rendered "contemplate." It implies an earnest attention, beholding with thoughtfulness, that every lineament of His face may be imprinted upon their souls. His once-marred visage, His pierced hands and side—all will be indelibly impressed upon them. When they thus learn that He who was spurned as a malefactor and a blasphemer was really the Lord of glory, their grief and repentance will know no bounds.

We have two New Testament pictures of this scene: Thomas the apostle, called Didymus (the twin), believed when he saw. In the remnant of Judah, the other twin—may I say?—will come to the front, equally unbelieving till the marks of spear and nails shall prove convincing.

Then in Saul of Tarsus we have a preeminent

picture of the same remnant. Hating the name of Jesus, he goes on his way, zealously persecuting all who love that name, till arrested by a light from heaven: his eyes, blinded to earth's glory, peer into the holiest; and there, upon the throne of God, he beholds the Nazarene! Thus he was one born before the time; that is, before the time when, by a similar sight, the remnant will be brought to cry, as he did, "Lord, what wilt Thou have me to do?"

His days and nights of darkness answer to the period of mourning here set forth. "In that day shall there be a great mourning in Jerusalem, as the mourning of Hadadrimmon in the valley of Megiddon" (ver. 11). The reference is generally supposed to be to the great grief that fell on Judah when Josiah was slain, in the same valley where the Lord is yet to appear for the judgment of the armies of the haters of His earthly people. Megiddon is, of course, Armageddon, the valley of slaughter, of Revelation 16:16.

In vers. 12 to 14 the people are distinguished into various classes. The family of the house of David, the royalty of Judah, mourn apart. The house of Nathan, the very prophet who once reproved David for his sin, mourn also apart. Then there are the families of Levi and of Shimei, or Simeon, once joined in iniquity, now each joining, though apart, in common confession because of sin.

So shall every family participate in the affliction of soul that extends to the glorious appearing of Him who long since entered into the heavenly sanctuary by His own blood.

Another feast closes the series in Lev. 23. Of that, chapter 14 of our prophet treats; so I leave it till we reach that portion.

CHAPTER XIII

THE FOUNTAIN OPENED AND THE SHEPHERD SMITTEN

IMMEDIATELY linked with the time when Israel shall have reached, in spirit, the day of atonement, the fountain is provided for cleansing from all defilement which the first verse of this chapter announces. When the Spirit of God has wrought repentance in the remnant, the word of God will at once be applied in cleansing.

It is *to* (not "in," as people often attempt to quote it) the house of David and to the inhabitants of Jerusalem that the fountain is opened in order that they may be morally cleansed from all sin and uncleanness, in accordance with the testimony of Ezekiel (chap. 36: 24-27): "For I will take you from among the heathen, and gather you out of all countries, and will bring you into your own land. *Then will I sprinkle clean water upon you,* and ye shall be clean: from all your filthiness, and from all your idols, will I cleanse you. A new heart also will I give you, and a new spirit will I put within you: and I will take away the stony heart out of your flesh, and I will give you a heart of flesh. And I will put My Spirit within you, and cause you to walk in My statutes, and ye shall keep My judgments, and do them."

The day of atonement brings them to the cross. The next step is the laver, to which the fountain answers. Observe well, it is not, as Christian poets have sung, "a fountain filled with *blood,*" but of living *water*—the word of God applied in the Spirit's power to their consciences. The same truth is taught in the Lord's washing His disciples' feet, the laver of regeneration, and the washing of water by the Word, but all in connection with the present dispensation. So from the side of the crucified Saviour flowed both blood and water — blood, to *expiate* sin before God; water, to *cleanse* the ways and keep the saint free from defilement.

As the power of the truth is brought home to the remnant, it will lead them to judge all iniquity and to put away all uncleanness. Idolatry will become as an evil dream when it is past, and deceivers of all kinds will "pass out of the land" (ver. 2).

As all prophecy will have come to its glorious fulfilment, the office of the prophet shall cease. Any essaying that rôle will be judged even by his own parents (vers. 3, 4).

But One there is in contrast to the false prophets in every way, even the One for whom they shall mourn when they are brought to see how they have sinned against Him. "He shall say, I am no prophet, I am a husbandman; for man acquired Me as a servant from My youth." Some have followed the rabbis in applying these words, and those following, to the deceivers; but it seems far clearer, and more in keeping with the context, to apply them to the Lord Jesus Christ. He was acquired as a servant from His youth, and, like the devoted slaves of Exod. 21, for love of His own He would not go out free. To Him the wondering remnant cry, "What are these wounds in Thy hands?" He replies, "Those with which I was wounded in the house of My friends." What grace, that He should so speak of Judah, who knew Him not when He came among them in lowliness (vers. 5, 6).

But He could never have been wounded by them, had it not been according to the purpose of God that He should be made a sin-offering. So at once we read, "Awake, O sword, against My Shepherd, and against the Man that is My Fellow, saith Jehovah: smite the Shepherd, and the sheep shall be scattered: and I will turn My hand upon the little ones" (ver. 7). Clearly the smitten Shepherd here is the wounded One of the preceding verses. There, it was man's treatment of Him that was emphasized. Here, it is the solemn fact that God's judgment fell upon Him when, for our sins, He was smitten on the cross. There, as the Good Shepherd, He gave His life for the sheep, and endured divine wrath, that all who trust in Him might be forever secure from the well-deserved vengeance of Jehovah's insulted throne. So the words are directly applied in Matt. 26:31. The Shepherd was smitten by Jehovah Himself. The sheep were for the moment scattered, but God's hand is turned in grace to the little ones who are lowly enough to own their guilt and trust in Him whose precious blood cleanseth from every stain. To the remnant, the value of His work will be made known when their blindness has passed away, and they will be numbered among the feeble and the poor in spirit who cast themselves upon redeeming grace.

Not all Israel, however, nor yet all of Judah, shall be saved. But of those restored to the land after the Church has been rapt away to heaven, two parts will be cut off in death during the time of Jacob's trouble. The third part will be brought through the fiery trials of the great tribulation, and will be refined as silver and purified as gold. They shall call upon Jehovah's name, and He will respond to them in grace and loving-kindness.

To them He will say, "It is My people," thus reversing the Lo-ammi sentence of Hosea, chap. 1; while they in turn shall cry with hearts uplifted at the thought of such abounding mercy, "Jehovah is my God!"

Their salvation will be thus of a double character, as was that of their fathers of old, wherever faith was in exercise, who were brought to God and saved from Egyptian bondage.

The closing chapter gives us the details of their deliverance from their enemies, and does not leave them till they are seen keeping the happiest feast of all the year—that of the tabernacles—with the assured sense of the favor of Jehovah.

CHAPTER XIV

THE TRUE FEAST OF TABERNACLES

DEEP indeed is the darkness with which this chapter opens, but gloriously brilliant the light at the close.

Of all Jerusalem's sieges in the past, none were more severe than that depicted in the first two verses. They describe conditions which careful students of history admit have never been known in any past destruction of the city, and can only apply to something yet future.

"Behold, the day of Jehovah cometh, and thy spoil shall be divided in the midst of thee. For I will gather all nations against Jerusalem to battle; and the city shall be taken, and the houses rifled, and the women ravished; and half of the city shall go forth into captivity, and the residue of the people shall not be cut off from the city" (vers. 1, 2). From east, west, north and south, the armies of the nations will have advanced upon Jerusalem, hating the people and city of God, but mutually hating each other.

Antichrist will be owned by the apostate Jews within the city as the Messiah and King of Judah. But against him the Assyrian, or king of the north, and the king of the south (terms used relative to Palestine), will pour their hordes into the land in one last desperate effort to wrest from this wicked king his brief authority. Behind the Assyrian power will be Gog, the last prince of Rosh, Meshech, and Tubal—undoubtedly the head of the vast Russian empire. Allied with him will apparently be the kings from the sun-rising, or the far east, whose armies will hasten to join him in his assault on Jerusalem.

On the other hand, the Beast, the elected emperor of the confederacy forming the revived Roman Empire, will be the sworn foe of all these hostile powers, and the arm upon which Antichrist will lean. From every part of western and southern Europe he will draw his vast armies, who will be imbued with equal hate against both the faithful remnant of Judah and the Assyrian coalition.

Between these conflicting powers Jerusalem's position will be a most pitiable one. Unable to maintain the dreadful struggle, the city will be taken, and the horrors of a sack be again undergone.

But when, as it would seem, no power, human or divine, could prevent its total extinction, the Lord shall go forth, staining all His raiment in the blood of the adversaries of His people, fighting as a mighty warrior in the day of battle (ver. 3). Before the eyes of the astonished armies of the world He will appear in glory, and He "shall stand upon the mount of Olives," from which He ascended to heaven when He had by Himself made purification for sins.

As His feet touch that sacred spot, a great earthquake will rend the mount asunder, which will depart to the east and to the west, opening up a deep valley, through which the remnant of His people shall flee for refuge unto Azal (a spot now unknown), which will be as a Zoar for the faithful residue, when judgment is about to sweep over the scene. Thus will they be hidden in the day of the Lord's anger till the indignation be overcast.

This section closes, if properly punctuated, with the declaration, "Yea, ye shall flee, like as ye fled from before the earthquake in the days of Uzziah king of Judah." Here there should be a full stop. Of this earthquake in the days of Uzziah we have no specific record, though it is generally supposed to be the one referred to in Amos 1:1. The reference to it here completes the dramatic account of the siege and the deliverance. A new beginning is made in the last clause of the 5th verse, which introduces an orderly account of the appearing in glory of the Lord Jesus and all His heavenly saints, and the blessed results that follow. "The Lord My God shall come, and all the holy ones with Thee!" Thus shall be ushered in that glorious kingdom which has been so long predicted. Not by the preaching of the gospel and the conversion of the world will this event be brought to pass. Nothing less than the personal presence of the Son of God will ever bring in the Millennium. The holy ones who will come with Him include all the heavenly hosts—angels, and redeemed sinners transformed into glorified saints. 1 Thess. 4 and 1 Cor. 15:51-57 make it plain that ere the time of trouble begins for Israel all the saved of every past dispensation will be caught up to meet their Lord in the air.

> "Dead and living, changed and rising,
> In the twinkling of an eye."

They will appear at His judgment-seat, to be rewarded according to the services rendered to

Himself while in this scene. Then the Church as the Bride, and all Old Testament saints as the called and chosen guests, will participate in the marriage supper of the Lamb, which is to be celebrated in the Father's house. After the happy nuptial rites, the Lord Jesus, accompanied by all His holy ones, will descend to take His earthly kingdom, and to deliver the remnant of Israel and Judah from their cruel and blasphemous adversaries.

This will take place on "one day which shall be known to Jehovah," a day which no human method of computation can determine. The exact meaning of verses 6 and 7 has puzzled the most scholarly; but this much seems clear, that it shall be a day diverse from every other, beginning in deepest gloom and darkness, but, brightened by the outshining of the Sun of Righteousness, "at evening time it shall be light." So will the morning without clouds have dawned upon this poor world, where night has held sway so long.

Probably as a result of the great earthquake, predicted in verses 4 and 5, will be the phenomena of verse 8. According to the word of the Lord given in Ezek. 47:1-12 and Joel 3:18, living waters shall go out from Jerusalem—a perennial stream of refreshment, dividing into two parts, half going toward the eastern sea and half toward the western. Of spiritual blessing likewise does this speak, for it sets before us also that river of God's pleasure, the Holy Spirit's testimony to the glories of Christ, which will be as a stream of life and joy to the saved nations.

Remarkable physical changes will take place in Palestine. The valleys exalted, and mountains leveled, the country will become as a great tableland from Geba on the north to Rimmon, south of Jerusalem. This sacred city will be inhabited in security, and her day of trembling be forever past, for the Lord shall be King over all the earth, and be everywhere owned as the one Jehovah, and His name one (vers. 9-11).

The nations who will have shown no mercy to Jerusalem will be dealt with in judgment without mercy, a plague consuming their flesh, and internecine strife, or civil feud, causing them to destroy each other. Satan himself was an anarchist in the beginning. His kingdom is a kingdom of anarchy, knowing neither love nor pity (vers. 12, 13).

Judah will become as the battle-axe of the Lord in that day of His power, victorious over every foe, and enriched by the spoil of those who would fain have spoiled them. Retributive justice will thus be visited on all oppressors when righteousness shall no longer suffer, but reign triumphant over every adversary (vers. 14, 15).

Then shall the last joyful feast of the Levitical calendar be actually reached (that of the tabernacles), which was to be observed after the ingathering for a full week, culminating in the holy convocation of the eighth day—looking on to eternity (Lev. 23: 33-43). The sowing, and the long period of waiting for the harvest, over, the reaping time will have come, when joy and praise will fill every heart and songs of thanksgiving be upon every lip.

Nor shall Israel keep her feast alone, but all the nations that are left for the kingdom shall go up from year to year to Jerusalem, there to worship the King, the Lord of hosts, and to join with His people (they themselves being numbered among them) in celebrating the glorious ingathering, as they dwell in booths of verdure, as of old it was written in the Book. It will be a sweet and lovely ending after centuries, yea, millenniums, of bitter strife and bloody warfare, when the noise of battle shall be no more heard, national hatreds shall be done away, and the era of peace on earth and God's good pleasure in men shall have in very deed arrived.

If, as seems to be intimated in verses 17 to 19, at the beginning, there be any dissentients who shall dare to refuse to wend their way to the city of the great King to worship before Him, immediate judgment shall fall upon them. The heavens will be closed so that their lands will be parched for lack of rain; that they may know that the time when God is directly governing the world shall have at last arrived. If the family of

Egypt go not up, who depend not on rain, but on the yearly inundation of the Nile for the fertilization and maturing of their crops, then a special visitation shall be theirs, a plague "wherewith the Lord shall smite the heathen that come not up to keep the feast of tabernacles."

In this age men may defy God and seem to prosper. In that, which is so soon to come, godliness and prosperity will be linked together. It will be the dispensation of the fulness of the seasons, when all things shall be headed up in Christ, and every knee must bow to Him—when men will no longer walk by faith, as now, but by the sight of their eyes, beholding on every hand the evidences of direct divine intervention in human affairs.

The last two verses form a fitting climax to the chapter and the book. "In that day shall there be upon the bells of the horses, HOLINESS UNTO THE LORD; and the pots in the Lord's house shall be like the bowls before the altar. Yea, every pot in Jerusalem and in Judah shall be holiness unto the Lord of hosts: and all they that sacrifice shall come and take of them, and seethe therein: and in that day there shall be no more the Canaanite in the house of the Lord of hosts." No longer will a distinction be made between sacred and secular; but men will have learned that anything worth doing at all should be done for the glory of God. The articles for temple service (used in the rebuilt temple of Ezek. 40 to 48) will be sacred to Jehovah. But so will also be every vessel used by the house-wife in Jerusalem and in Judah; while the very bells upon the horses will tinkle His praises. This is the lovely ideal the Holy Ghost portrays for Christians living in the present age; as it is written, "Let the word of Christ dwell in you richly in all wisdom; teaching and admonishing one another in psalms and hymns and spiritual songs, singing with grace in your hearts to the Lord. And whatsoever ye do in word or deed, do all in the name of the Lord Jesus, giving thanks to God and the Father by Him" (Col. 3: 16, 17). And, again, we are told, "Whether therefore ye eat, or drink, or whatsoever ye do, do all to the glory of God" (1 Cor. 10: 31). He who thus has God's glory ever before Him, even in the smallest details of life, will anticipate the Millennium, and already enter into what shall by-and-by be true of restored Israel under the reign of the Lord Jesus Christ.

There will be no drudgery then, no mere working for reward, for the Canaanite will have ceased out of the land in that day. Undoubtedly the name refers to the ancient enemy who ever contested Israel's possession of the promised inheritance; but it bears the meaning of "trafficker," or "bargainer," to whom, in Hos. 12:7, we have seen the sons of Jacob are compared. When ill feeling between Abraham and Lot was so narrowly averted through the generosity of the former, it is significantly stated that "the Canaanite . . . dwelt then in the land" (Gen. 13:7). When all strife and bitterness shall be done away in Abraham's redeemed seed, the Canaanite will have passed out of the scene for all time to come.

This is Israel's hope: the possession of the land pledged to their fathers, under the sway of Him whom David called,

> "A righteous Ruler over men,
> A Ruler in the fear of God!"

even our adorable Lord Jesus Christ; when in His own times He shall show, who is that blessed and only Potentate, King of kings, and Lord of lords. Ours is a higher and holier portion, even to be the Bride of Him who is then to reign. We look to heaven, not to earth, for our inheritance, from whence we expect that very soon now "the Lord Himself shall descend . . . with a shout, with the voice of the archangel, and with the trump of God: and the dead in Christ shall rise first: then we which are alive and remain shall be caught up together with them in the clouds, to meet the Lord in the air: and so shall we ever be with the Lord" (1 Thess. 4:16, 17).

Thus the two callings are clearly distinguished in Scripture. Israel is the wife of Jehovah, now divorced because of her sin, but to be brought back to Himself in grace and made to dwell in her former land in the day when the kingdom is displayed. The Church of the present dispensation is the Bride of the Lamb, whose nuptial hour is drawing near, and who will be one with her Redeemer throughout all the ages to come. Old Testament saints, and tribulation saints who are taken away by death ere the kingdom is set up, will be, as was John the Baptizer, friends of the Bridegroom, "called" to the marriage-supper of the Lamb, to participate in their Lord's rejoicing, and able also to share in Jehovah's joy when the earthly Bride shall return to His arms of love and compassion. In heaven their position will be analogous to that of the spared of the nations on earth, who will rejoice with Israel when they see the place she will have in the millennial kingdom.

Thus are there various companies and varied glories in heaven and upon earth; but when the authority of the Lord Jesus is owned in both spheres, and every enemy has been banished and rendered powerless, all redeemed creation will delight to ascribe blessing and honor and glory and power to our God and to the Lamb that was slain, world without end. Amen.

Notes on the PROPHECY OF MALACHI

CHAPTER I

THE FAILED REMNANT

WE know nothing whatever of the writer of this book. His name, Malachi, meaning "My messenger," occurs in verse 1; but we read of him nowhere else in Scripture, and we get no particulars concerning him here. He was the last of the prophetic band, and his book appropriately closes the Old Testament canon. Till the advent of John the Baptist, of whose coming he prophesied, no other messenger was directly sent to Judah from God.

The conditions he describes fit in well with what is recorded of the state of the returned remnant in the latter period of Nehemiah's governorship. So it is quite likely that he lived and ministered the word of Jehovah either during that time, or a little later.

The divisions are not very pronounced. In this first chapter, and going on to the 9th verse of the next, the prophet gives a message to the priests, while the balance of the book is addressed to the people, but includes more than the remnant, and really amounts to an indictment of all Judah.

Chapters 3 and 4 tell of the coming of the day of the Lord, to be preceded by the one who, like Malachi himself, will in a distinctive sense bear the title of "My messenger."

A striking feature of the prophecy is the eightfold controversy of Jehovah with His people. Notice chapter 1, verses 2, 6 and 7; chapter 2, verses 14 and 17; chapter 3, verses 7, 8, and 13. Again and again they are solemnly charged with gravest departure in heart from the Lord whom they outwardly professed to serve, and each time with brazen effrontery, they dare to contradict God's testimony to their state, ask for proofs, and manifest an utterly calloused conscience.

All this has a voice of exceeding seriousness for us, particularly if in any measure we seek to take the ground they did. Almost at the end of a dispensation, there had been an outward return to God and to His word; but there was not a corresponding subjective state. They became occupied rather with *place* and *position* than with vital godliness. As a result, we have the gross Phariseeism of our Lord's day, which was simply the outgrowth of the conditions described by Malachi.

Sad as Judah's state had become, it is of love, not of judgment, that the opening chapters treat. "I have loved you, saith the Lord." What could be more tender, more calculated to touch the hearts of His people, if indeed they had any heart left, and were not altogether hardened and unconcerned! Unchanging was that mighty love of His, whatever the perversity of their ways. Yet, with supreme contempt, they impudently retort, "Wherein hast Thou loved us?" They looked for temporal prosperity and worldly glory as the proof of His love. Bereft of both, they called His affection in question, utterly ignoring the prolonged course of carelessness and infidelity to Himself, for which He had chastened them. Patiently He deigns to reply to their caviling query: "Was not Esau Jacob's brother? saith the Lord; yet I loved Jacob, and I hated Esau." And He goes on to picture the desolations of Edom, and to declare that they shall never be retrieved, for the seed of Esau are "the people against whom the Lord hath indignation forever." On the other hand, though Israel's blessing seem to tarry, it shall surely come at last, so that all nations shall confess, "The Lord will be magnified from the border of Israel" (vers. 1-5).

It is His dealings with Jacob and Esau after long centuries had shown what they really were that are referred to. The phrase, "Jacob have I loved, but Esau have I hated," is quoted triumphantly by the apostle in Rom. 9: 13 to prove the wisdom of God's choice made before the children were born, when He said, "The elder shall serve the younger." Carefully observe, there is no hyper-Calvinistic question here of reprobation for hell and predestination for heaven. It is Jehovah's inalienable right to dispose of His creatures as He will, that the apostle is contending for; and He manifests with holy joy that He *wills* to show mercy to those who deserved only wrath. Jacob and Esau are cited as illustrations. Before either was born, God chose Jacob to be superior to Esau, nationally. The elder was to serve the younger, and thus own the superiority of God's choice. Then, when the whole Old Testament history had come to a close, He sums up all, and says, "I have loved Jacob, and hated Esau." The grace which took the poor heel-catcher up at first, was shown to his seed to the very end.

But what return had He received from Israel for all this? It is clear duty for a son to honor his father, and a servant his master; but what honor had He received as a Father, or what reverence as a Master? Even the very priests in the newly-restored temple despised His name. But when the charge is brought, they superciliously inquire, "Wherein have we despised Thy name?" (ver. 6).

Solemnly He brings their sins before them, declaring that polluted bread was offered on His altar, thus failing to own His holiness, and ignoring His claims. Again they are ready to answer back, ere the reply to their former question is complete, asking, "Wherein have we polluted Thee?" On His part there is amazing patience and grace; on theirs, almost incomprehensible insensibility and levity. They practically said, "The table of Jehovah is contemptible;" for they offered the blind, the lame and the sick to Him in sacrifice, and kept the best for themselves. Would they dare to so act toward their governor, or any other earthly ruler? Yet He, the great King, they could treat in a manner so unbecoming. But He pleads with them to repent, and cry to Him for that grace they were ignoring, yet needed so much. Covetousness was the root-sin that was leading them daily farther astray. The priests would not so much as shut the temple doors save for wages, nor kindle the altar-fire except for gain. True love for Himself was lacking, and their holy office had been prostituted to a mere worldly profession, and used as a means of enrichment. Because of this, He could have no pleasure in them, nor accept an offering at their hands (vers. 9, 10).

It seems almost unnecessary to attempt to draw attention to the similar state prevailing in so many places at the present time. Is it not patent to even the least spiritual that worldliness and covetousness are the characteristic features in the professing Church, and godliness and true devotion the exceptions?

Even where there has been a measure of revival and return to what is written in the word of God, the same evil principles have crept in insidiously, and are doing their deadly work in many quarters. Nothing but a spirit of prayerfulness, coupled with careful watchfulness, will keep any from being carried away by the unholy current.

But it is blessed to know that, whatever the present failure, God shall yet be fully glorified; so we read, "From the rising of the sun even unto the going down of the same, My name shall be great among the nations; and in every place incense shall be offered unto My name, and a pure offering: for My name shall be great among the nations, saith the Lord of hosts" (ver. 11). It is hardly the present work of grace among the Gentiles that is here contemplated, but rather that wonderful era of blessing which is still in the future — the times of restitution of all things spoken by the mouth of all the holy prophets since the ages began. Then shall Jehovah's name be honored and His word obeyed throughout the whole earth, when all nations shall bask in the sunshine of His favor.

In the next verse the prophet reverts to the serious charge made above. Judah profaned the table of the Lord, characterizing it as a thing polluted, and its meat contemptible. They declared it a weariness to attend upon its service, and made light of what should have been both sacred and precious. Their wretched thoughts were manifested by the unsuitable offerings they brought, which He would not accept, but, instead, invoked a curse upon the deceiver who brought Him that which was corrupt, while keeping the better for himself. Was it thus they would treat the King of kings, whose name was to be reverenced among the heathen? (vers. 13, 14). They who had known so much of His power and grace had proven altogether unworthy of His love. But the nations who had been passed by during the time of Israel's special favor were yet to bow at His feet and own His greatness and glory.

They who have never learned the distinctive character of the Spirit's work in this dispensation invariably apply such passages to the present outgoing of the gospel to the Gentiles; but while they may indeed, and do, prove that the call of the nations now is not out of harmony with the scriptures of the prophets, all these promises will have their complete and literal fulfilment in the Millennium. We wait in faith for brighter and more glorious hopes to be consummated.

Let shame be upon us if our state be in any wise like that depicted in the solemn chapter we have thus briefly gone over!

CHAPTER II

THE SIN OF THE PRIESTS

IN a fuller and more pointed manner are the sins of the priesthood brought home to their consciences in this second chapter. Anointed for temple service, set apart to holiness, and devoted to the most sacred of all offices, "ordained for men, in things pertaining to God, to offer gifts and sacrifices," they had proved recreant to their sacred trust, and thought only of their own profit. "Supposing that gain is godliness," they lost no opportunity of ministering to their own desires, while neglecting their holy calling.

There is no such official sacerdotal order recognized by God in the present dispensation, but all believers are now anointed priests, both holy and royal, having immediate access to the holiest in virtue of the blood of Jesus. As worshipers they go in to God to offer up spiritual sacrifices. As royal priests separated to Himself, they come out to show His praises to a needy world, and as holy priests they are appointed to intercede on behalf of those who pray not for themselves. What cause, then, for shame and humiliation when our feet stumble and our paths are crooked! All that is here said to the earthly priesthood may well be pondered by the heavenly company, as we challenge our consciences as to whether we too have not failed grievously, as they did.

"O ye priests, this commandment is for you." Thus clearly and distinctly the hierarchy is addressed in verse 1. If they refused to hear and heed the word so solemnly given, the Lord would send a grievous curse upon them, cursing their blessings, as He had already begun to do. Their seed should be rejected, and thus the family of Levi set aside from their appointed place of privilege, as has been the case ever since the rending of the veil, though only manifestly since Jerusalem's destruction by the Romans under Titus. Their solemn feasts too should be polluted, and they themselves rendered unclean, ceremonially, to set forth the uncleanness of their hearts and hands (vers. 2, 3).

Of old His covenant of life and peace had been with Levi, when he was separated from his brethren to find his all in God. For the fear wherewith he feared Jehovah, when Israel made the calf in the wilderness (Exod. 32:25-29), an everlasting covenant had been confirmed to him; but this should not hinder the outpouring of divine wrath during the season of Israel's dispersion because of their sins. No longer were they afraid before His name, as they had been in those days of the wilderness. Then the law of truth was in their mouths and iniquity was not found in their lips, when in singleness of heart they walked with God in peace and equity, and were His honored instruments in executing judgment upon evil (vers.

4-6). It is a lovely description of true devotion to the Lord. Only as the priest thus keeps his heart and guards his ways will God be glorified in his life. To talk of separation and holding the truth while neglecting what is here set forth is mere sham and hypocrisy.

The priest's lips should keep knowledge and men should seek the law at his mouth, thus approving himself as the messenger of the Lord of hosts (ver. 7). Therefore the need of earnest, prayerful study of the whole word of God, with a view to bringing all the life into practical subjection thereto. The servant of God in the New Testament is exhorted to "study to show thyself approved unto God, a workman that needeth not to be ashamed, rightly dividing the word of truth" (2 Tim. 2: 15). It is not a question of following some favorite teacher or cleaving to a particular line of doctrines, but giving the Holy Scriptures, in their entirety, that honored place which God intended they should hold as the complete guide for His people and the suited food for their souls.

Nor is it merely Bible study that is enjoined, but we are called to be "*doers* of the Word," allowing no portion of it to be a dead letter to us, but giving it all its due weight and authority over our hearts and consciences, seeking to walk in all that is written therein.

This, the priests addressed by Malachi utterly ignored. Having departed from the path of obedience themselves, they caused the simple to stumble at the law, and to go astray from the word of the Lord. Therefore the covenant of Levi had become corrupted, as they had shown themselves to be anything but the moral seed of Phinehas, whose javelin had stayed the plague, and whose faithfulness would be remembered to all generations. Contemning the law, these recreant priests had been made contemptible themselves, and they should be despised by the people they had misled. Their ways testified against them, so the Lord refused their service (vers. 8, 9).

The tenth verse is the beginning of the second division of the book, which goes on to the end of the prophecy. It is now the people of Judah as a whole who are addressed in the last message they were ever to get directly from God until the coming of the Just One, the Amen, the faithful and true Witness, preceded as to public ministry by John, the messenger whose coming is predicted in the first verse of chapter 3.

They had all sprung from one common father, Abraham, and were created by one God, Jehovah of hosts. Why then should brethren deal treacherously with each other by profaning the covenant of their fathers? (ver. 10). It is not the so-called "Fatherhood of God" that is here declared. There is not the slightest evidence that "one father" refers to the Deity. It was the Lord Jesus who made known the Father. Only in a national sense could Israel say, "Doubtless Thou art our Father." Individually they all had one father, however, in whom they gloried, even Abraham, whose seed they all were. Thus they were a nation of brethren. But, alas, how unbrotherly had they acted!

What can be more shocking than to be called by a name so suggestive of love and tenderness (even as Abraham himself said to Lot, "We be brethren"), and yet to treat one another with callous indifference and cold-heartedness, amounting at times even to enmity and hatred. "Who are these brethren?" one is reported to have asked, concerning certain companies of factious saints. "They are people," was the reply, "'who are very particular about breaking bread, and very careless about breaking hearts!" What a crying shame that such a testimony concerning any Christians should ever be more than an evil calumny invented by the father of lies! "Let brotherly love continue" is God's admonition to us all. And let us bear in mind that, since our Head has gone back to the glory, we manifest our love to Him by love to His members here upon the earth.

The feeble remnant, returned to the place of the Name, separated from the nations, surely needed the strength to be derived from heart-unity and each other's love and brotherly encouragement. Outside, the wolves raged and snarled.

Inside, the sheep were biting and devouring one another! It is a pitiable picture. Alas, it has been often duplicated by Christ's sheep since. It was not the outside opposition that wounded the heart of Nehemiah: but when he found the separated people exacting usury of one another, and treating their brethren with cruelty and rigor, his great soul was moved to its depths. That the evil had never been really departed from, only temporarily checked, Malachi makes evident.

Dealing treacherously every man against his brother, it was only to be expected that they would prove traitors to their God. And this the prophet charges directly upon all Judah and Israel. They had profaned the holiness of Jehovah, that holiness "which He loved" (how striking the expression!), and had been united in marriage to the daughters of strange gods (ver. 11). These mixed marriages are also mentioned in Nehemiah and Ezra, thus helping us to decide as to the true time of Malachi's ministry. Neither true to each other nor to the Lord, they defiled themselves by forming unholy alliances with the idolatrous people around them. When brotherly love is lacking, true godly separation will soon be only a name, and none need be surprised if the rising generation turn to the world for their companions when they have seen bickerings and variance among those professedly separated to the one only Name.

But God's face is against all those who so act, and He will cut them off. He could not accept offerings from a people so indifferent to His holy character, whatever the outward expression of grief and penitence (vers. 12, 13).

The manner in which they inquired, "Wherefore?" in response to words of such pathos and solemnity, exhibits the actual state of their souls. He is not slow to reply. He was the witness to all their evil-doing. Forbidden to enter into marriages with the heathen, He had made of twain one flesh among His own people. But they had violated their nuptial pledges by adding to their households outlandish women who were leading them away from Himself. It was that He might seek a godly seed that He had thus decreed concerning their family relationships. But laxity as to divorce, and mixed marriages, were fast corrupting the seed of God (vers. 14, 15).

The practice of setting aside their wives (so common, alas, in our own degenerate times) to gratify a passing whim was detestable in His eyes. He hates putting away. Hidden violence would all be searched out, and could not remain forever covered. All must come to light in due time. "Therefore take heed to your spirit," was His word, "that ye deal not treacherously" (ver. 16).

We need only to turn to the nineteenth chapter of Matthew to see how little effect this remonstrance had upon them. Divorces were granted on most trifling and absurd pretences, and meantime all their lawlessness was covered with a cloak of extreme punctiliousness in outward religious observances. How easy it is to make much of externals while habitually careless as to the true piety and sincere obedience to the weightier matters of the word of God!

The Lord was wearied with their empty religiousness—mere words from the lips, and not the genuine utterance of the heart acceptable in His sight. But again they answer Him with a caviling question, saying, "Wherein have we wearied Thee?" He replies, "When ye say, Every one that doeth evil is good in the sight of the Lord, and He delighteth in them; or, Where is the God of judgment?" (ver. 17). It was thus they were setting aside His revealed Word and congratulating themselves on being Abraham's seed, and therefore in the line of promise. The merits of the fathers were made to cover all possible delinquencies in their own lives. It could not be, thought they, that God would visit in judgment those in whose veins flowed the blood of Abraham, Isaac and Jacob. Thus they dwelt negligently in a fool's paradise, having already forgotten the lesson of the Babylonish captivity. Nor has it been otherwise with the Church. Ruin and disaster early came in, because of departure from the living God. For centuries spiritual Babylon held sway over the consciences of His children, and kept them in bondage and ignorance.

At last, through the recovery of the word of God, came deliverance and blessing, followed, even in the lifetime of the Reformers, by a lifeless orthodoxy, coupled with relaxation of morals and indifference to that Word so graciously entrusted to them.

Since then, there have been various revival periods when the special work of the Spirit has been to emphasize practical godliness and devotion to Christ. Each successive movement has begun with more or less loyalty to God and to His word. But decay and disintegration have soon followed. At last the truth of the mystery of Christ and the Church was brought to light, and the name of Jesus became the rallying-standard for many of His people, wearied of the failing systems of men. But again have pride and self-will wrought sad havoc; and it remains now to be seen how far there will be a judging of what has thus marred the lovely testimony raised up to the excellency of the peerless name of the Lord.

The hour is late. The Judge is at the door. The coming of the Lord draweth nigh. Lowliness and self-judgment become us all. May we have grace given to discern the signs of the times, and to bow our hearts to His Word.

CHAPTER III

PREPARATION FOR THE MESSENGER OF THE COVENANT

MALACHI means, "My messenger." It was through him Jehovah declared, "Behold, I will send My messenger (using the same word as the prophet's name), and he shall prepare the way before ME: and the Lord, whom ye seek, shall suddenly come to His temple, even the Messenger of the covenant, whom ye delight in: behold, He shall come, saith the Lord of hosts" (ver. 1). Thus was John's coming predicted as the herald of the King, Messiah, but in such a way as to make it plain that Messiah Himself was identified with Jehovah; for the word is, "He shall prepare the way before Me." (See Matt. 11: 10; Mark 1: 2; and Luke 1: 76; 7: 28).

It is also of importance to notice that "angel" and "messenger" are one in the Hebrew. So John was the angel of Jesus, but Jesus Himself was the Covenant-Angel of whom Jehovah had said long ago, "My name is in Him" (Exod. 23: 20, 21). To the very temple but lately rebuilt by Zerubbabel, though afterwards enlarged and beautified by Herod, did He suddenly come as the Nazarene, only to be despised, rejected, and crucified.

But another coming is clearly foretold here; for when it actually takes place, the unholy will not be able to abide it, nor to stand in His presence. As a refiner and purifier He shall sit to purify and purge the Levitical family, setting apart for Himself the sons of Zadok (Ezek. 48: 11), who shall have turned to Him, owning their guilt and judging themselves for their share in the sins of the priesthood. Upon the rest judgment must burn like fire (vers. 2 and 3).

It seems plain from verse 4, as also the 43rd chapter of Ezekiel, that in the days when the kingdom is established over all the earth, sacrifices and offerings will be reinstituted in Jerusalem and the land of Judah, though only as commemorative of the one great sacrifice of the cross; thus sustaining to millennial saints the same relationship that the Lord's Supper now occupies among Christians.

The evil-doers will be weeded out from among the people, and a righteous remnant alone be preserved, "For I am Jehovah, I change not; therefore ye sons of Jacob are not consumed" (vers. 5, 6).

Never had they kept His ordinances in a completely scriptural manner. But from the days of their fathers they had departed from what He had caused to be written for their guidance. So, in view of the advent of the Messenger of the covenant, He bids them return unto Him in heart, that He may return unto them with blessing and loving favor. But, as so often before, they arrogantly ask, "Wherein shall we return?" (ver. 7). There was no sense of need or of failure. Quite the contrary; they were self-satisfied and content. So long as outward forms and ceremonies were attended to, they saw no reason to search and try their ways.

So their sinfulness has to be pressed upon them more strongly still. "Will a man rob God?" Yet they had deliberately robbed Him. With amazing effrontery, they ask, "Wherein have we robbed Thee?" He replies, "In tithes and offerings," and declares that the curse of the violated law rested upon the whole nation. It is a question which was the most solemn — their sinful course, or their calm indifference concerning it. Conscience seemed completely gone; and when a good conscience has been put away, anything can be indulged in with a degree of self-assurance that seems inexplicable (vers. 8, 9).

Still, terrible as their failure had been, it is not too late yet to repent. He calls upon them to bring all the tithes into the storehouse, in this way acknowledge their stewardship under Him, and that needful provision may be made for those who served in the temple, thus releasing them from attention to carnal things; and they are promised abundant blessing if they but heed His voice. He would have them prove Him, and see if He would not open the windows of heaven and pour out upon them such a shower of spiritual refreshment that they would be straitened as to storing it. The devourer, too, He would rebuke for their sakes, causing their enemies to cease from molesting them, that in peace and quietness they might enjoy the abundant fruits of their labor. Blessed with all that heart could desire, both spiritually and temporally, all nations would call them the happy people, and theirs should be a land of delight (vers. 10-12).

All this is to be literally fulfilled when the spirit of grace and supplication is poured out upon the future repentant remnant, and they return to God with their whole heart. Everything waits upon this, even as the Lord Jesus Himself declared, "Ye shall not see Me henceforth till ye shall say, Blessed is He that cometh in the name of the Lord."

But for saints of every dispensation an important principle is here enunciated—blessing waits on true devotion of heart. Let all that is due to the Lord, long withheld because of our selfishness, be rendered to Him—all the tithes brought in, and He will rejoice to pour down showers of blessing upon His waiting and expectant people. God delights to give; but our low, earthly-minded state so frequently hinders His visiting us with a gracious revival. "Let us search and try our ways, and turn again to the Lord" (Lam. 3: 40) is a word in season at the present solemn moment in the Church's history.

For Judah, the era of blessing had not yet dawned, nor has it ever really come since; for they knew not the time of their visitation. Their words were stout, or strong, against God; yet, when He challenged them as to this, for the eighth time, they brazenly challenged Him in return, inquiring, "What have we spoken so much against Thee?" (ver. 13). No appeal, entreaty, or warning, seemed to move them, or to turn them in the slightest degree from their self-complacency and egoism.

Yet they had said, "It is vain to serve God," for they blindly estimated things by the standard of worldly prosperity; and as they contrasted their lowly lot with the proud surrounding nations, they considered there had been no profit in keeping Jehovah's word and seeking to obey His voice. What they did not take into account was that they were part of a failed nation, and still reaping the sad fruit of their fathers' evil sowing, So they were stumbled at the prosperity of the wicked, but did not, like Asaph, enter with unshod feet into the sanctuary, that they might understand the end of the enemies of the Lord. (See Ps. 73.)

Nevertheless all were not thus insensate and gainsaying. A remnant is distinguished in vers. 16 to 18 that may well be a shining example to us. In the midst of all the declension and cold-heartedness of the mass, a few there were who feared Jehovah, and sought each other out in the dark and cloudy day, speaking often one to another of the precious and serious things pertaining to a walk with God. The Lord took pleasure in this feeble company, and hearkened, and heard their communings and their confessions, and entered their despised names in a book of remembrance, which will soon be opened at the judgment-seat of Christ: "And they shall be Mine, saith the Lord of hosts, in that day when I make up My peculiar treasure;" for as they had found their treasure in *Him*, He found His in *them*. In the day when He shall visit upon the wicked their iniquities He will spare the remnant, discerning between those who truly served Him, and those who had no heart for His Word. It is a striking and beautiful passage, that is rich in the ministry of comfort and cheer to the tried and tested ones who value fellowship with God above all else.

Occupation with the evil can only weaken the hand and distress the spirit. But occupation with Him who sits in peace above all the mists of earth will strengthen and cheer, and prove the only real power for practical holiness and victory over all the might of the enemy.

CHAPTER IV

THE SUN-RISING

THE break between these two chapters seems unfortunate, and helps to divert the mind from what has just been presented. The fact is that verse 1 of chapter 4 is but a continuation of what has gone before. The Lord is going to discern between the righteous and the wicked. When? In the coming day that shall burn as an oven, the day of the Lord toward which all prophecy points as to the time when all the wrongs of the ages are to be put right. For, be it remembered, "the day" is not a brief period of twenty-four hours, but a day that will embrace the entire Millennium, concluding with the passing away of the earth and the heavens, thus introducing the day of eternity, or the day of God, as set forth in Peter's second letter (3:10-12). The present season is called "*man's* day," for it is the time (of undefined duration) when man is doing his own will (1 Cor. 4:3; marginal reading, "day," in place of "judgment"). For the heavenly saints, "the day of *Christ*" will immediately follow, when, caught up to meet their Lord in the air, they shall be manifested before His judgment-seat (Phil. 1:6, 10). The day of the *Lord* then begins for Israel and the nations, embracing the judgments to be visited on the earth and the reign of righteousness, closing when the kingdom is delivered up to the Father, and God (Father, Son, and Spirit) will be all in all throughout the never-ending "day of *God*," the eternal state.

It is then, of the day when the Lord Jesus returns in manifested glory to visit judgment on all who have refused the everlasting gospel, that the opening verse treats. That day will "burn as an oven; and all the proud, yea, and all that do wickedly, shall be stubble: and the day that cometh shall burn them up, saith the Lord of hosts, that it shall leave them neither root nor branch." Thus will men be made to know the wrath of the Lamb, when He shall be revealed from heaven in flaming fire, taking vengeance on those who know not God.

But in that day of thick darkness and gloominess, for a preserved remnant light shall break forth in overwhelming glory. "Unto you that fear My name shall the Sun of Righteousness arise with healing in His wings; and ye shall go forth, and grow up as calves of the stall. And ye shall tread down the wicked; for they shall be ashes under the soles of your feet in the day that I shall do this, saith the Lord of hosts" (vers. 2, 3). This is very different from the hope of the Church. *We* wait for the shining-forth of the Morning Star, not the rising of the Sun of Righteousness, which latter is distinctively Israel's hope. The Morning Star is the herald of the dawn, and rises ere the Sun is yet visible. So will the Lord Jesus descend from heaven with a shout, and translate the heavenly saints to the Father's house prior to the time of Jacob's trouble, the great tribulation, which takes place upon the earth in a brief interval between the coming of Christ for the Church and His appearing with His holy ones in glorious majesty, for the relief of the remnant of Judah, and Israel, in the day of their sore trial as a result of their rejection of the Lord when He came before in grace. This is the shining-forth of the Sun of Righteousness, whose beams will bring healing for His own, but will consume the wicked with their intensity. It will not be the Church, but Israel, who will then tread down the evil-doers as ashes beneath their feet, in accordance with the universal testimony of the prophets.

It should be plain to all thoughtful students of the word of God that this passage completely nullifies the theory of a converted world at the coming of Christ. Where, then, would be the wicked who are to be trodden down? The fact is that Scripture knows nothing of this favorite system of modern divines. There will be no Millennium till Christ appears, for He must first act in power for the destruction of all who have refused to own His claims, thus purging the scene for the establishment of His kingdom.

Much has been made of these three opening verses by annihilationists of every school. They suppose the prophet to refer to the final day of judgment, and the ultimate destruction of the lost in the lake of fire. Their argument is that as the wicked will then be burnt up root and branch, and be ashes under the feet of the righteous, they will have ceased entirely to exist, and thus will have been effectually blotted out of God's universe.

The mistake is made by failing to observe that it is *temporal* judgment which is here foretold, of which that which fell upon Sodom and Gomorrah was a sample. Fire from heaven will consume the *bodies* of the wicked on the earth before the millennial kingdom is set up, and thus become ashes under the feet of the righteous. But there is no hint here as to what will become of the soul and spirit. We learn elsewhere in Scripture of judgment *after* death, though the body be burned to ashes. Our Lord tells us that it shall be more tolerable for Sodom and Gomorrah in the day of judgment than for certain of the cities in which His mighty works had been performed but He Himself had been rejected.

Nearly forty centuries have elapsed since the wicked dwellers in the cities of the plain were burned up root and branch. Had Abraham or Lot walked over the sites of those destroyed places a few days after the fire fell from heaven, the wicked would have been ashes under the soles of their feet. But were they then annihilated? Far from it. They have yet to stand before the Great White Throne for judgment where they will be dealt with in accordance with the light they had, and which they refused.

The same may be said of "the proud, and all that do wickedly," spoken of here by Malachi. Destroyed utterly as to their bodies and place on earth, they yet exist in the world of spirits, and will prove that "it is appointed unto men once to die, and after this the judgment." For, as our Lord Jesus said, "God is not a God of the dead, but of the living; for *all* live unto Him" (Luke 20: 38). Let not the reader, if unsaved, be lulled to sleep by the devil's gospel of final extinction. Abiding wrath and eternal judgment are terrible realities from which the precious blood of Christ alone can deliver.

In Gen. 1: 16 the sun is first introduced, the type of the Lord Jesus from whom His Church gets all her light, even as the moon reflects the glory of the sun. Ere Malachi closes the Old Testament canon, he reverts to that first type, and presents the same glorious person as "the Sun of Righteousness."

In view of all the expostulation that has gone before, the last three verses take on a most solemn character. Judah is exhorted to remember the law of Moses, which God had commanded for all Israel, but which they had violated from the first, and were now filling up the cup of their iniquities. To call them back to Himself, He would send them Elijah the prophet, ere the coming of that great and dreadful day of the Lord which we have been contemplating. We know from Matt. 17: 10-13, and Mark 9: 11-13, that, for faith, John the Baptist was that Elijah; but the nation received him not as such; therefore the ministry here referred to is yet future. As Moses and Elijah are coupled together in these verses (the lawgiver and the restorer), so we see the signs of each wrought by the two witnesses of Revelation 11, which would seem to make plain the character of the ministry to be raised up as a testimony in Jerusalem at the time of the end.

Elijah is to turn the heart of the fathers to the children, and the heart of the children to the fathers, thus bringing all the remnant into subjection to the revealed will of God, that He may not come and smite the earth with a curse.

And so with this solemn word, CURSE, the Old Testament abruptly comes to a close. The law had been violated in every particular. On the ground of the legal covenant the people had no hope whatever. Wrath like a dark cloud was lowering over their heads. The awful *curse* of that broken law was all they had earned after long ages of trial. But a Redeemer had been promised; and where there was faith, in any who felt the seriousness of their condition, they looked on to the coming of the Seed of the woman who was to bruise the serpent's head, and Himself be made a curse, that all who put their trust in Him might be redeemed from the doom they had so long and fully deserved. *"To Him give all the prophets witness, that through His name whosoever believeth in Him shall receive remission of sins"* (Acts 10: 43). Through Him alone can guilty men, who own their lost estate and trust His grace, be delivered from the *"curse."*

POSTSCRIPT

AFTER many months of intermittent labor, I have been, through grace, enabled to complete this volume; and I send it forth with the earnest prayer that God may use it—imperfect in many respects as I know it to be—to the glory of His great name and the blessing of many of His people.

Everywhere we have found the same great facts emphasized. Man in his best estate is altogether vanity; but grace abounds over all our sin and failure.

If at times the notes seem pessimistic, and unduly burdened with a sense of the failure of the testimony committed to man, it is not intentional, but rather an evidence of human frailty and imperfection. For the prophets, rightly read, lead to optimism of the brightest hue, occupying the soul with evil only that it may be judged in oneself, but pointing on to the glad morning without clouds when He for whom we wait shall come down like rain upon the mown grass, and His displayed kingdom shall be like clear shining after the storm has passed.

Evil is but transitory, and has sway only for a moment. The good shall abide forever, when the last remains of sin will be banished to the lake of fire, and there shall be new heavens and a new earth, wherein dwelleth righteousness.

"Wherefore, beloved, seeing that ye look for such things, be diligent that ye may be found of Him in peace, without spot, and blameless . . . Therefore, beloved, seeing ye know these things before, beware lest ye also, being led away with the error of the wicked, fall from your own stedfastness. But grow in grace, and in the knowledge of our Lord and Saviour Jesus Christ. To Him be glory both now and forever. Amen" (2 Peter 3: 14, 17, 18).